TO JIM MARSH ON HIS BIRTHDAY — BEST WISHES!

Ed Rankin, Jr.

Hugh Morton

Charlie Choo Choo Justice

January 21, 1989

Dedicated

to

Julia Taylor Morton

and

Frances Wallace Rankin

Library of Congress Catalogue Card Number: 88-82050

Hardcover ISBN: 0-942399-06-4

Printed by Everbest Printing Company, LtD., Hong Kong,
through Four Colour Imports, Louisville, KY.

Produced and distributed by Lightworks, 6005 Chapel Hill Road,
Raleigh, N.C. 27607.

Making A Difference In North Carolina

Hugh M. Morton

Edward L. Rankin, Jr.

All photographs in this book were made by Hugh M. Morton
unless otherwise designated.

Each chapter's text is initialed by its author.

Design by Avery Designs

Published by Lightworks

CONTENTS

SAM J. ERVIN, JR.
U.S. Senator, Watergate Superstar

Hugh Morton and I were fortunate to have a taped interview with Sam Ervin, Jr., at his home in Morganton only a few weeks before his death in April 1985. Seated in a wheelchair, obviously diminished in body, "Senator Sam" was mentally alert, in good spirits and kept a flow of commentary and humorous anecdotes going for over an hour. Most of his comments were about past experiences, North Carolina, its history and its people. Here are a few highlights:

How He Was Appointed

"I was asked to meet Governor Umstead at the executive mansion, and we sat on one of the side porches and talked about the Senate vacancy. Finally Bill said, 'Percy Reade (his former law partner) says I should appoint you to the Senate. Now, I'm not going to tell I'm going to appoint you, but I want to find out if I offered it to you, would you accept?' I told him I had never thought about it, but here was my reply: I was trained for the law. I love the law. I love judging and I had figured I'd spend my life in that field. I hope you won't offer it to me because if you do I would accept it as a matter of duty." (The telephone call and offer came the next day.)

An Earlier Experience With William Umstead

"When I was a freshman at Chapel Hill, Bill Umstead was a sophomore and had organized a Bible class on campus. He proselyted me into attending and on the first meeting he looked at me and said, 'Ervin, lead us in prayer.' I had never prayed in public in my life, and all I said was 'Lord, help us, amen.' I stayed after class and told Bill never to call on me to lead in prayer . . . it was embarrassing to me. Bill replied, 'Sam, I've heard preachers harangue the Lord for 40 minutes and say no more than you did in just a few words.' "

Susie Sharp for U.S. Supreme Court

"Everett Jordan and I tried to get President Nixon to appoint Susie Sharp (then Associate Justice, North Carolina Supreme Court) to the United States Supreme Court, but he chose Judge Harold Carswell (who was not confirmed). Later I was at the White House and I told the president that if he had had the good enough judgment to take our advice and put Susie Sharp up, she would have been confirmed . . . and would have been a good judge. Nixon replied, quite seriously, 'In retrospect, I have to concede that your recommendation sounds more sensible than I thought at the time.' After my second try for Susie, she said she did not want to go up there with that bunch. I told her that was why I want you up there . . . they need someone like you to straighten them out!"

On Good Government in North Carolina

"Our people have been pretty loyal to intelligent leaders throughout our history. Demagoguery never flourished in North Carolina like it did in the deep south. If our people had a leader in whom they had confidence, they stuck with him. The constitutional prohibition on extra terms for governors and lieutenant governors meant they had to be statesmen in their first terms. I opposed the change feebly . . . and I hope the people will repeal the dern thing. The lack of a veto has stood governors in good stead. On that question, I say 'if it ain't broke, don't fix it.' "

On the Greatest President

"Harry S Truman was the greatest president with whom I served. He was not overeducated but had common sense. He had great courage as symbolized by the sign on his desk: The Buck Stops Here. He made such great decisions as the one to drop the atom bomb on Hiroshima. I was a great admirer of him. He was the first man of standing to stand up to Senator McCarthy. And he always appreciated the fact that I was on the committee that voted to censure McCarthy. We had a good relationship despite my misgivings about his stand on civil rights."

On Presidents Who Were Not Great

"Lyndon B. Johnson and Richard M. Nixon were too much alike. They stood for what was politically expedient. Johnson would have made a good president if Sam Rayburn (Speaker of the House) had lived . . . but, unfortunately, he didn't. He had implicit confidence in Rayburn. Johnson had a great weakness . . . he wanted everybody to love him. A man in public life who stands for anything is not going to have everybody love him. There are going to be a few against him, in any event."

Advice to Young People on Public Service

"Government touches people at so many points of their lives today that I think everybody should be vitally interested in government—out of self-defense if for no other reason. Young people should study the United States Constitution, study constitutional law and qualify for public office. I think the greatest thing they can do is to serve their country in a public office." *ELR*

Samuel James Ervin, Jr., a man for all seasons, was one of the best-known North Carolinians of this century. His life was filled with achievements as a student and scholar, World War I hero, talented lawyer, state legislator, congressman, distinguished judge, leader in the United States Senate for 20 years, and, above all, an acknowledged authority on the United States Constitution . . . and one of its most steadfast and effective defenders.

Delegate Wayland Spruill, a veteran North Carolina legislator, was not pleased with any of the front runners being promoted at the 1956 Democratic national convention in Chicago. So he rose in a meeting of the North Carolina delegation to nominate Senator Sam Ervin, Jr., as a "favorite son" nominee for President of the United States. Noted for his folksy humor, "Cousin Wayland," as he was widely known, had the delegation and "Senator Sam" roaring with laughter at his light-hearted comments. Seated next to the Senator is Mrs. John (Mary Laurens) Richardson, long-time worker and leader in the Democratic party. The Senator said later that when Spruill compared Ervin with the other candidates, "Wayland may have been damming me with faint praise."

A gifted speaker, who used his encyclopedic memory to quote with ease from the Bible, William Shakespeare, great philosophers, poems and innumerable other sources, Ervin speaks at a community-wide meeting in Morganton honoring him for his service to the nation as chairman of the Watergate Committee. At his left is Governor Terry Sanford, the principal speaker. Seated at his right is Margaret Bell Ervin, his wife. In his autobiography he wrote, "Margaret is a strong and gentle spirit who is loved and respected by all who know her. Since our marriage she has stood beside me, in sunshine and in shadow, with steadfast love and constant inspiration."

Just appointed to the United States Senate by Governor William B. Umstead, Senator Sam Ervin, Jr., came to Wilmington in 1954 to inspect the damages wrought by Hurricane Hazel, and also to speak to the Wilmington Chamber of Commerce at the invitation of Hugh Morton. Ervin was then 58 years of age. He recalled later that Julia Morton, Hugh's wife, admonished him after his speech for saying, "No one is qualified (because of the magnitude of the responsibility) to be a United States Senator." She said, "Don't ever say you are not qualified to be a United States Senator. When you run for election an opponent may use your own words against you."

ON THE IMPORTANCE OF HUMOR

"Observation and experience as a practicing lawyer, legislator, and judge . . . taught me that an ounce of revealing humor often has more convincing power than a ton of erudite argument . . ."—Senator Ervin, in his autobiography, Preserving The Constitution.

The Senator's sister, Jean Conyers Ervin, reveals that the importance of humor came much earlier to her brother than practicing law. In her remarks on the occasion of the Senator's acceptance of the North Caroliniana Society Award (1980) and the celebration of the 56th anniversary of his marriage to "Miss Margaret", Jean Ervin relates:

"Even at a very young age Sam saw the funny side of things and knew what would provoke laughter in his contemporaries. In those days pupils answered the roll with Bible verses and one day Sam answered the roll with Solomon's words, 'I have more understanding than all my teachers.' He had to stay after school.

"Sam has always taken such a delight in reciting poems that I have thought he memorized poetry just for fun, but this is not correct. The real reason for his vast memorized collection of poetry is that he talked in school, and for this misdemeanor had to remain after school and memorize poetry. He must have talked a lot. He still does."

The chairman of the Senate Watergate Committee holds his "straight as an arrow" walking stick soon after President Richard M. Nixon made his speech with the much quoted statement, "I am not a crook." The photo was made at the Sir Walter Hotel, Raleigh, the political hub of North Carolina for decades. As Watergate chairman, Ervin gained national and international recognition and fame in 1973 during this constitutional crisis and bitter chapter in American history. Columnist James J. Kilpatrick described Ervin as "the last of the Founding Fathers."

Senator Ervin chats with Democratic party notables (left to right) Estes Kefauver, candidate for vice president on the 1956 ticket with Adlai Stevenson, and United States Senator from Tennessee; Mrs. Enrest (Buffie) Ives of Pinehurst, sister of Governor Stevenson; Mrs. Nancy Kefauver, wife of Senator Kefauver; and Alton Lennon of Wilmington, N.C. 7th District Congressman and a former United States Senator. The photo was made in Blowing Rock at the home of Mrs. and Mrs. Jimmy Harris, long-time residents of Charlotte.

A PERSONAL TRIBUTE FROM AN OLD FRIEND

Albert Coates, Professor Emeritus of Law at the University of North Carolina at Chapel Hill and founder of the Institute of Government there, wrote a tribute about his friend and classmate (1917) following the Senator's death. Here is an excerpt:

"If I had to pick out what, to my way of thinking, is the finest accolade of a lifetime it would be the tribute of the Majority Leader of the United States Senate on the 8th day of February 1973 in picking him to head the most important Senate committee of this generation—the Senate Select Committee on the Watergate Affair—giving as his reason: 'We are looking for a good, fair, impartial investigation, and Sam Ervin is the only man we could have picked on either side of the aisle who would have the respect of the Senate as a whole.'

"That statement was rooted in a 20-year record of day-to-day work by Sam Ervin with his fellow senators who knew him well in committee and on the floor. They had found that he knew his business, loved it, and tended to it. That he moved in his own orbit—full of common sense and mother wit. That he was all of a piece—not a lot of planks nailed together, but a growing tree with the sap rising through it. That he would vote and act from forces welling up in the man himself and not from any outside influence or external pressure.

"If I had to pick out one sentence from all his sayings characteristic of Sam Ervin throughout the comings and goings of his life, it would be a sentence which he didn't have to think up—it came to him from the certitude of his own being while he was talking to his homefolks in Morganton on returning from World War I. He had been reported as 'missing in action' on the western front, and his neighbors were telling him they were so glad he had been found. 'I was never lost,' he told them. 'I knew where I was all the time.' And so it has been from that day to this."

Author's Note: *Comments by Jean Conyers Ervin and Albert Coates are reprinted with permission from* The Sam Ervin I Knew *(North Caroliniana Society Imprints Number 4).*

A genial and popular man, Sam Ervin was an astute politician who won his elective contests handily throughout his long career in public office. He is shown here in the midst of the North Carolina delegation at the 1956 Democratic national convention at Chicago. Delegate Zeno Ponder displays a local newspaper with the latest news about the battle for nomination to the presidency. Delegate Dan Stewart is behind Ponder.

B. Everett Jordan (left) and Sam J. Ervin, Jr. served together in the United States Senate for about 15 years. They pause at the State Ports Authority docks in Wilmington for a picture. Members of the North Carolina congressional delegation came for an inspection trip and briefing on the state's efforts to improve and increase world-wide shipping from facilities at Wilmington and Morehead City.

SENATOR SAM'S PARTING WORDS

Excerpt from his last weekly newsletter:

WASHINGTON—It is impossible to over-magnify the importance of seeking truth. This is so because truth alone can make us free. The men who established constitutional government in America knew this. They knew the verity which Justice Oliver Wendell Holmes subsequently stated when he said that "the best test of truth is the power of the thought to get itself accepted in the competition of the market." They knew that false opinions cannot possibly be dangerous to a country if truth is left free to combat error.

They wrote into the Bill of Rights the great freedoms which secure to each American the right to think and speak his thoughts concerning all things under the sun. Their ultimate purpose in so doing was to create the only kind of society in which individual personality can develop and survive.

We discover truth in fragments and must piece it together like a picture puzzle. As a consequence, the search for truth requires much study and observation and meditation. It requires an attitude of mind which makes us wish to be on the side of truth as well as to have truth on our side. We can best achieve this attitude by taking and keeping the oath phrased by Thomas Jefferson in these challenging words:

"I have sworn upon the altar of God eternal hostility against every form of tyranny over the mind of man."

HURRICANE HAZEL
Brings Record Deaths, Destruction

When Hurricane Hazel struck the North Carolina coast on October 15, 1954, it did not behave like hurricanes are supposed to behave when they move inland. Instead of losing its punch, Hazel confounded the weather experts and civil defense people by moving with undiminished ferocity across the coastal plain, lashing everything in its path. Fayetteville and Raleigh felt its raw power before Hazel went into Virginia and up the eastern seaboard where damages continued to mount. Leaving the U.S., it crossed the North Atlantic and ended its trail of death and destruction in Western Europe.

In North Carolina, the toll: 19 people killed; 15,000 homes or other buildings completely destroyed or with major damages; 39,000 homes or other buildings with minor damage. Total property losses: $125 million.

Unfortunately, Hazel was the precursor of three other hurricanes to follow in quick succession in 1955. While not following Hazel's path across the state, Connie (August 12), Diane (August 18) and Ione (September 20) battered the coast, compounding earlier damages caused by Hazel. This was especially true in agriculture where streams and drainage canals still clogged from Hazel could not accommodate rainfall from three more hurricanes. One area, for example, received 15.25 inches in a 24-hour period. Total crop and other losses to farmers: $131 million.

What were the total losses from the four hurricanes? Governor Luther H. Hodges gave the answer in testimony to the U.S. Senate Appropriation Committee in 1956: $326 million. It is unlikely that North Carolina has ever received— and survived—a more disastrous blow from Mother Nature in its recorded history. *ELR*

What is it like to experience the howling winds, pounding waves and awesome destruction of a world-class hurricane? Hugh Morton and a small group of newsmen witnessed and recorded the full fury of Hazel when it struck the North Carolina coast on October 15, 1954. Shown struggling against the storm at Carolina Beach is Julian Scheer, *Charlotte News* reporter. The houses behind Scheer are being pushed off their foundations by the surging sea. Flames of unknown origin help complete the destruction. Hugh's photo won first prize for spot news in N.C. Press Photographers Association competition that year.

The incredible might of Hazel is clearly shown here. These large cabin cruisers were tossed, like giant toys, into the middle of the highway on Harbor Island, far from where they had been moored or anchored in Wrightsville Sound. Over 150,000 insurance claims for losses were filed with insurance companies as a result of Hazel.

Hurricane Connie, which struck August 12, 1955, unearthed these Civil War projectiles at Fort Fisher. Connie, Diane and Ione all compounded the earlier damages of Hazel.

A local teenager ventures out at Carolina Beach as the storm's wind and water began to slacken. Coastal residents quickly recovered from their shock, helped first those who needed it most and began picking up the pieces of their lives. Ralph Howland, *Charlotte Observer* correspondent, wrote, "As a people untutored in great disasters, Carolinians did mighty well. They learned quickly and acted swiftly. They aren't soft, nor do they surrender easily. Their fortitude may be their best secret weapon."

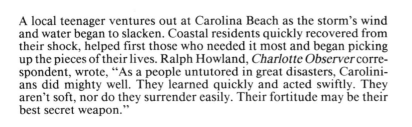

Long Beach in Brunswick County was among the coastal communities hardest hit by Hazel. This Long Beach house, which had been completely swept away by wind and water, is being relocated on its original lot weeks later. Ed Rankin, then private secretary to Governor William B. Umstead, first saw the damage during a low level flight in a National Guard aircraft shortly after the hurricane struck. "Long Beach was largely swept clean," he says. "It was like a giant hand moving in from the sea, clearing the beach of all signs of human habitation . . . and jamming what had been there back into the marshes and mainland forests. In the center of the island a deep inlet was created, dividing Long Beach into two parts. The inlet was not closed until about four years later."

Alice Strickland, town clerk of Carolina Beach, gives instructions to two local workers as the hurricane abates. An indomitable person, not cowed by the raging storm, she remained in the tiny town hall during Hazel. Newsmen and others found her a reliable source of information, calmly answering questions while sea water swirled around her knees.

Dawn came bright and clear the day after Hazel. Here is how the beachfront at Wrightsville Beach looked. Local governments, stunned by the magnitude of the destruction, quickly asked and received assistance of state and federal governments. The State Highway Patrol and 11 North Carolina National Guard units promptly helped local law enforcement officials in protecting areas with the most damage, controlling traffic and preventing looting. Other resources—state highway forces, electric utility crews, U.S. Army engineers, to mention a few—streamed into the coastal region as rapidly as they could. The American Red Cross, for example, gave direct assistance to over 1200 families in need.

DR. BILLY GRAHAM
The World Is His Parish

There is a popular perception of competition between religious denominations for members, and rivalry among individual evangelists for the financial support of followers and potential followers. There is some truth to this notion, but it absolutely does not apply to Dr. Billy Graham. Since the first day of his ministry it has been his purpose to draw people into the local church . . . regardless of denomination. He feels that anything that does not help the local church becomes a parasite on it. Billy Graham makes an earnest effort to support all churches.

For example, he is scheduled to be in Russia in 1988 for the 1,000th anniversary of the Russian Orthodox Church. His staff helped organize the recent visit to Columbia, S.C., of His Holiness Pope John Paul. He has used his influence and contacts behind the scenes to gain the release of Jews imprisoned behind the Iron Curtain in eastern Europe. Dr. Billy Graham's parish is the world, and helping churches within his parish, irrespective of denomination, is his objective. It is this philosophy, supported by deed, that has brought him the worldwide respect that he deserves and has received.

T.W. Wilson

The Reverend T.W. Wilson believes that only God will ever know the tremendous impact of Dr. Billy Graham's good work in this country, and in nation after nation around the world. Wilson, a childhood friend of Billy Graham, has been in evangelism with Graham for the past 43 years. He reports that when Reverend Billy Kim of South Korea was in the Graham offices in Montreat recently Kim reported that Billy Graham's ministry had changed the whole country of South Korea through growth in the churches and increased church attendance.

In a Japanese city the size of Atlanta, GA, the number of people who made a profession of faith on the occasion of a Graham Crusade there was greater than the entire Christian population of the city prior to that time, Wilson said. The same story could be told over and over again in almost every corner of the globe.

Billy Graham has never endorsed a political candidate. This is contrary to what some people think, and different from what some writers have written. Dr. Graham believes it is fitting and appropriate to be friends with people in both of America's major political parties, and he has followed such a policy without partiality. Wilson says that the closest Graham came to an endorsement was in the case of Richard Nixon, but there was no endorsement.

At times Billy Graham has served as liaison between the leaders of the major political parties. The last night that the Lyndon B. Johnson family spent in the White House, Dr. Graham was their house guest. The next day, Billy Graham was to speak at President Nixon's inauguration. As both Johnson and Graham prepared to leave the White House, LBJ said, "Billy, I want you to tell Dick Nixon something for me. You tell him he won't be in office 30 days until he'll realize that he ain't running this country. You tell him there is nothing in this world for him to do except be like a jackass in a hail storm, and stand there and take it."

Wilson accompanied Billy Graham to Charlottesville, VA, to visit President Lyndon B. Johnson in the hospital there following Johnson's heart attack. Wilson heard Johnson tell Dr. Graham, "Billy, you know the thing that gave me my heart attack, I went over to Buford Ellington's funeral (Ellington was former Governor of Tennessee) and that preacher never even mentioned his name. When I die, I want you to preach my funeral, but I want you to at least call my name, and if you can, in a clear conscience, tell at least one good thing I've done."

LBJ's last wish was granted. Dr. Billy Graham did preach President Johnson's funeral, under a big tree on the Johnson ranch in Texas. Dr. Graham mentioned him by name, and he recalled not one good thing, but several, that President Johnson had done.

Wilson says Billy Graham rarely goes into an airport, hotel lobby, or any public place without captains of airplanes, stewardesses, or someone telling him they were converted to Christ under his ministry. Graham, in Wilson's view, is a crusade evangelist who happens to televise some of his crusades, as opposed to being a television evangelist with regularly scheduled programs.

Wilson says a recent poll showed that some of the TV evangelists spend as much as 50 percent of their air time soliciting money, but that Graham "will

Jean and Leighton Ford

A youthful Dr. Billy Graham is the speaker at the annual convention of the North Carolina Press Association at the Grove Park Inn in Asheville on July 13, 1956.

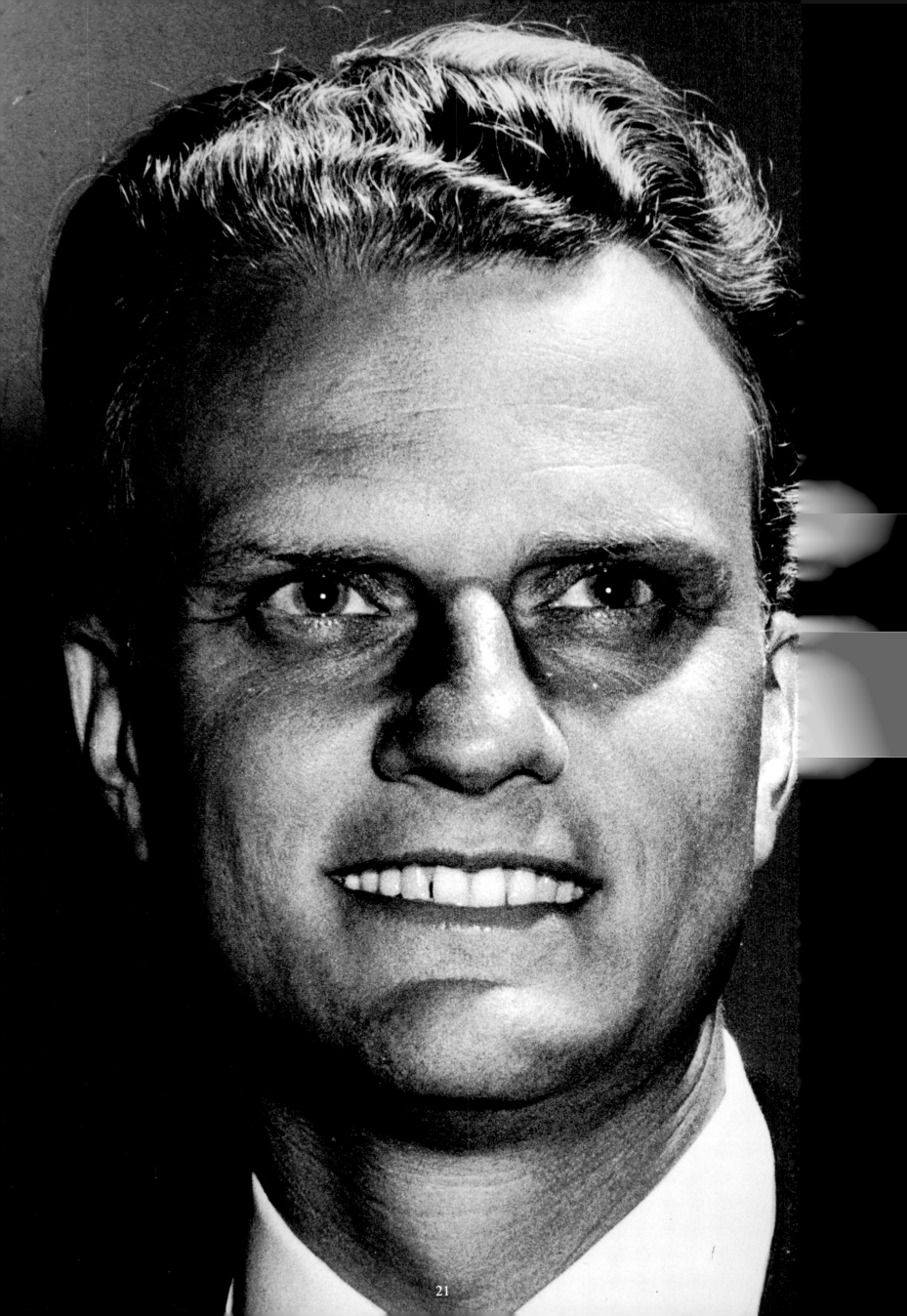

Dr. Billy Graham is the principal speaker at the North Carolina tribute to slain President John F. Kennedy in Kenan Stadium in Chapel Hill where early in his administration the President had appeared to receive an honorary degree. Tickets to the event were sold in every county in North Carolina, and the funds raised went toward the state's contribution to the John Fitzgerald Kennedy Library. Ted Kennedy is at the rostrum, and seated are U.S. Secretary of Commerce Luther H. Hodges, N.C. Republican Party Chairman J. Herman Saxon, Dr. Graham, and former Lt. Gov. L.Y. "Stag" Ballentine.

The jam-packed Charlotte Coliseum cheers as the great singer Ethel Waters is escorted to the stage by Ty Boyd to sing *His Eye Is On The Sparrow*, her musical tribute to Dr. Billy Graham in the celebration Charlotte sponsored to honor its most distinguished native son. Norman Prevatte, producer of the program for the Chamber of Commerce, stands at the bottom of the steps at the left. Reverend Grady Wilson is facing Miss Waters at the right.

President Richard M. Nixon unveils the historical marker which is now erected in front of the IBM building on Park Road where the Graham homeplace once stood. Beside the marker (left to right) are Mrs. Pat Nixon, Mrs. Ruth Graham, President Nixon, and Dr. Graham. Elsewhere in the photograph in the Charlotte Coliseum are Governor Robert W. Scott, Senator Everett Jordan, Charles H. Crutchfield, Senator Strom Thurmond, Former Texas Governor John Connally, Cliff Barrows, Rep. Charles R. Jonas, Senator Sam J. Ervin, Jr., George Beverly Shea, and County Commission Chairman James G. Martin, later Congressman and Governor of North Carolina and John Belk, Mayor of Charlotte.

quit the ministry before he goes to begging." Graham's appeals are brief and extremely soft-sell, usually associated with the offer of a free book. If the person writing for the book wants to contribute to underwriting the expense of telecasting the crusade, Graham tells his audience that will be welcomed.

Billy Graham is a perfectionist and runs a highly disciplined organization that operates smoothly most times, but this is not to say that human error does not occur on occasion. While in Memphis, TN, he noted that the City Hall had huge signs facing highways in four directions stating the number of days the city had gone without a traffic death. Dr. Graham said in his opening remarks at the crusade there, "You people in Memphis are to be congratulated. On the way here to the stadium tonight I looked there at City Hall and I see you have gone 157 days without a fertility." The audience went wild with laughter.

Jane Austin Graham

Back home in North Carolina, Billy Graham conducted the wedding ceremony of his younger sister, Jean, in her marriage to Reverend Leighton Ford. Jean and Leighton exchanged rings and pledged their own vows to one another, whereupon Dr. Graham said, "By having given and received these wings. . . ." When Wilson walked up to Billy Graham at the wedding reception following the ceremony, his leader jokingly said, "If you say anything to me about wings I'll kill you." It may be the only time that God-fearing, peace-loving Dr. Billy Graham has been known to threaten violence.

Reverend William Franklin Graham III, Billy Graham's son who is known as Franklin, heads Samaritan's Purse and World Medical Mission, Inc., headquartered in Boone. Both organizations are successful, concentrating in Third World countries where they supply medical and other support, including on-the-job training in ways for people to help themselves. Franklin is a great encouragement to his mother and father, and has become an effective Christian leader.

The physical resemblance between Billy and Franklin is striking. Facial likeness is strong, and their mannerisms in speaking bear remarkable similarity. Each has a superb, supportive wife. On the subject of Billy's wife, Wilson says, "I do not believe there would be a Billy Graham as we know him today had it not been for Ruth. I have heard him say that she has been his greatest critic, his chief counselor and advisor. She has given Billy some of his best sermon material. Ruth has been a stabilizing influence."

As for Franklin's charming wife, Jane Austin, she is also the busy mother of their three boys and an infant girl. When the original Graham home in Charlotte was to be demolished to make way for the IBM building, Jim Bakker seized the opportunity to move the house to Heritage Village in Rock Hill, S.C. Jane Austin wanted to see the home at its new location, and the three boys wanted to test Bakker's water slide. After water sliding first, the boys looked so disheveled that Jane Austin admonished the youngsters, "Don't tell anyone who you are, don't sign the register, and don't touch anything."

At the house the boys asked their mother lots of questions in hushed voices, and everything was fine until Roy bellowed from the top of the steps, "Mama, which room did Mother Graham die in?" Then the crowning blow came to the incognito visit when another son hollered from upstairs, "Mama, which was Daddy Bill's room?" In Jane Austin's words, "The boys were really good, but they blew it." *HMM*

Just before Dr. Billy Graham began speaking at the 1963 "Singing On The Mountain" at Grandfather Mountain, the State Highway Patrol announced that U.S. 221 passing the Singing Grounds was blocked bumper to bumper from Marion to Blowing Rock, a distance of 55 miles. Everyone was cautioned not to be in a hurry returning home. Including those who tried to reach the event as well as those who did, it was possibly the largest crowd ever to assemble in Western North Carolina.

Even on a rainy evening as shown in this photograph, huge throngs gather in Carter Stadium each night of the week-long Billy Graham Raleigh Crusade. Dr. Graham is in the spotlight at upper left.

Billy and Ruth Graham are in Raleigh in November 1986 for Dr. Graham to receive the North Carolina Award For Public Service, the state's highest honor.

Reverend Franklin Graham (right) and his father, Dr. Billy Graham, are all smiles for the 1987 dedication of the world head-quarters of the Samaritan's Purse Ministry which Franklin heads in Boone. The younger Reverend William Franklin Graham is following Dad's footsteps by supplying doctors, medical supplies, and self-help leadership to needy people all over the world.

MICHAEL JORDAN
Tar Heel, Olympian, NBA Superstar

The Heart Fund in Greensboro held a Michael Jordan Golf Tournament that Hugh Morton, Jr., helped organize, and it raised about $20,000. Michael played one hole with each of 18 foursomes, and my assignment was to ride with Michael and make a photograph of him with each of the foursomes, who later received prints. When we arrived at the 18th hole we found a television crew with cue cards and a bunch of little boys ready to be filmed with Michael in a public service spot for the Heart Fund. I saw the word "cardiovascular" on the cue cards, not part of my normal vocabulary, and I said, "Michael, won't you have trouble with that word?" He looked straight at me with a twinkle in his eye and said, "Mr. Morton, you've got to remember, I graduated from Carolina. I didn't go to State."

There are many who believe Michael Jordan is the best basketball player in the world, so it was startling to be talking with NBC's basketball analyst Al McGuire and hear him say, "Michael is a better person than he is a ball player. There are qualities in Michael that people are not aware of, because all they see is the Nike shoe eight feet above the floor, the dollars, and so on. When you strip all that away, and you take a walk with him on the golf course for three or four holes, you'll find out he's a beautiful guy."

Michael Jordan's UNC coach, Dean Smith, says, "I can't imagine the improvement yearly from his junior year in high school, it's just remarkable. You have a tremendously talented individual in athletic ability. Now you couple that with an amazing determination to get better. Then you put with that an unbelievable competitive spirit, and that's what you see as a basketball player. He was raised right by his parents, and then he chose to do what he was supposed to as far as going to school and working very hard academically. He took equal pride in his academic work as he did in basketball."

Buzz Peterson, Jordan's college roommate and UNC best friend, says, "If anybody ever lived a dream life wanting to grow up to go through college and win the national championship, play on the Olympic team, and have fame and fortune in the NBA, Michael's lived it. He's lived the perfect life. But he's the same guy, he's the same person. He has not changed a bit."

Lou Bello, ex-referee now radio newsman, says, "Michael puts out 100 percent, and of course he has the God-given ability that he can do things other mere mortals cannot do, a 360 in the air, a backward dunk. Then of course the fellow is so nice, so pleasant. He recognizes you. A lot of guys go on to great fame. They don't remember referees, they don't remember friends, they don't remember people. Michael's got that smile and handshake. I think he enjoys being alive, being an American citizen."

On the subject of remembering people, Buzz Peterson was injured and out for the season in his and Jordan's sophomore year at UNC. Coach Smith would not allow the players to visit Peterson's hospital room. Carolina was to play Villanova on television, and Jordan phoned the hospital room to advise Buzz that he would wear a wrist band high on his arm, just below the elbow, saying, "The wrist band lets you know I'm thinking about you." Peterson was deeply touched as he watched the game on television. He is even more moved now, six years later, because Jordan still wears the wrist band just below the elbow, and it still honors his ex-roommate. Hundreds of high school players around the nation, and some college players, can be seen wearing wrist bands just below the elbow, just because Michael Jordan does it. Few, if any, realize that they are joining in paying tribute to Buzz Peterson, assistant basketball coach, Appalachian State University.

Bobby Jones of Charlotte, former All-America at Chapel Hill and standout for the Philadelphia Seventy-Sixers in the NBA, says, "Michael is a very special athlete. He is a man who has been gifted with unique abilities. I have played against a lot of ball players who can jump high and run fast, and do all the different things, but he has a combination of quickness and jumping ability, and intelligence on the court, that is very, very rare. I played against him two years in the NBA. Really, every time we played against him we would have somebody pick him up at half court, and the coach would say, 'after he beats that guy, then somebody else will go get him, and after he beats him, the third guy will come and run after him.' We in effect would triple team him, and would not have any success. Michael is a player who comes out every night and plays his hardest. He plays above the rim, and wants to win. People say he is a great offensive player, but his defense is outstanding also. He led the league in steals at his position, had a tremendous amount of blocked shots, and plays an all around game which a lot of people overlook." (Note: Jordan was named the 1988 NBA Defensive Player of the Year.)

The world may not have seen a more highly disciplined athlete than Michael Jordan. He sets goals for himself, then goes about doing exactly what he has plans to do. As of the early part of 1988, the athletic plan remained as it had been for a couple of years. Michael intends to play basketball for eight more years, and by that time he believes he will be good enough at golf to join the PGA tour. That is the plan. That is what he is working toward. Buzz Peterson, just returned from visiting Jordan and his parents in Chicago, says, "I tell you this, he loves the game of golf. He loves it. He has every athletic ability to play it. I have played with him every summer since he has been gone, and he has improved so much each year. This time I played with him at Briarwood Country Club, one of the hardest courses in Chicago. He shot a legit 75 on a tough golf course. To be a good golfer I believe you have to play every day. When he gets through with basketball, it's going to take him a year or two. Curtiss Strange is helping him, and it has really improved his game a lot. If he gets it in his mind to do it, he'll do it. He is so competitive. He's getting better, there is no doubt."

If Jordan winds up with anything near the $28 million contract mentioned in an April 1988 Associated Press article, some of the thousands of his fans fear it could lead to his ruin. Buzz Peterson does not see it that way. He keeps saying it is the same old Michael as when they entered UNC together in 1981. Peterson's fears for Jordan are not drugs and alcohol, for he says Michael will not even drink a beer. Peterson says, "I tell you one thing, I would rather ride in a car with an 85-year-old blind lady driving than ride with Michael. I cannot stand the way he drives. He drives too fast. Something is going to happen. He's going to have a bad accident if he doesn't slow down."

Peterson's visit with Jordan in Chicago was during the 1988 NBA playoff series between Michael's Bulls and Brad Daughtery's Cleveland Cavaliers. At UNC Peterson had roomed two years with Jordan and one year with Daugherty, which made the games extremely interesting to Buzz. Ron Harper, starting guard for Cleveland, was injured and did not play Thursday night, so Jordan, who scored 51 points, was guarded by Craig Ehlo. Harper was quoted in the paper Friday, according to Buzz, as saying that he would not let Jordan score 50 points on him on Sunday. *continued*

Michael Jordan takes to the air over Larry Bird and Robert Parrish of the Boston Celtics. Gene Banks, Chicago team mate and former Duke star, is beneath the basket.

Coach Dean Smith, always looking out for his players, consulted Jack Nicklaus for advice on how Michael Jordan might sufficiently improve in golf to join the PGA tour following his basketball career. The Golden Bear recommended that Jordan's whole golf game be thoroughly analyzed at the high-tech Jack Nicklaus Academy of Golf at Grand Cypress resort as a first step toward achieving the basketball star's goal.

Three of North Carolina's starting five on the 1982 NCAA National Championship team—James Worthy, Michael Jordan, and Sam Perkins—are among the top players in the NBA, while Jimmy Black is in coaching and Matt Doherty is a stockbroker, Worthy, Jordan, and Perkins treasure their friendship developed at Carolina, but when Los Angeles, Chicago, or Dallas meet each other on a NBA court, no Tar Heel spares the other in the effort to win.

The original Air Jordan shoes, the footwear that almost every kid in the country longs for, launched Michael Jordan toward his basketball and business success. Dean Smith helped Michael arrange his original connection with the Pro-Serv, Inc., business agents, and Smith monitored the situation to make sure his former star was treated fairly.

Buzz Peterson

Jordan is also friends with Otis Wilson, linebacker with the Chicago Bears football team, and just before the Sunday Bulls—Cavaliers game Wilson called to Jordan, "get my jersey for me, Michael." (Wilson's jersey is 55.) Although it was almost an impossible goal, 55 became the magic number Jordan hoped to achieve, and he told Peterson, "When you see me lick my chops, you know I'm on my way." Harper, the Cleveland guard, could not contain Jordan, and as the game drew closer to the buzzer, Peterson said Jordan made two jumpers in a row, turned and looked to him on the sidelines, then "licked his chops." With two seconds left in the game, Jordan turned to Otis Wilson in the stands, spread the fingers of one hand twice, signaling 55. Ron Harper was exactly right. Jordan did not score 50 points on him. He scored 55, and Chicago won the game. As quickly as they could make it to the golf course, Buzz Peterson, Otis Wilson, and Michael Jordan had an extremely happy 18-hole round together, but that time nobody scored 55. *HMM*

Michael Jordan—Tar Heel

Michael Jordan knows that anyone who played basketball at Chapel Hill is bound to be a friend, even when it is the opposing coach of the Philadelphia Seventy-Sixers, Billy Cunningham.

Michael Jordan—Olympian

Michael Jordan—Chicago Bull

Everyone who knows Michael Jordan gives credit to his mother, Deloris, and his father, James, for bringing him up right. They are a devoted family. His parents are firm in their belief that Michael knows right from wrong, and that he will remain a model citizen in spite of the pressures of success. Deloris has difficulty not crying when she mentions Michael giving her his Olympic Gold Medal.

Clyde Roark Hoey, senior United States Senator from North Carolina, looks up, with his genial smile, from reading his mail at his Washington office. Dressed in his customary cutaway coat, wing collar, cravat, flower in his lapel, Clyde Hoey was perhaps the last of his generation in North Carolina politics. The photograph was made for the cover of *The State* magazine, one of a series of North Carolina elected officials. A tall, courtly man, noted for his skillful oratory, he was one of the state's most popular elected officials. While serving as governor, he would usually leave his office in the Capitol each day at 10:00 a.m. for a stroll down Fayetteville Street to a nearby drugstore for a Coca-Cola, his favorite beverage.

CLYDE R. HOEY
Courtly Governor, U.S. Senator

Clyde Roark Hoey got his start early in life as a printer's devil in Shelby. He quickly learned the trade and became owner of a small newspaper, *The Cleveland Star*. Not content with this success, Hoey read law, as it was done in those days, and with little formal education but plenty of hard work and intelligence he became an attorney. Later he served in the House and Senate of the North Carolina General Assembly.

Clyde Hoey was representative of an era when state political leaders were, primarily, achievers and leaders in their vocations who were also active in political affairs. He was recognized as an outstanding attorney, leader in community and state affairs, Baptist layman and, not to be overlooked, brother-in-law of O. Max Gardner, former governor and leader of the formidable "Shelby dynasty."

Young people seeking careers in politics or elective office were usually advised to make their mark first in their vocation, become active in the dominant Democratic Party and hope that their labors and contributions would be noted and rewarded later.

When Hoey campaigned for governor in 1936 North Carolina was gripped, like the rest of the nation, by the Great Depression. Times were hard, jobs were scarce and Hoey spoke often of better, brighter days ahead. An effective campaigner, Hoey had an unusual gift of oratory and folksy humor. For example, he would tell the story of the old man who believed in an everlasting heaven but not an everlasting hell. Why not hell? The man said, "I don't believe a man's constitution could stand it!"

As governor, Hoey proved to be a sound manager of state funds and programs. He supported free textbooks for elementary schools, a 30 percent increase in expenditures for public schools, an expanded highway system and a state advertising program to attract tourists and industry to North Carolina.

After completing his term as governor, Hoey returned to the practice of law until 1945 when he was elected to the United States Senate and served there with distinction until his death May 12, 1954 at age 76. *ELR*

President Harry S Truman came to Raleigh on October 19, 1948 to participate in ceremonies for the unveiling of a large monument to the three presidents North Carolina has given the nation. A huge crowd filled Capitol Square to witness the event and the President greeted them with a wave of his hat. Others shown (left to right) are Willis Smith of Raleigh, program chairman; Kenneth Royall, Secretary of War; Governor R. Gregg Cherry; and Clyde R. Hoey, senior United States Senator, who helped arrange for the Truman visit.

A state-owned and operated port facility was a long-time dream of Wilmington and southeastern North Carolina. When the General Assembly approved a State Ports Authority, Senator Hoey attended the dedication of the new state facility representing President Truman who could not attend. Shown standing on the dock at Wilmington are (left to right) former U.S. Senator William B. Umstead, Senator Hoey, Director George Ross of the State Department of Conservation and Development and Governor W. Kerr Scott, who also actively supported the port project.

The Carolina Motor Club, AAA Affiliate for North Carolina and South Carolina, cherishes this photograph of its emblem gracing Governor Hoey's official limousine in 1940. From the look of the bumper and tag it is obvious that the governor did not acquire a new limousine every other year as governors did later.

'CARBINE' WILLIAMS PREPARES TO TEST FIRE

In October 1950 Collier's Magazine assigned me to go to Godwin, N.C., to photograph Marshall Williams, who invented guns. The assignment editor said to be sure to take pictures of Williams standing in the doorway of his workshop, test firing one of his guns into the cotton field out back. That is all I was told, and when Williams picked up a standard U.S. Army Carbine to test fire, I said, "No, Mr. Williams, not that Army Carbine, I want you with one of your guns." He gave me a withering stare and said, "I invented it." The story ran in the March 3, 1951 issue, and only then did I learn that David Marshall "Carbine" Williams was a national hero for inventing the Carbine while serving a prison sentence because a revenue officer was killed in a raid on a whiskey still said to be owned by Marshall Williams. Williams was a firearms genius who held dozens of patents, and although hardened by prison, he was fiercely loyal to the United States government responsible for his confinement. The Carbine was one of the main small arms weapons used by the United States in World War II. Williams is holding one of the many other guns he invented. *HMM*

UTILITY LEADER FOR WHOM LAKE NORMAN WAS NAMED
Norman A. Cocke (center), shown with his wife Mary, was one of North Carolina's great citizens. As President of Duke Power Company, Chairman of the Board of the Duke University Board of Trustees, and as Trustee of the Morehead Foundation at Chapel Hill, he played an important role in the state's progress for 50 years. Lake Norman, largest lake in the state, is named for Norman Cocke. One day I had opportunity to photograph Mr. and Mrs. Cocke at the Linville Golf Club with their house guest, Charles E. Wilson (left), President of the General Electric Company. The two men wore caps that were casting bad shadows on their faces, so I decided to use a flash bulb to fill the shadow. Thankfully the bulbs in my case were GE bulbs, and I called it to the attention of Mr. Wilson, who responded, "Yes, son, and there's nothing better but God's own sunlight." *HMM*

The intense Wake Forest coach follows the action in a game with the University of North Carolina at Chapel Hill. Shown behind him are Red O'Quinn (No. 30) and Tom Fetzer (suit). Wallace Wade of Duke University, another legendary coach, recommended Peahead for the job at Wake Forest. Coach Walker stayed 14 years, earned a record of 77 wins, 51 losses, six ties, and was inducted into the North Carolina Sports Hall of Fame in 1968.

'PEAHEAD' WALKER
The Deacon Giant Killer

Rarely has a football coach in North Carolina captured more attention and respect of sports fans and sportswriters than Douglas Clyde (Peahead) Walker who directed the football program at Wake Forest College (now University) for 14 years.

As the head coach of the small Baptist school, Peahead was often described as "The Deacon Giant Killer" because he had a habit of kicking the daylights out of such powerhouses as Duke, Tennessee, Georgia and North Carolina. He delighted in the role of being a David among the Goliaths of the Southern Conference.

The late sportswriter Bob Quincy was correct when he wrote: "It is difficult to chronicle Walker in one story. He actually plays the role of two individuals; D.C. Walker, a serious, demanding and creative student of football; and, a man with a drawl, a rakish smile and a ready witticism for the subject of the moment.

"...Walker was a man of many moods. He could pose as a banker in his dark, smartly tailored suits. He would also be perfectly at home down on a Charleston wharf teaching old salts a thing or two about how to get the most out of their vocabulary. Foremost, he is a man's man and worthy of a chapter in any history written about the game of football."

William Friday, UNC president emeritus, relates this story about Coach Walker and the North Carolina Tar Heels. It was Wake Forest's last game when they had to face Charlie Justice, the great Carolina back. Playing on their home field, the Deacons could not stop Justice and were losing. Late in the game Wake pursuers tackled Justice out of bounds and pushed him into a concrete wall. Justice was not injured and the Tar Heels went on to win the game.

Several days later, Friday and Billy Carmichael, the UNC controller, were dining in a Raleigh cafeteria when they saw Peahead across the room. Carmichael, an ardent Carolina fan and close friend of Justice, went over to Walker and complained, in a playful way, about the out-of-bounds tackle. Peahead listened calmly and replied, "You have no cause to complain, Mr. Carmichael. It was the only time all day we put a hand on him."

Dick Herbert, former sports editor of *The News & Observer*, Raleigh, and a close friend of the Deacon coach, recalls that in Peahead's last year at Wake Forest the Deacons were undefeated for the season, with only arch rival Clemson to be played. In the closing minutes of this crucial game, Wake had a second down on the Tigers' four-yard line and had a perfect season almost within its grasp. The Deacon quarterback, who was calling the plays, called a pass, which was intercepted and Clemson went on to win 7-6. What did Peahead Walker, noted for his volcanic temper, say when his quarterback came to the sidelines? Only "Why didn't you quick kick?" *continued*

41

After a season in which Walker defeated Wally Butts of Georgia, Wallace Wade of Duke and Colonel Bob Neyland of Tennessee, the Deacon coach asked Jim Weaver, the athletic director, for a raise. He was making $7,500 a year. Weaver indicated he thought Peahead deserved a significant raise. However, President Harold Tribble demurred, finally agreeing to an $800 increase. Walker resigned, accepted a coaching position with Herman Hickman at Yale . . . and the Wake Forest football program slid into a decline.

At Yale, the coach found a very different environment. "We didn't have scholarship boys," he told Bob Quincy. "Most of our players had more spending money than Herman (Hickman) and I drew in salaries. When I wanted a man to center the ball in practice, I'd politely suggest, 'Mr. Van Swank, please assume the pivot position.' " Quincy said that at Wake Forest the coach would have bellowed, "Get the hell over the ball." Peahead left Yale to coach the Montreal Alouettes of the Canadian Football League for eight seasons.

The legendary Douglas Clyde (Peahead) Walker, who could always spot promising football talent, closed out his career serving as a scout for the New York Giants of the National Football League. He lived in Charlotte and traveled widely for the Giants until his death in 1970.

ELR

A clowning Frank Howard, football coach of the Clemson University Tigers, models (left) a toupee lifted, without permission, from Bobby Batson at a conference party. The balding Frank Howard, long-time friendly foe of Peahead Walker, is at right. The two coaches were headliners at sports-related dinners where they kept the audiences laughing with their friendly insults and stories. Here's a typical exchange: *Howard*—"I remember you as a boy in Alabama. You didn't have an underwear change then, and two-tone shoes to you were a pair of black brogans with red clay on the soles." *Walker*—"I often wondered why Mrs. Howard accompanied her husband on all his trips. Then I found out why. He is so ugly she'd rather go with him than have to kiss him goodbye."

A gathering of football coaches in the Atlantic Coast Conference enjoys a yarn by Coach Jim Tatum of Maryland. They are (left to right) Peahead Walker, Wake Forest; Beattie Feathers, N. C. State; Tatum; Wallace Wade, Duke; George Barclay, Crowell Little and Carl Snavely, all North Carolina. Barclay and Little were assistants to Snavely. Coach Wade was one of Peahead's lifelong heroes. Wade built a 110-36-7 record, coaching the Blue Devils from 1931 to 1941 and 1946 through 1950. He coached two Duke teams into the Rose Bowl, and brought the 1942 game to Durham, when large crowds were discouraged on the West Coast for fear of a Japanese attack.

Quarterback Tom Fetzer listens carefully to Coach Walker during a practice session. Peahead's reputation for using fiery language with his players caused some concern at the Baptist college. When questions were asked at a campus meeting of Baptist ministers during football season, a small committee was sent to the practice field to discover the truth of such allegations. The committee hid behind some bushes, observed what took place and returned with its report. "Well, did the coach use curse words?" they were asked. "Yes, he did," was the reply, "and if you had seen how the team played, you would have cursed, too!"

One of Coach Walker's greatest talents was the ability to evaluate raw talent and recruit these young men to play at Wake Forest. John Polanski (left), a powerful fullback, was a typical example of the talent that Peahead brought to his school from Pennsylvania and other northeastern states. Coach Frank Howard of Clemson would say, "Peahead runs his recruits through the woods. Those big enough to run straight over trees, he put in the line. Those who ran around trees, he put in the backfield." Polanski probably could have done both.

Coach Peahead Walker of Wake Forest and Coach Jim Tatum of UNC (former coach at Maryland) swap stories at a meeting with sportswriters. In earlier years Peahead and Tatum had played minor league baseball together for Snow Hill in the Coastal Plains League. A playing manager, Peahead said he would have gladly traded Tatum for a beagle hound and two pairs of wool socks, but nobody wanted him. In 1959, Jim Tatum recruited Jesse Jackson to be UNC's first black football player, but the confusion following Tatum's unexpected death that summer led to Jackson enrolling at North Carolina A&T in Greesnboro. It was eight years later that Ricky Lanier became the first UNC black football player.

Douglas Clyde (Peahead) Walker, who coached football at Wake Forest in the 1940s, came to Wake at a salary of $4,000 a year and had the smallest athletic budget in the Big Four (others: North Carolina, N.C. State and Duke). But what he lacked in budget and staff he made up with hard work and an unrelenting drive for perfection in play. A tough, demanding coach, Walker worked his players so hard at practice that they looked forward, with relief, to Saturday and only having to face their opponents.

Another famous Wake Forest coach was Horace (Bones) McKinney, who directed the Deacon basketball program for 13 years. He is shown at the 1942 Southern Conference Tournament where, as a member of the victorious N.C. State Wolfpack, he was named to the All-Tournament team. The tournament was played before a packed house of 3,200 people at Raleigh Memorial Auditorium. While McKinney was head coach, the Deacons won the 1959 Dixie Classic, the ACC championships in 1961 and 1962 and played for the ACC championship five straight years. McKinney's record as a player may never be matched for variety: Durham High School (won 69 consecutive games), N.C. State (named to All-Southern Conference team as sophomore), UNC-Chapel Hill (member of 1946 team, runner-up for national championship), four years with Washington Caps, NBA, and two years with Boston Celtics (All-Pro two years). Best known in recent years for his witty color commentary on ACC basketball telecasts, McKinney was inducted into the North Carolina Sports Hall of Fame in 1971, and into the Wake Forest University Sports Hall of Fame in 1973.

The Governor of North Carolina is expected to attend and participate in many events and activities in the life of the state. Governor Broughton is shown speaking during halftime at the University of North Carolina—University of South Carolina football game at Kenan Stadium, Chapel Hill, in 1942. The young men, shown with their dates, are (left) Truman M. Hobbs, then president of the student body who later became a Federal judge in Alabama, and J. Stevenson Peck (right) who was then president of the University Club and later became a prominent banker in Maryland.

J. M. BROUGHTON
Raleigh's First Governor, U.S. Senator

The first member of his family came to Wake County a century before James Melville Broughton was born November 17, 1888 in Raleigh. The son of a prominent businessman, young Broughton had the advantage of growing up in a well-established family with many community ties. A Raleigh senior high school is named after his uncle, Needham B. Broughton.

Broughton graduated from Wake Forest College, studied law at Wake Forest and attended Harvard Law School. Although best known as an accomplished attorney with a large law practice, Broughton earlier worked briefly as a school principal in Franklin County and as a staff reporter on the *Winston-Salem Journal.*

Active in civic, political and religious life of Raleigh and the state, he served as school board member, city attorney, state senator, president of the Wake and State Bar Associations and was the keynote speaker at the Democratic state convention in 1936. An active Baptist layman, he taught a men's Bible class regularly for 25 years.

Before Governor Broughton had completed his first year in office, the Japanese attack on Pearl Harbor brought the U.S. into World War II. State government was called upon to assume an important role in the war effort and to organize its civilian defense system.

Early in his administration Governor and Mrs. Broughton attended the commissioning of the U.S.S. *North Carolina* (B.B. 55). They brought to the great battleship the historic, magnificent silver service from the State of North Carolina which had been used on an earlier battleship named after the state, and also on the U.S.S. *Raleigh*, a cruiser which made a good-will cruise around the world. The silver service had been returned to the executive mansion in 1930 and remained in use there until the new B.B. 55 was commissioned in 1941. (See Chapter 17).

There was excellent cooperation between Broughton and members of the General Assembly of 1941 and 1943, and all his major recommendations were approved and enacted into law.

Broughton was a popular chief executive, an able speaker and traveled widely across North Carolina attending public events large and small. During his term he was invited to speak to major events in more than 15 states. At the 1944 Democratic National Convention in Chicago, the governor was nominated as a candidate for Vice President of the United States and of the 16 nominees finished sixth on the first ballot.

Following success in the Democratic primary and fall election, Broughton began a full term of six years on January 3, 1949 as North Carolina's junior United States Senator. He looked forward with joy and enthusiasm to many years of service in that powerful legislative body. Unfortunately, he died suddenly on March 6, only 63 days after taking office, at age 60. *ELR*

Joseph Melville Broughton, the first Raleigh native to occupy the executive mansion, had the difficult task of leading North Carolina during World War II. A tall, impressive figure, Broughton was a popular governor, receiving the largest vote ever given a candidate for governor at that time in the history of the State. The state government was called upon to assume an important part in the war effort while at the same time reducing its own program of construction and keeping any expansion to a minimum. All major recommendations made by the Governor to the General Assembly were approved, including State support for extending the public school term from eight to nine months, and in adding the 12th grade.

As wartime governor, Broughton was faced with many national priorities impacting on state government. In February 1942, he attended a state-wide conference on "The Classroom Teacher in the Emergency" at Chapel Hill. Conference leaders shown are (left to right) *front row:* Dr. Donald DuShane, Washington, D.C., Mrs. Annie Laurie McDonald, Hickory, the Governor, State Superintendent of Public Instruction Clyde A. Erwin, Mrs. Mae Campbell; *back row:* T. S. Johnson, Raleigh, Mrs. Helen Smith, Rocky Mount, Dr. J. Henry Highsmith, Sidney Marsh, Dr. T. E. Browne, John Lang, all of Raleigh. (Photo identification courtesy the research of Dr. Charles F. Carroll, retired State Superintendent of Public Instruction.)

'The Governor Is Going To Let Me Go Down'

The young newspaper reporter stood quietly in a cell on death row listening intently to farewell remarks by a condemned felon. Convicted of the brutal murder of his wife, the prisoner was scheduled to die in the gas chamber at Central Prison, Raleigh, the next morning.

Speaking from his cell to other death row inmates he could not see, the prisoner calmly said, "The governor is going to let me go down. I hope you fellows have better luck." Words of encouragement were called out from the other cells. It was the evening religious service held before an execution, and the prison chaplain closed the service with a prayer.

The prison warden had allowed the newsman to attend the service because he was assigned to cover the prisoner's execution. The subsequent newspaper story, which made front page of *The News & Observer*, included an earlier in-depth interview with the prisoner, quoted his farewell message and described in graphic detail his execution in the gas chamber.

The following day the reporter was summoned to the governor's office for a heart-to-heart talk with Governor Broughton. Obviously troubled by what he had read, the governor patiently explained his legal responsibilities as chief executive, how he decided on whether to intervene in death cases, and how difficult it was to make these decisions. It was Broughton's first year in office, and may have been his first death case to consider.

"Your story was well done for your readers," the governor said, shaking his head, "but it certainly does not make my job any easier." *ELR*

Mrs. Eleanor Roosevelt, the peripatetic First Lady and popular speaker on college campuses, addresses students at the University of North Carolina at Chapel Hill. (She received an honorary degree there in 1935. Her husband, President Franklin Delano Roosevelt, had to wait until 1938 for his UNC honorary degree). Shown on the platform (left to right) are Louis Harris, a student who became a famous political pollster, an unidentified student, Dr. Frank P. Graham, University President, and Governor and Mrs. Broughton. Alice Willson Broughton, the First Lady of North Carolina, often traveled with her husband. She was an attractive, charming and intelligent woman who kept the Executive Mansion a busy center of entertainment and warm hospitality.

'The Prisoner Is A Baptist'

In earlier years, prominent church or denominational affiliation was considered a valuable asset for gubernatorial candidates. Governor Broughton, for example, was an active Baptist layman and leader in the state and Southern Baptist conventions.

Broughton was meeting one day in his office with a delegation seeking parole for a state prisoner. Each visitor identified himself as a minister and requested leniency for the prisoner. When all had been heard, the Governor noted that the ministers represented major Protestant faiths—Methodist, Presbyterian, Lutheran and Episcopal. "Who," he asked with a smile, "represents my church, the Baptists?"

"The prisoner does, your Excellency," came the reply. "He is a Baptist." *ELR*

JEFFERSON-PILOT
Life Insurance Leader, TV Pioneer

Grady Cole, WBT Radio's greatest star (and money maker), was an original, laid-back performer who dominated the morning air waves for over 25 years. "He talked *with* people . . . not at them," says Charles H. Crutchfield, "and listeners believed in him and whatever he was selling. He was the most unpredictably intelligent man I've ever known. And he was a genius for knowing and understanding politics inside out. I got much credit for building this company, but I think Grady Cole is the guy who really built this company. We made more money from 5-9 a.m. with him than we did the rest of the day and night." Cole retired from his show in 1961 to become assistant general manager.

In the past 80 years a small, home-grown life insurance company has become the mighty Jefferson-Pilot Corporation, a powerful force in life insurance, financial services, news and broadcast management and public service. Its leaders have been a parade of prominent businessmen, including P.D. Gold, Charles W. Gold, Albert G. Myers, George A. Grimsley, Julian Price, Joseph M. Bryan and Howard "Chick" Holderness.

Since 1967 the company's leader has been W. Roger Soles, whose brilliant performance as president and chief executive officer has propelled Jeff-Pilot to the most rapid expansion in its history. A farm boy from Columbus County and a World War II combat veteran, Soles has spent his entire business career with the company. He joined the securities department in 1947 following graduation from UNC-Chapel Hill.

Jefferson Standard pioneered in providing capital funds to newspapers, and later to broadcast properties. Julian Price and Joe Bryan believed that good management judgment, editorial acumen and favorable markets could qualify a newspaper property as a good earning risk. Before World War II, Jefferson Standard became a chief source of financial backing for newspapers.

Since acquiring WBT/WBTV, its flagship broadcast operations, Jeff-Pilot has purchased and operates television and radio stations in many states, a production company and a computer services company. Jefferson-Pilot Broadcasting is known nationwide for the quality of its management, programming, news and public service. *ELR*

W. Roger Soles is a man who clearly knows how to manage a giant life insurance company—and most successfully. A recent business magazine article headlined, "Sailing with The Pilot, you'll find Roger Soles at the wheel." It has been Roger Soles' skilled, talented and powerful hands guiding The Jefferson-Pilot Corporation as president and chief executive officer since 1967. Noted for his keen financial judgment, Soles provided key financial analyses in earlier years to President Julian Price and Senior Vice President Joseph M. Bryan encouraging them to increase Jefferson Standard investments in news media companies which led to the purchase of WBT Radio and WBTV in Charlotte and other media properties.

WBT Radio chose Ty Boyd to fill the large void left when Grady Cole left the air for a management position at the station. "When I took his seat at WBT, I felt mighty small," Boyd says. "No one ever filled his footprints — or could." A youthful and fresh talent, Boyd attracted his own audience, became a major on-the-air personality at WBTV and stayed 14 years. He left in 1978 to form his own company in Charlotte, and now speaks before 120 audiences a year across the U.S. and world.

Howard Holderness led Jefferson Standard as president for 17 years (1950-67) and the company achieved startling growth, tripling in size. Known as "Chick" to all, Holderness had served for many years as vice president and treasurer before taking the presidency. He recalls the early years when he married his wife, Adelaide Fortune, "I was making $3,600 a year—and got an increase of $50 per month for being married." The son of George A. Holderness, a vice president and member of the Board of Directors of Jefferson Standard, Chick Holderness grew up in a company environment. He also served as a director of Burlington Industries, Duke Power Company and other major North Carolina corporations. In 1984 the Board of Governors of the University of North Carolina presented Mr. and Mrs. Holderness with the University Award, its highest honor.

While Charles H. Crutchfield is intensely proud of the commercial success of WBT/WBTV during his 44 years there, he also likes to recall other achievements in public service:

—With the help of Coach Wallace Wade of Duke University, WBT Radio convinced the Southern Conference to permit the first play-by-play radio coverage of its football games. The schools feared that fans would stay at home to listen and not fill the stadium seats as paying customers. Crutchfield was the first play-by-play announcer for those games.

—Postmaster Jim Farley named Charlotte Postmaster Paul Younts to promote Air Mail Week. When Younts asked WBT to help, Crutchfield gained national and international attention by having his staff fly around the world recording messages of good will from world leaders. The historic recording disc, now in gold, is in the Library of Congress.

—At request of State Department, Crutchfield went to Greece for four months in 1951 to set up a radio network and improve U.S. broadcasting into this critical region.

—He was one of 48 American businessmen who toured the Soviet Union in 1956 to promote good relations between the U.S. and Soviet Union. As result of this trip, and after listening to effectiveness of Soviet English-language propaganda, he initiated a weekly radio program, Radio Moscow, to refute the Soviet propaganda. Written and produced by Alan Newcomb and Rupert Gillette, the program attracted a large audience, won prestigious awards and was syndicated nationally in 1960.

—When H. Ross Perot led a national campaign to send food and medicine to U.S. prisoners in North Vietnam, Jeff-Pilot Broadcasting supported the effort so successfully that WBTV received 175,000 letters in its "Write Hanoi" campaign. Crutchfield flew staff to Paris with the letters, and they tried to deliver the letters to the North Vietnam embassy. When this effort was rejected at the main gate, the WBTV staff quickly obtained a ladder, climbed to the top of the embassy wall and dumped all 175,000 letters into the embassy courtyard. Cmdr. Paul E. Galanti, USN, one of the U.S. prisoners, later wrote Crutchfield that WBTV had participated in "probably the most magnificent propaganda effort in U.S. history . . . you got the Communists' attention . . . and I feel strongly that the campaign helped tremendously to bring us home."

—U.S. Senator Sam J. Ervin, Jr. said that Crutchfield "familiarized the nation with the seriousness of the crime problem by telecasting his own comments upon it, and by dramatizing Jenkin Lloyd Jones' eloquent oration 'Weep for the Innocent.' By making a special telecast in Washington, D.C. of these comments and this oration to members of the United States Senate, he did much to secure the enactment of 'The Omnibus Safe Streets and Crime Act of 1968.'"

—Crutchfield chaired the radio/television committee to gain public support for the Governor's Committee for Public School Amendment (The Pearsall Plan) in 1956. It passed with an overwhelming margin of approval. *ELR*

Joseph M. Bryan, whose life could be described as an American epic, likes to dig in early and start something of value. He has been doing it for most of his 90 plus years. In 1961 he retired after 30 years as a senior executive with Jeff-Pilot. Before joining the insurance company he fought in World War I, rode horseback in Haiti as a cotton trader, made a success in the New York cotton exchange and then met Kathleen Price, daughter of President Julian Price of Jefferson Standard. They were married in 1927 and Joe Bryan joined the company in 1931. The Bryans have been generous benefactors to the City of Greensboro, to cultural and youth organizations and to programs at many colleges and universities in North Carolina.

When Jefferson Standard purchased WBT Radio, Charlotte, in 1945, Charles H. Crutchfield, 33, was employed as general manager. This decision launched Crutchfield on a 44-year career there in broadcasting and telecasting, which included serving as president of Jefferson-Pilot Broadcasting for 14 years. Under his talented leadership, WBT became a 24-hour operation, WBT-AM was signed on, WBTV made its debut (1949) and its power was increased to 100,000 watts, and innovative programming and public service reached national and international audiences. As head of a strong affiliate, Crutchfield, who held equally strong opinions, did not hesitate to battle the CBS network and CBS News on many public and broadcast issues over the years. He retired in 1977.

Following duty in the U.S. Marines in World War II, Wallace Jorgenson applied for a network position in the Chicago sales office of the Columbia Broadcasting System. Before going into service his only experience had been with a small radio station in Minnesota. CBS told Jorgenson that he needed more work experience, that he could get it by working for a smaller affiliate station, and informed him that WBT, Charlotte, had an opening. He won the job as a local sales rep for $75 per week—and never went back. After working his way up through the management ranks, Jorgenson was named president of Jefferson-Pilot Broadcasting in 1978. Active in community, state and national affairs, he began reading WBTV's editorials on the air in 1983 because the opinions had more impact when delivered by the president of the company. In 1987 he was elected president of the National Association of Broadcasters.

Lee Kirby (left), popular announcer and commentator, interviews
Mayor Phil Van Every of Charlotte during an early public service
telecast at WBTV. Kirby came to Charlotte aboard a special train ex-
hibiting pharmaceutical products, serving as host and announcer.
Charlie Crutchfield liked his appearance and voice and hired him as a
staff announcer.

The original Arthur Smith group of musicians and entertainers, with
Clyde "Cloudy" McLean serving as announcer. Beginning in 1943 as
"Arthur Smith and his Cracker-Jacks," the group quickly became an
all-time headliner for WBT Radio and WBTV. Shown (left to right)
are Arthur Smith, Brother Ralph Smith, Clyde McLean, Sonny Smith,
Tommy Faile and Don Reno. A talented musician and composer,
Smith captured national fame with two of his compositions: *Guitar
Boogie* and *Dueling Banjos*. Charlie Crutchfield, who had announced
for The Briarhoppers for years, says Smith had "the common touch
with people in the Carolinas . . . and was one of the station's best assets." McLean went on to become one of the station's best-known and
most popular weathermen.

If you like the television coverage of ACC basketball, here are the people most responsible for the delivery of this popular sports programming. Shown (left to right) at the ACC Tournament in Greensboro are Dee Ray, president of Raycom, Inc., James G. Babb, executive vice president of Jefferson-Pilot Communications Company, and Rick Ray, CEO of Raycom. The Rays are married and their company is now in its 10th season of sports/entertainment productions. Jeff Pilot and Raycom, Inc., have been in a joint venture since 1982 to produce and market ACC basketball games. A 32-year veteran with WBTV, Charlotte, Jim Babb has many more responsibilities than basketball coverage. He has operational responsibility for Jeff-Pilot Communications' 16 divisions in Charlotte, Atlanta, Richmond, Denver, Miami, San Diego, Memphis and New York City. The operations include television and radio stations, TV syndication, sports news network and computer software services.

MARSHALL & WESTMORELAND
World Class Generals

In the past 50 years, the two largest and most costly wars in which the United States took part were World War II and the Vietnam War. And the two generals who headed the nation's Armies in those wars were men with strong North Carolina ties.

General of the Army George C. Marshall was Chief of Staff of the U.S. Army in World War II. Later he was Secretary of Defense, and helped lead the economic recovery of Western Europe by formulating the history-making Marshall Plan while serving as Secretary of State.

General William C. Westmoreland, former Commanding General of Fort Bragg, was the senior United States military officer in the Vietnam War. Since retirement he has devoted much of his time seeking proper recognition for the servicemen and servicewomen who fought in that bitter, costly and difficult conflict.

Even in World War II, when overwhelming public support for the war effort limited criticism of U.S. military leaders, very few of them escaped the editorial barbs of *Time* magazine. The miniature overseas edition I read as a serviceman in the Pacific kept me in touch with the news magazine. If my memory is correct, General Marshall was the only U.S. or Allied leader covered in depth by *Time* who received only the highest accolades for the performance of his duties.

In my opinion, General Marshall was the leading hero of the World War II era, and the accolades and honors received before and after his death are well deserved. Following retirement from his several distinguished careers, General and Mrs. Marshall settled in Pinehurst, much to the delight of North Carolinians. The residents of Pinehurst welcomed their neighbors and respected their desire for privacy. However, the Marshalls were friendly people who frequently took part in Pinehurst community activities when they were in town. As might be expected of a retired General of the Army and Secretary of State, Marshall was often called to Washington for consultations.

The Azalea Festival in Wilmington, in its second year, was fortunate to have General and Mrs. Marshall as guests of honor. Although Mrs. Marshall needed a nap after the drive from Pinehurst, and the General was recovering from a recent operation, they took an active part in the festival schedule. Marshall joked about his drive to Wilmington as being over "early American concrete."

After returning to Pinehurst, General Marshall wrote a note of thanks to his hosts, Bishop and Mrs. Thomas H. Wright, and said he cherished the following letter he received from a lady who attended the festival parade:

"Dear General and Mrs. Marshall. I want you to know I have never been so thrilled in all my life when I saw you in the parade in Wilmington. I believe you could see me, too, because you gave me a special acknowledgement. I was among the thou-sands of spectators watching the parade, but I bet I was the only one that did not see the Beauty Queen or remember specially the lovely floats—just you."

General Westmoreland was born in Spartanburg County, S.C., and is married to Katherine Van Deusen of Fayetteville, N.C., known to her friends as Kitsy. An alumna of UNC-Greensboro, Kitsy loves to tell of being a college freshman courted by the handsome Colonel Westmoreland, with other girls leaning out dormitory windows to get a glimpse of him. The Westmoreland's summer home is in Linville, N.C., and their winter home is in Charleston, S.C.

During his career, Westmoreland served three different tours of duty at Fort Bragg. I first met him on November 11, 1963 when he attended the Veterans Day program aboard the U.S.S. *North Carolina* Battleship Memorial at Wilmington. The General had made the Fort Bragg band available for the event, and he was obviously impressed with the memorial, the program and with Bill Mauldin, the World War II cartoonist, who was the speaker. After the program ended, Westmoreland offered the Battleship Commission any support he could give as CG at Fort Bragg. However, within a few months, President Lyndon Johnson ordered Westmoreland to take command of the U.S. forces in Vietnam.

When he returned from Vietnam, Westmoreland concluded that the war and the conduct of U.S. armed forces were not fairly represented or understood by the American people. There was a shocking lack of understanding and appreciation of the service rendered in Vietnam by U.S. soldiers, marines and sailors under extremely difficult circumstances. As their former commander, Westmoreland felt an obligation to correct the mistaken impressions left by critics and others.

The general became a lecturer on the Vietnam war, and felt he was making good progress toward his goal when he was, in his words, "ambushed" by the highly controversial CBS News documentary in 1982 which eventually led to an epic legal battle between Westmoreland and the network. Charles H. Crutchfield, retired president of Jefferson Standard Broadcasting Company, was one of many Westmoreland friends who came to his defense. WBTV has been a respected CBS affiliate station for many years.

Crutchfield did his best to head off the litigation, urging CBS to acknowledge that Westmoreland's entire life had been dedicated to the loyal service of his country, and that he deserved to enjoy retirement with honor. In 1988, six years after the CBS show, Crutchfield said there was still deep division within the network because many CBS affiliates believe the zealous news team had been unfair and misleading in their documentary.

In retrospect, the excesses of CBS and other vociferous critics of the Vietnam War may have helped rally the nation behind its Vietnam veterans with support not fully given while the conflict was in progress. The national Vietnam War Memorial in Washington is one example of well-deserved recognition and appreciation. Many

continued

General George C. Marshall, one of the most distinguished Allied leaders of World War II, was considered by many to be America's most respected citizen when he and his wife, Katherine, journeyed from their Pinehurst home to Wilmington for the Azalea Festival in April 1949.

General and Mrs. Marshall were hosted in Wilmington by Right Reverend Thomas H. Wright, Bishop of the Episcopal Diocese of East Carolina, and his wife, Hannah. The flowers were the main attraction for the Marshalls, and they enjoyed them immensely at Greenfield Gardens and other gardens in the area.

General William Westmoreland, one of America's best-known military leaders during Vietnam era, dressed as a pioneer frontiersman at Quaker Meadows near Morganton to take part in the re-enactment march of North Carolina patriots who trudged from the Blue Ridge Mountains to Kings Mountain to hand the British one of the most stunning defeats of the American Revolution. The Overmountain Victory Trail was one of the highlights of North Carolina's observance of America's Bicentennial in 1976.

states, including North Carolina, have taken steps to honor Vietnam veterans.

On the lawn of the State Capitol in Raleigh, a handsome and dramatic new bronze statue honors the men and women who served in the Vietnam war. General Westmoreland is grateful for this and for all the recognition given the U.S. armed forces who served under his command.

The courageous general may also have served his country well by causing television journalism to re-examine carefully its basic responsibilities in reporting and covering the news, especially in times of tumult and dissent.

One book in particular, *Reckless Disregard*, by Ranada Adler, a *New Yorker* magazine writer, has been most gratifying to "Westy." The book and the unfolding of history leaves General William C. Westmoreland standing tall. *HMM*

My wife, Julia, was placed in the seat of honor beside General Marshall by his hostess, Hannah Wright (back to camera) at a dinner in the Cornwallis House in Wilmington. The event was a memorable one for everyone attending.

The Westmoreland libel lawsuit against CBS was a public relations battle as well as a test of law, with both sides trying to win public favor with the help of high-powered PR firms. Westmoreland's PR folks asked me for pictures of him doing ordinary chores, not dressed in uniform. The General's sweet wife, Kitsy, threatened to expose the General and me as "complete frauds," because she said, "West never brought in a load of wood in his life."

Fred Rhoads, cartoonist who for years drew the Army character Sad Sack for the comics, decided that Westmoreland's portrait at Grandfather Mountain with Mildred The Bear and Sad Sack should show the General with nine stars on his shoulders instead of four. As for the General's medals, there was not room for the decorations Rhoads was willing to award.

It was two well-known, four-star Generals on the Blue Ridge Parkway as General Westmoreland gave a guided tour of the Linn Cove Viaduct to General Matthew B. Ridgeway, who at some time in his career held every major command in the United States Army.

R. GREGG CHERRY
'The Iron Major' Governor

The visitor to the State Capitol asked an old custodian who had observed many sessions of the General Assembly, "Who is the best man in the General Assembly?"

"Well," said the custodian, "for a rough and tumble man, I gives it to Mr. Cherry."

And that wise remark would have found much agreement with friend or foe of Robert Gregg Cherry, 1937 Speaker of the House of Representatives. Known as "The Iron Major" since his combat service in World War I, Gregg Cherry could deal with the most complex legislative debate, keep a disputatious House in check and on schedule, and earn the respect of everyone with his personal warmth, wit, honesty and courage.

Cherry's performance as an outstanding House Speaker marked him as an excellent bet for the governor's office. He served effectively in four sessions of the House and two in the Senate, all from Gaston County.

Elected governor in 1944 at age 53, Cherry found the post-war problems of World War II more difficult and vexing than the war years. North Carolina was plagued by shortages of material, equipment and personnel while a vast log-jam of public and private needs cried out for attention.

Cherry and his administration attacked the challenging issues with vigor and determination. He marshalled public support with great skill. His experience as a legislator, especially during the Depression years, proved invaluable. Taking advantage of sharp increases in state revenues, while American industry was switching over to civilian goods and services, he convinced the General Assembly to pay off most of the state's debts.

One day Cherry strolled over to a meeting of the State Highway Commission, unannounced, and gave his appointees a brief, pointed message on the need to pave and improve rural roads. "Farmers can't ride on promises and blueprints and plans," he said. "Let the roads stay where they are and fix 'em up so folks can use 'em." And so he launched many rural road projects which were not actually completed until well after his term had ended.

A tobacco-chewing, straight-talking man, Gregg Cherry knew about and understood the needs of ordinary folks. An orphan child—his mother died while he was an infant and his father died when Gregg was seven—Cherry grew up with relatives in Gastonia. He was a man of uncompromising honesty, with an acute sense of duty and responsibility.

After earning undergraduate and law degrees from Trinity (now Duke University), he practiced law in Gastonia, became active in civic and political affairs and was elected mayor of the city. He married Mildred Stafford of Greensboro, a lovely woman with a keen intellect, gentle grace and charm, who later served with distinction as First Lady of North Carolina.

In one of his last speeches as Governor, Cherry said, "No government which has been satisfied with the status quo has long endured. We live in a changing world, and our efforts must be directed toward sensing what that change will be and exerting our best energy in molding our present institutions to meet future needs." *ELR*

Harry Truman's famous prediction, which later came true, did not appear to bother Governor Cherry as he read his newspaper on the floor at the 1956 Democratic national convention. A veteran legislator and former Speaker of the House, the governor was a skillful political leader and chief executive. Cherry was noted for a quick and keen sense of humor and enjoyed telling stories and jokes, often about himself. He was a special favorite of the Honorary Tar Heels, a group of national news people who had demonstrated a special affection for the state.

Crowning of the first Azalea Festival Queen made history in an unexpected way. As a capacity crowd watches in Lumina Ballroom, Wrightsville Beach, and the beautiful starlet Jacqueline White awaits her crown, Governor Cherry manages to put the crown on upside down. Carl Goerch (at microphone), publisher of *The State* magazine and master of ceremonies, looks on in astonishment. The Queen kept her poise amid the laughter, the crown was correctly placed, and the festival went on to be a great success. Queen Jacqueline, who became a successful movie actress, returned for the twentieth festival.

Governor Cherry, a loyal and partisan Democrat, pauses in the midst of the 1956 Democratic convention in Chicago for a photo with fellow delegates from North Carolina. He is with (left to right) an unidentified delegate, Harold Makepeace of Lee County, Capus Waynick of Guilford County and David McConnell of Mecklenburg County.

President Harry S Truman and Governor Cherry chuckle at the sight of a "Hoover Cart" parked at the State Fairgrounds, Raleigh, during a Truman visit in 1948. The two-wheel cart, pulled by horse or mule, was named by Democrats for Republican President Herbert Hoover, seeking to blame Hoover for the Great Depression of the 1930s. Editor Jonathan Daniels of *The News & Observer,* a highly partisan Democrat and ardent Truman supporter, arranged for the cart to be displayed during the visit by Truman, who was then in the midst of his heated campaign against Governor Thomas Dewey. Truman and Cherry were both World War I veterans, plain spoken and unpretentious men who enjoyed each other's company.

THE HUMAN SIDE OF CHERRY

Gregg Cherry liked to walk. He walked from the executive mansion to his office at the State Capitol almost every day, weather permitting, and usually alone. A burly, friendly person, he would stop and chat with people along the way.

He frequently talked with the peanut vendor on Capitol Square, a familiar fixture there for many years. One day the vendor told Cherry, "The thing I like about you, Governor, is that you have never lost touch with the common people. In fact, you're common as any of us."

Each Governor has thousands of appointments to make during his term. Cherry liked to speak of his appointees as "patriots." When asked at a press conference about a pending appointment, he would smile and say, "I guess I'll find me a patriot somewhere."

A job hunter heard about the death of a Cherry appointee, and called the Governor immediately to tell him about the death. Then the caller asked, "Do you think I can take his place?" With typical Cherry wit, the Governor replied, "It's all right with me if you can arrange it with the undertaker."

Cherry received a letter from an irate school teacher who vowed, "I would not vote for you again if you were the Angel Gabriel." Replied Cherry, "If I were the Angel Gabriel you couldn't vote for me. You wouldn't even be in my precinct."

A compassionate man and lawyer, Cherry studied carefully each death case before deciding whether or not to use his authority as governor to intervene in the case. In one case a man was con-

victed of a brutal crime and sentenced to die after conflicting testimony at the trial on whether he was sane or insane. Shortly before the date of execution, Cherry went unannounced to Central Prison, entered death row and personally talked with the condemned prisoner. From this interview he decided not to stop the execution.

Each spring thousands of school children travel to Raleigh to visit the State Capitol and other attractions. For decades it was the custom for the governor to receive these groups and personally shake hands with each child and teacher. Cherry particularly enjoyed these visits, and was known to have spent as much as three hours in a day to meet these groups. Although the Cherrys had no children, the governor loved children and insisted that any school boy or girl in North Carolina who wanted to come to Raleigh and see the Capitol had a right to visit his or her governor.

Gregg Cherry stood firm at the 1948 Democratic national convention as a southern Democrat, not as a Dixiecrat. He refused to be drawn into the ranks of rebellious southern governors and others who objected to the nomination of Harry S Truman for president. The North Carolina delegation also stood firm with its governor. As a result, Cherry and North Carolina received much credit for Truman's nomination and election. Kerr Scott, Cherry's successor, said, "I've heard many people refer to Gregg Cherry as 'The Iron Major.' But he's known to me as the Rock of Gibraltar of that convention."

ELR

A VISIT BACKSTAIRS AT THE WHITE HOUSE

When David Haywood heard the news, he could scarcely believe his ears. The President of the United States was inviting him to visit the White House. David Haywood was so pleased that he could only smile and bob his head with pleasure when friends congratulated him.

An elderly black man, known affectionately to many as "Uncle Dave," Haywood had served as butler and majordomo to at least 14 North Carolina governors during their residence in the stately executive mansion at Raleigh. He was intensely proud of his more than 50 years of service in the mansion.

It was a very special invitation intended to fulfill the life-long ambition of a dying man. Haywood's physician had discovered the week before that the slender wisp of a man was incurably ill and that time was running out for him. When this news reached Governor R. Gregg Cherry, a warm-hearted man, he picked up the telephone and called his close friend, William B. Umstead, the junior United States Senator from North Carolina.

Haywood was extremely proud of the beautiful silverware, china and linen which was used to serve the governors, their families and guests. Polishing the state silver was his job, and he resented anyone shining a fork while his back was turned. Haywood had often said that someday he hoped to visit the White House so he could make his own comparison with the facilities available for serving the presidents.

Governor Cherry asked Senator Umstead to help Haywood realize his ambition for a backstairs White House visit before time ran out. The Senator quickly agreed to help and assigned me the job of working out the details. I was then an administrative assistant to the Senator.

I was dismayed to find that the White House had just been closed to all visitors. It was August, 1947, and President and Mrs. Truman were preparing to move across the street to Blair House so that massive renovations could be made to the historic residence of presidents.

When I made my plea to the top presidential assistant, he was sympathetic but adamant. "We have made no exceptions to the rule," he said. "Furthermore, visitors are never allowed backstairs in the food service areas." Only the president and Mrs. Truman could permit such a visit, he added. I immediately requested this final appeal.

Within a few hours a message came from the White House. The president and Mrs. Truman cordially invited David Haywood to visit the White House at the earliest possible moment. The door to all service quarters would be open for his full inspection.

Arrangements were swiftly made for Haywood, his wife and daughter to make the trip to Washington. They were met by Senator Umstead at his office, given a warm welcome and handed to my charge for the White House visit. The guest of honor proudly wore his brass-buttoned butler's uniform with 14 narrow gold stripes on the sleeve—one for each governor served. He first entered service at the mansion when he was 19. Now at 71, frail and white-haired, he was prepared to tour the White House.

We entered the White House grounds through a small, side gate. Under the guidance of a Secret Service agent, the tour began at the locked, stainless steel door of the kitchen. Haywood and our small party entered the large, hotel-type kitchen where a neatly dressed dietician, wearing a huge ring of keys, explained the methods of food preparation and storage. Her keys were used to unlock refrigerator doors and cabinets where all foodstuffs were securely stored.

Next came the pantries where all the china, linen and silverware were stored separately. The head butler in charge of each pantry greeted Haywood cordially, showed him all the items under his charge and answered all questions politely and fully. David Haywood's expression never changed. He was pleasant, alert and dignified. He made a careful examination of everything shown him.

After each inspection, the majordomo would gravely thank his informant and then comment, "It's mighty nice, but I don't think it's a bit better than what we have down in Raleigh."

The final stop was in the private dining room used by the President and his family. Haywood and our group stood in silence while the White House service butler explained where the President sat, where Mrs. Truman sat and described in detail how the meals were served.

"Is this the chair where President Roosevelt once sat down to eat?" Uncle Dave finally asked, pointing to the head of the table.

"Yes, sir," the butler replied. "That's the very chair."

"And is this the same chair where President Truman now eats?"

"Yes, sir. It is."

With this answer, the old man slowly walked over to the table, knelt and reverently kissed an arm of the historic chair.

Not one word was spoken. But the sight of that gentle man paying homage in his own simple, dignified way filled everyone's eyes with tears—mine included.

David Haywood passed to his reward a few months after his return to Raleigh. He died a man full of years, with his life-long ambition realized—thanks to the kindness of the Governor of North Carolina, a United States Senator and the President of the United States. *ELR*

Author's Note: *Reprinted with permission from March 1969 issue of* We the People of NORTH CAROLINA, *official publication of the North Carolina Citizens for Business and Industry.*

GREAT SWING MUSICIANS
Performing in North Carolina

One of the big reasons for my enthusiasm for photography when I was a teenager was my interest in swing bands. There was no television in the 1930's, so to see a band it had to be seen in person. While some of my friends were collecting autographs, I collected photographs of my favorite swing musicians. My parents did not mind the photography; they thought that was great. They clearly wondered about the swing music, however, in much the same way that I am puzzled by some of the rock music that is popular today.

Benny Goodman, with his stars Lionel Hampton, Harry James, Gene Krupa, Teddy Wilson, Jess Stacy, Fletcher Henderson, Martha Tilton, and others was my favorite band. Goodman achieved a level of excellence in the '30s and '40s that still sounds good to many in my generation. Tommy Dorsey, Glenn Miller, Artie Shaw, and Glen Gray and the Casa Loma Orchestra were close seconds on my favorites list. Duke Ellington, Larry Clinton, Fats Waller, Count Basie, and Jimmie Lunceford brought me great pleasure when I listened to their records and saw them in person. I followed them, as well as individual stars like Billie Holiday, to many parts of the eastern United States.

Illustrative of my loyalty to Benny Goodman, I saw him and his band in the '30s and '40s in Washington, D.C., Baltimore, Detroit, New York, and Raleigh, and in 1979 in Greensboro and 1983 in Wilmington. Each time I took pictures, and I deeply regret the cameras and the film in the early days did not measure up. It was virtually impossible to snap candid shots that are up to today's standards.

If a musician was good, I liked him or her, white or black. From my standpoint Louis Armstrong, in his own charming way, did as much for better race relations as any individual in this century. Another "Satchelmouth" admirer, Nick Ponos of Wilmington, whose son is shown with the masterful trumpeter in these pages, recently wrote: "Louis Armstrong was without a doubt one of the greatest musicians and personalities that ever walked upon the earth. I truly believe that if he walked through no-man's land playing his horn between two armies that were in battle, the firing would cease to hear him through. He was indeed an ambassador—gifted of God."

In my teens in the '30s and early '40s and before I had a car, it was a real adventure just getting to some of the swing band performances. I rode trains and buses, hitch-hiked, and did a lot of walking. Traveling to Wilson for the Glenn Miller dance in the Watson Warehouse was no problem. Half of Chapel Hill was there, and there were plenty of rides. My 8 o'clock class the next morning was the major hitch. I made pictures of the great Glenn Miller and his folks, including Tex Beneke, but that was a night I got no sleep at all. Except for taking pictures, I was typical of many kids my age.

Some of my early swing band negatives were scorched beyond use when my mother's home in Wilmington burned in 1950. Ruined were shots of one of North Carolina's greatest, Hal Kemp and his Orchestra, featuring Saxie Dowell and Skinny Ennis, photographed at Lumina Ballroom on Wrightsville Beach. Incidentally, my mother told me she named Lumina while she was a student at Vassar after my grandfather, Hugh MacRae, had founded the Tidewater Power Company that owned both Lumina and the street car line. The best bands were booked into Lumina, and the best way then to get to the island was aboard the street car. The other choice was by boat.

continued

Benny Goodman, "The King of Swing," in concert with the Greensboro Symphony Orchestra, tunes his clarinet backstage.

The great Louis Armstrong traded trumpets for this picture with 5-year-old John Ponos in Wilmington in 1967.

Glenn Miller signs autographs in Watson Tobacco Warehouse in Wilson in 1940.

Tex Beneke, star saxophonist and vocalist in the Glenn Miller band, headed the group following Miller's death in a World War II plane crash.

Jack Teagarden, best of the swing band trombonists, plays a Raleigh dance engagement in 1940.

Bunny Berigan poses for this picture in the Wilrick Hotel in Sanford, the day he played a tobacco warehouse dance there in 1941.

Cab Calloway, scat singer unexcelled, led bands that brought to prominence several stars of the swing band era. He is shown performing one of his famous numbers at the Azalea Festival in Wilmington.

Gene Krupa, the best of the swing band drummers, gained fame with Benny Goodman. He is shown in Lumina Ballroom at Wrightsville Beach with his own band after World War II.

Lionel Hampton, another famed Benny Goodman alumnus, displays his remarkable talents at a dance at Grandfather Country Club, Linville.

There were some marvelous college swing bands in that day and earlier. The "Old Professor," Kay Kyser, started at UNC, and in my time at Chapel Hill excellent bands were headed by Freddie Johnson, Charlie Wood, Skipper Bowles, Tiny Hutton, and Johnny Satterfield. Jimmy Poyner led a top notch band with its origin at NC State. Les Brown and Johnny Long launched their nationally known bands at Duke.

John Scott Trotter of Charlotte, who was arranger for Hal Kemp's orchestra, earned much of his fame when he moved to Hollywood to be music director for 30 years for the great Bing Crosby. Bruce Snyder left Chapel Hill to join Tommy Dorsey, and John Best of Shelby played trumpet in several top bands. North Carolina musicians had a big hand in making the nation swing.

Allan and Margaret Preyer invited me to sit at their front row table in the Greensboro Coliseum in 1979 for the Benny Goodman concert with the Greensboro Symphony, and it was a meaningful experience. I was so afraid Goodman would not be the superlative best that he was when I had seen him last nearly 40 years before. A few years later in Wilmington when I was able to talk with him, it was my intention to pay him the highest sort of compliment. I said, "you know, Mr. Goodman, in Greensboro you were exactly as good as you were 40 years ago." Benny Goodman's response was the best possible reply for all perfectionists to use under the circumstances. He said, "What, no better?" *HMM*

Tommy Dorsey, "The Sentimental Gentleman of Swing," slides his trombone for the Pied Pipers featuring Jo Stafford and Frank Sinatra (right) at a UNC dance in 1941. Buddy Rich at the drums is in the background (left). The event was in the Tin Can, the University's ancient gymnasium.

Ziggy Elman swings *And The Angels Sing* on trumpet, with Buddy Rich on drums, in the Tommy Dorsey band's appearance in Chapel Hill in 1941.

Thomas H. Wright, Jr., of Wilmington (right), who was head of a UNC dance committee, treasures this photograph standing by Helen O'Connell, songstress known for *Green Eyes* and *Amapola* with the Jimmy Dorsey band. Jimmy Dorsey is at left.

They called themselves modestly "The World's Greatest Jazz Band," and few could argue that they were not when they played the Azalea Festival in Wilmington in 1971. Left to right: Bud Freeman, Yank Lawson, Billy Butterfield, and Ed Hubble.

Bob Haggart played bass for "The World's Greatest Jazz Band," having gained fame as a member of Bob Crosby's Bobcats with the number *Big Noise From Winnetka.*

Ella Fitzgerald, at age 18, sings *A Tisket, A Tasket* with Chick Webb's Orchestra. They played in North Carolina, but this photo is in the Howard Theatre in Washington, D.C.

Dean Hudson (right) played more dance halls, warehouses, high school gyms, and college campuses in North Carolina than any other band leader in the late thirties and early forties.

The Glen Gray and the Casa Loma Orchestra performs at Chapel Hill, with Gray (right) and Clarence Hutchenrider soloing on clarinet with *Smoke Rings.*

Star saxophonist Boots Randolph perforoms at the Azalea Festival.

ROBERT M. HANES/ WACHOVIA BANK

Tough-minded Visionary, Great Citizen

(Photo credit unavailable)

Following Robert Hanes' example, Wachovia executives were instrumental in making the Research Triangle concept a reality. Archie K. Davis, who served as president and chairman of the Research Triangle Foundation for many years, is shown speaking at the ground-breaking of the National Humanities Center in April 1977. In 32 days Davis raised $1.5 million in private funds to build the Center building. The building was named in Davis' honor. Others are (left to right) Chancellor Joab Thomas, North Carolina State University; Chancellor Ferebee Taylor, UNC-Chapel Hill; President Terry Sanford, Duke University; Fred A. Coe, Jr., president/chairman of Burroughs Wellcome Co.; and President William Friday, University of North Carolina System.

Founded in 1879, Wachovia Bank & Trust Company has had many outstanding leaders but none more dynamic and courageous than Robert M. Hanes. He became president in July 1931 when the nation was in the midst of the Great Depression. More than 1200 banks had closed and another 5000 would follow.

Under his strong and innovative leadership, Wachovia did not close, absorbed its losses and kept operating at a critical time when North Carolina desperately needed sound banking leadership. A tough-minded visionary, Hanes viewed economic adversity as an opportunity to move out and build for better times ahead.

His life and banking career reflected the solid Moravian principles taught him by his family and the community in which he grew up. Accepting responsibility for his life, his family and community service was second nature to him.

His associates describe him as highly intelligent, strongly motivated, having a generous heart, a keen sense of humor, a powerful force for good in North Carolina, and a leader who believed that the best of banking was always in the public interest.

As a banker, he pioneered in state-wide banking, in installment credit, auto loans and other consumer services, and in many other advances in banking.

However, he also served as a state legislator, as a Marshall Plan administrator in western Europe following World War II, as a civilian aide to Secretary of Army Robert T. Stevens, as president of the American Bankers Association, as a promoter of small businesses, and as a trusted adviser to many North Carolina governors.

An indomitable man, Robert Hanes never stopped working for his beloved North Carolina and for the many causes in which he believed. Terminally ill, he called a business leader to ask for an appointment and told the man he would ask for a contribution to the Research Triangle Park. The person called said he had a bad cold and would have to see him later. Hanes quickly replied, "Look, my friend, I am dying of cancer and I need to see you now." He got the appointment and a generous contribution.

At his funeral on March 2, 1959, his pastor, Dr. Mark Depp, said, "I leave it to others to speak of Robert Hanes as a banker and financier, he was that . . . as an illustrious citizen of the state and nation, he was that. But I am content to speak of him today as a good man—for he was that, too." *ELR*

Pride in Winston-Salem glows in the smile of Robert Hanes, a native son, always ready to promote his home town and its products. Hanes had close business and personal ties with R.J. Reynolds Tobacco Company of Winston-Salem, a pioneer North Carolina manufacturer and producer of the two famous cigarette brands.

"Methods and equipment may change but the fundamental principles of sound banking remain the same. Integrity, sound loan policies, able management, a proper appreciation of the depositors' interests—these are the necessary foundations of any lasting banking structure."
—*Robert M. Hanes, 1933.*

Clad in a fringed bedspread, full Indian headdress and war paint, Robert Hanes reads a humorous proclamation at a summer meeting of the State Board of Conservation and Development. In the midst of a social hour, board members, spouses and staff were surprised at the unexpected appearance of the state's best-known banker in Indian regalia, and overcome with laughter at his impromptu and witty performance. Hanes was an active member of the state board, attacking his assignments with the same energy, zeal and intelligence he displayed in working for Wachovia Bank.

On a cold, blustery day in March 1960, Governor Luther H. Hodges breaks ground for the Robert M. Hanes Memorial Building in the Research Triangle Park. Hodges said that Hanes, who died in 1959, "was the guiding and leading mind and spirit that gave cohesion to the efforts of all of us involved in the Triangle." Mrs. Robert (Mildred Borden) Hanes and other members of the family stand in background. They include Mrs. Anne Hanes Willis, Frank Borden Hanes, Mr. and Mrs. Gordon Hanes, James G. Hanes and James G. Hanes III.

More than 50 years of top executive experience in banking and finance is represented (left to right) by John F. Watlington, Jr., John G. Medlin, Jr., and Archie K. Davis. They have continued Wachovia's strong growth and development since Robert Hanes's retirement in 1956. Watlington served as Wachovia Bank president/chief executive officer, 1956-76. Medlin became president/CEO in 1977 and is president/CEO of First Wachovia Corporation, a leading interstate banking organization in southeastern U.S. Davis served as Wachovia chairman of board, 1956-74.

"Wachovia's style is to emphasize substance more then form and to be more than to seem. Our personality and reputation are sometimes characterized as low key and conservative, but competitors and customers will provide witness that we are also quite aggressive and enterprising. Our approach is to develop close and personalized customer relationships which have a better probability of growing, enduring and making money over the years." —*John G. Medlin, Jr., 1983.*

Wachovians say that John G. Medlin, Jr., has much in common with the presidents before him, but he is also the product of his own time and of his own experiences. He grew up on a tobacco farm in eastern North Carolina in the lean years of the Great Depression where he learned, in his words, "that even the best people experience hard times . . . you learn to have faith in others and in yourself . . . and, most of all, you learn the best way to accomplish something is to work persistently and carefully for it." Medlin stands in front of the Robert Hanes portrait in the Wachovia board room, Winston-Salem.

W. KERR SCOTT

Governor, U.S. Senator, Friend of Rural People

Known as the Squire of Haw River, W. Kerr Scott was often described as controversial, stubborn, tenacious, unpredictable, a hard worker, a good listener, a restless and sentimental man, and a tough fighter for his causes. He served as governor 1949-1953.

He had a keen understanding and appreciation of rural people and the common man. One of his notable political assets was a sharp disdain for the existing power structure in state politics, government and business. Proud of his Scottish ancestry and farm heritage, Scott was described by some observers as a jet-propelled plowboy.

He frequently expressed his philosophy as, "What is bad for any large segment or group of people is bad for all the people." Despite his populist appeal and his differences with the existing power structure, Governor Scott was not really that much of an outsider. After all, he was a successful farmer and dairyman, and had served many years as State Commissioner of Agriculture.

His knowledge and experience with agriculture, agribusiness, the state's economy, state government and the General Assembly contributed greatly to his ultimate success as governor. Scott also spoke with ease and was a good storyteller, using his humor, rustic and unvarnished at times, to make his points with audiences, large or small. Soon after he was elected, he told a gathering of rural folks, "I'm still not sure what it takes to be governor. To be inaugurated, I had to buy a suit of clothes that cost as much as a fine calf."

Scott firmly believed that his upset victory over the heavily favored Charlie Johnson gave him a clear mandate from the people for his program for the next four years. He also understood that he had an uphill battle with the General Assembly, where many legislative leaders had not supported him for governor and actively opposed his legislative program.

In his first address to the General Assembly, he met these issues head on, "We must take courage rather than fear in advancing . . . we are in a period of readjustment following the end of World War II as shortages end . . . our economy is moving from a sellers to a buyers market . . . so we can look forward to a period of greatest prosperity ever in this state. . . ."

He then proposed a 15-point GO FORWARD program for North Carolina, including recommending a $200 million bond issue to build a network of all-weather rural roads across the state. Despite heavy opposition, Scott won in the General Assembly and with the voters with his argument that North Carolina needed all-weather rural roads to wipe out the "mud tax" which was holding back rural areas, rural people and preventing badly needed economic development and growth.

The Squire of Haw River's many contributions as State Commissioner of Agriculture, Governor of North Carolina and as United States Senator left an enduring and progressive mark on state government and politics for generations to come. *ELR*

The happy warrior is W. Kerr Scott, United States Senator and former Governor of North Carolina sporting an Adlai Stevenson hat and badge at the 1956 Democratic national convention in Chicago. A robust, cigar-smoking campaigner, Scott enjoyed a good political fight. There was a split in the North Carolina delegation over whether or not to support Stevenson, some of whose forebears came from North Carolina, but Scott and other delegates kept North Carolina Democrats for Stevenson.

The Scott GO FORWARD program included $7.5 million in bonds to provide facilities for ocean-going vessels at state port facilities at Wilmington and Morehead City. The governor is shown breaking ground at the State Ports Authority, Wilmington, in 1950. Others (left to right) are Albert Myers Sr., SPA chairman, Colonel George Gillette, SPA executive director, and Colonel Royce McClelland, mayor of Wilmington.

Dr. Henry Jordan, a dentist and textile manufacturer from Randolph County, was responsible for carrying out the Scott road program, including the paving of over 15,000 miles of roads. An affable, practical man who enjoyed working with people, Dr. Jordan was a valuable member of the Scott team. He was a brother of B. Everett Jordan, long-time Democratic party leader and later United States senator. Henry Jordan was frequently mentioned as a possible candidate for governor.

While visiting at Nags Head, Governor Scott chats with two small guests at The Carolinian Hotel. A warm-hearted family man, the governor readily agreed to pose with the Easter Bunny and the children.

ROBERT SCOTT SPEAKS OF HIS FATHER AND MOTHER

When Robert Walter Scott was elected in 1968, it was the first time the son of a former governor was elected governor by popular vote in North Carolina. In an interview with Bob Scott, now President of the North Carolina Community College system, he spoke about his father, W. Kerr Scott, and his mother, Mary White (Miss Mary) Scott:

Plain Folks. "My father could identify with the average person. He always had time for average folks. The truck driver and waitress were just as important to him as the corporate executive or person in high public office."

Straight Talk. "He always told me to be straight forward, straight up, say what you think. That caused grief, as you might expect, more than one time for me and him. But that habit of speaking directly comes naturally in our family. He also liked to make decisions and move on. Don't dwell on them, right or wrong."

Sense of Humor. "My father, his brother Ralph and the other Scott brothers who were not so well known in public life, all had a sense of humor. They believed you should be able to laugh at yourself . . . don't take yourself too seriously. It was a natural humor—not contrived. I don't have it, unfortunately. It's a gift. You either have it or you don't."

Love of Farming. "My father and mother had their roots very deep in the soil of Alamance County and in their farm and the community. During all his years as Commissioner of Agriculture, he lived at Haw River and drove back and forth to Raleigh each work day. As a youngster I recall he would meet with the farm employees at 7 a.m. sharp each work day, go over the work to be done that day, and about 7:15 a.m. get in his car and head to Raleigh. Unless he had a night meeting, my father would be back between 6:00—6:30 p.m. and would expect a full report on what had been done on the farm."

The Home Place. "Like so many North Carolina farmers, he was an entrepreneur. He and my mother took some old land grown up with sassafras sprouts and covered with gulleys, and literally built up its fertility over the years. We have some old photos of my parents standing in deep, washed-out gulleys above their heads. When you build something like that you put your soul in it and you don't give it up. Even when he went to Washington as a U.S. Senator, he craved to come home and did at every opportunity. My mother said that having to live in an apartment up there hastened his death."

Sense of Community. "During World War II, when gas was rationed, my father would walk from home to Hawfield Presbyterian Church each Sunday morning, a distance of about three miles. As he walked, other men along the route would join him and they would walk together, talking of farming, crops, news of the day, politics, etc. By the time they had arrived at church in time for Sunday school, there would be a small troop of men who had, in a way, the world's problems pretty well settled."

Family Ties. "People say I am more like my mother than my dad. I know I am in looks. She had a gentleness about her that was a counter balance to his roughness. She had a great appreciation for history, and I learned from her the same appreciation of history."

Appointment of "Dr. Frank." "Following my father's death, I asked my mother to tell me how he made the decision to appoint Dr. Frank Graham to the U.S. Senate. What I had heard was that my father had under consideration a number of names as a possible replacement for Senator Broughton, who had died in office. My father was at home seated at the breakfast table, having a cup of coffee, while my mother prepared breakfast. He told her that he had to make the appointment. She asked, 'Who are you going to appoint?' He pulled from his pocket an envelope with a list of names on it and read them to her. She replied, 'You haven't called the name of my candidate yet.' When he asked who that was, she said, 'Dr. Frank Graham.' My father made no comment. So when I asked my mother, 'Was this story true?' she never answered me . . . she just smiled. And to this day I don't know. But that smile made me think it was true." *ELR*

U.S. Senator W. Kerr Scott helps lead the attack against proposed tolls on the Blue Ridge Parkway in a hearing conducted by Secretary of Interior Fred Seaton, and National Park Director Conrad Wirth (seated together at left). Scott emphasized, among other objections, that the Blue Ridge Parkway was not built as a toll highway and that the scheme was impractical. Hugh Morton said this photo was made shortly before the senator's unexpected death on April 16, 1958. The opposition presented at the hearing, plus the direct intervention of President Dwight D. Eisenhower, caused the National Park Service to withdraw the proposal. Others shown in the picture include Congressman George Shuford, Governor Luther H. Hodges, Senator Sam J. Ervin, Congressman L. H. Fountain, Don Elias, publisher of the *Asheville Citizen-Times,* Spencer Robbins of Blowing Rock, and Asheville City Manager Weldon Weir.

Kerr Scott, whose populist ideas and political strength were more closely identified with rural areas, chats with Ben E. Douglas (right), former mayor of Charlotte, and a successful businessman. He later served as director of C&D in the administration of Governor William B. Umstead. Known affectionately to many as "Uncle Ben," Douglas was a large, avuncular man whose unremitting support for the Charlotte Municipal Airport is recognized now in the daily announcements heard by thousands of arriving air travelers, "Welcome to Charlotte International *Douglas* Airport." Grady Cole, the legendary morning announcer at WBT Radio, ridiculed naming the aiport after Douglas. Cole would rail, "It's Charlotte Municipal Airport, Charlotte, North Carolina . . . not Douglas Municipal Airport, Douglas, North Carolina!" But Cole's efforts failed and the Douglas name remains.

CASTLEMAN D. CHESLEY
Premier Sports Telecaster

Castleman D. Chesley (right) personally supervised many of his basketball telecasts, especially those in the ACC. At the 1977 ACC Tournament in Greensboro he is playing "mother hen" to Bones McKinney, Billy Packer, and Jim Thacker.

Billy Packer says, "Other than my own father, I cannot think of anyone who has been more helpful to me than Ches. He was a tremendous individual, a brilliant businessman, and a guy I grew to enjoy more the more I knew him. There was a period in time when I really thought he probably wasn't so smart. One of the great things about guys of his calibre, the more you know them the smarter they become."

Comparisons always fuel arguments, but many people believe that Billy Packer on CBS is the best analyst of college basketball in the nation. His discovery by C.D. Chesley can best be described as accidental. Packer says Marvin "Skeeter" Francis of the ACC was asked by Chesley to provide a fill-in for Dan Daniel who would not be available for a specific game, and Skeeter forgot until the last moment, when Packer was the only person handy.

Packer was given a free ride to N.C. State University, taken into the TV truck to meet Chesley for the first time, and told to broadcast the game with Chesley's leading play-by-play man, Jim Thacker. It was Billy Packer's first time on television, and he says, "being with Jim Thacker was very helpful, because Thacker is a good professional." They became the Thacker-Packer team, fondly remembered and yet to be equaled in the eyes of thousands of ACC basketball fans.

Eugene Corrigan, now ACC Commissioner, worked in the conference office in the early days when Chesley was just beginning his basketball coverage. Corrigan became athletic director at Virginia, then athletic director at Notre Dame, and at both places he continued to do business with Chesley. Corrigan says, "A lot of people have said the ACC is the best conference. Chesley had a hand in that. He was the guy who had the nerve and the guts to start syndicating college basketball when no one else did. He was a pioneer. We had some great negotiating sessions. He would slap his hand on his head. He would swear to us we were taking every cent he had. He was a great negotiator."

Corrigan has high admiration for Jim Weaver, the ACC's first commissioner, and the likely reason Chesley and Weaver did business so well was that each had a splendid sense of humor. Corrigan's favorite Jim Weaver story goes like this: There were lots of fights during games in the early 60s between the North Carolina Tar Heels and the Deacons when Bones McKinney was coaching at Wake Forest, and one of the guys always in the middle of it was Wake's big, handsome Dave Budd.

Weaver called Wake Forest and said, "Bring that young man to my office at the King Cotton Hotel, Greensboro, and I will decide whether he will ever play another game of basketball in this conference, because I am sick and tired of this." Wake Forest officials brought him over, and they brought the chaplain, the dean, the president of the student body, and the athletic director. Everyone praised Dave Budd, said what a great person he was and described him in the most glowing terms. The dean said Dave was a fine student, and that his brother was also a fine student. But when the

continued

ACC Commissioner Bob James (right) and Assistant Commissioner Marvin "Skeeter" Francis (left) represent the universities of the Atlantic Coast Conference in a 1977 ACC halftime ceremony paying tribute to C.D. Chesley for his vision and enterprise in establishing the ACC Television Network.

Jim Weaver, formerly Athletic Director at Wake Forest College, was
the Atlantic Coast Conference's first commissioner. Although Chesley
was chiefly associated with ACC basketball, his first contracts were ne-
gotiated by Jim Weaver for football.

chaplain began to extol Dave's parents as wonderful people, Jim Weaver interrupted to say, "That's enough, I don't want to hear any more. I don't want to breed him. I just want him to stop fighting."

Castleman deTolley Chesley was born in Washington, D.C., and lived many years in Pennsylvania. His later years were spent at Grandfather Country Club in North Carolina, and he is buried at Linville. In 1987 he was posthumously voted into the North Carolina Sports Hall of Fame, with an emotional induction speech delivered by Gene Corrigan.

Chesley came to UNC on a football scholarship, but after a year he transferred to the University of Pennsylvania. At Penn he performed with the Mask and Wig Drama Club, and he discovered that show business was in his blood. It never left him. Chesley graduated from the Wharton School of Finance, and was an intelligence officer in World War II. A man of enormous will power, he stubbornly learned to talk again, though it was in a hoarse whisper, after he lost his natural baritone voice to throat cancer and a laryngectomy in 1959. Soon after the operation his doctor said he would never whistle again, and that the hole in his throat would cause him to drown if he went swimming. He whistled for the doctor before he left the office. Within a few days, Ches found a swimming pool, and sticking his finger in the hole in his throat, he jumped in the pool and swam.

Jim Thacker's most vivid memory of C.D. Chesley was at the Southern Conference Tournament in Charlotte in 1964. Lefty Driesell's hot Davidson team was figured to play West Virginia in the Southern Conference finals. Chesley alerted his sponsors to expect a huge audience, but it did not come off that way. VMI beat Davidson in the semi-finals, then George Washington defeated West Virginia, leaving Chesley with a much smaller audience than he expected for the finals. The Coliseum was nearly empty, and to make matters worse, Chesley was already committed on his network to an extra 30 minutes after the game so Jim Thacker and Jay Randolph could interview the top players and coaches from Davidson and West Virginia who now were not there.

The place emptied in a hurry, and there was nothing for the TV camera to shoot while the announcers rehashed the game. Suddenly a man appeared in the upper stands, apparently drunk and fumbling through the seats looking for his hat. Director Frank Slingland trained the cameras on the man's antics for more than 15 minutes while Thacker and Randolph droned on. Yes, the "drunk" was C.D. Chesley, always the showman, ever wanting his viewers and sponsors to have the best entertainment he could offer. *continued*

Gene Corrigan, ACC Commissioner.

Dean Smith, distinguished coach who has been around the ACC longest, says, "Chesley is the one who got interest in basketball started in the ACC. People who are football fans started looking in. He had to have a product that was exciting, and basketball is unbelievable excitement for television. The athletic directors were very loyal to Mr. Chesley. When Eddie Einhorn and others wanted to come in, they did not even put it up for bids because Chesley meant so much to the conference."

Colorful ex-referee Lou Bello recalls there were no required TV timeouts in the early days, and Chesley would ask officials for time to squeeze in his commercials. The officials would cooperate, but would rib Chesley by asking if he wanted them to wear Pepsi signs on their backs. Then Bello said, "Here's what kind of a guy he was. So Lou Bello with his big mouth, I would kid C.D., 'Hey, I've got a wife and three kids, a dog and a cat, are you going to take care of them?' That summer in Raleigh a big Pepsi-Cola truck drove in our driveway. I didn't know what it was all about. The driver unloaded crates, crates of Pepsi-Cola for the Lou Bello family. I asked him what's going on, and the driver said it was from C.D. Chesley. What a guy! I personally cried down there last year when he was put into the Hall of Fame, because I had a friend, C.D. Chesley, Hall of Famer, who made ACC basketball what it is today." *HMM*

Everett Case (right), on the bench with his former star player and later assistant coach, Vic Bubas, became head basketball coach at N.C. State in 1946. Case coached N.C. State to six consecutive conference championships in the old Southern Conference, and the first three championships in the new Atlantic Coast Conference. Case's leadership and dominance forced other ACC institutions to raise their standards of basketball play and become more competitive. When C.D. Chesley brought television to the scene in the late fifties, he knew he had a good product.

C.D. Chesley enjoyed his work and was usually pleasant to be around, and these happy qualities contributed immeasurably to the high morale and efficiency of his television crews.

Ches and Ruthie, a devoted couple who truly enjoyed life together. Ruthie's name for Chesley was "Adorable."

Chesley's other major project was a football television network for the University of Notre Dame, with noted sportscaster Lindsay Nelson doing the play-by-play and former Irish quarterback Paul Hornung on color sidelights. Shown (left to right) are Hornung, Chesley and Nelson.

Always the showman, Castleman D. Chesley entertains his crew with his own patented facial expression when the winning basket is scored at the buzzer.

ORVILLE CAMPBELL
AND FRIENDS
Newspaper Publisher/Hero Worshiper

Orville Campbell considers Dr. William B. Aycock, retired law professor and former UNC Chancellor, to be his best friend in Chapel Hill.

Orville Campbell (center) wrote the words and Hank Beebe (at piano) wrote the music to *All The Way Choo Choo* in honor of football hero Charlie Justice (left).

One of Orville Campbell's earliest successes came when he ran for the job of editor of *The Daily Tar Heel*, the student newspaper at UNC. Campbell won by a handful of votes over pollster Louis Harris, with all-time great basketball star George Glamack (right) serving as manager of the Campbell campaign.

William D. Carmichael, comptroller of UNC, always has been Orville Campbell's most admired hero. He was a second father to Campbell.

Four of Orville Campbell's good friends, left to right: bandleader and church leader Kay Kyser; newsman Billy Arthur; Metropolitan Opera star Norman Cordon; and the secretary of the North Carolina Press Association, Beatrice Cobb. The scene is the Press Photographers Southern Short Course banquet, where "Old Professor" Kay Kyser and Billy Arthur discussed experiences when each was head cheerleader at UNC.

When the Duke of Argyll, World Chief of the Clan Campbell, was honor guest with his Duchess at the Grandfather Mountain Highland Games, his loyal clansman Orville Campbell and wife Dudley were there to pay tribute to the titled visitors.

The headline in the entertainment industry trade journal, *Variety,* read: "COUNTRY HICK BRINGS BACK TALKING RECORDS." Reference was being made to "What It Was Was Football," but the hick being talked about was not Andy Griffith, it was the many-faceted Orville Campbell, Chapel Hill printer, newspaperman, record producer, and civic leader who has assembled as varied and talented a collection of friends through the years as possibly any North Carolinian.

Variety was excited because there had not been a successful talking record in America since "The Two Black Crows," which was a long time ago. As an interesting follow-up, within five years of the football hit there were 50 talking records produced by comedians across the nation, and yet no verbal recording met with the success of the record Andy Griffith and Orville Campbell produced.

Hero worship is a key part of the Orville Campbell personality, and he freely admits it, saying, "I think everybody living should be a hero worshiper. Every human being should have someone they respect and look up to, someone whose good qualities they would like to attain."

Campbell grew up in Hickory, and he credits a Duke University football star in his hometown, Norman "Pinky" James, who roomed with Duke's great All-American Freddy Crawford, as being his first hero who gave him his original intense interest in athletics. Pinky James and his wife Inez gave young Orville twenty Horatio Alger books one Christmas, and when asked recently whether he read all of them, Campbell's answer was, "Damn right!"

Everyone's basketball hero at UNC in the early 1940s was George Glamack, "The Blind Bomber," who in that day of low-scoring basketball games set a record unheard of in the south by scoring 45 points against Clemson. Campbell and Glamack taught a church school class together, and since UNC basketball games were not crowded in those days, they were able to have the youngsters from their class at the game the night Glamack scored 45 points. After the game Orville and George celebrated by taking all of the kids to the UNC dining hall for a five cent ice cream cone.

When Campbell ran for editor of the campus newspaper, *The Daily Tar Heel,* George Glamack was his campaign manager. George personally escorted Campbell through every dormitory and Orville won by a margin of seven votes over present-day famous pollster Louis Harris. Glamack was a native of Yugoslavia, and after the United States entered World War II, there were preliminary steps taken for Glamack, whose full name was Juro Gregorvith Glamaclij, to return to Belgrade, Yugoslavia as an undercover agent for the U.S. government. As the war appeared to be drawing to a close, however, plans changed and Glamack played basketball for the U.S. Navy at Great Lakes Naval Training Station. After Navy service he played for the Rochester, N.Y., professional basketball team.

While it had been hero worshiper Orville Campbell who had become friends with George Glamack, it was talent scout Orville Campbell who became friends with 18-year-old UNC freshman George Hamilton IV, and who launched Hamilton on a musical career that has taken him to stardom in country music on the Grand Old Opry in Nashville. Hamilton had been told in high school that if he wanted a career in the music business, he needed a hit record, so he began calling at Campbell's office in Chapel Hill as soon as he enrolled in the University. Each time Campbell put him off, Hamilton would come back again a few days later. Hamilton says, "Orville was friendly, but he wasn't as excited about me as I was. He said we needed some original material. He finally told me that I didn't sing so good, but that I was the most persistent young fellow he had ever met, and that I deserved a chance."

Finally they found a song, *A Rose And A Baby Ruth,* written by John D. Loudermilk, a young commercial artist at WTVD, Durham. While both artists were too polite to come right out and say it, songwriter Loudermilk thought Hamilton was about the worst singer he had ever heard, and Hamilton thought *A Rose And A Baby Ruth* was the worst song he had ever heard. However, they allowed a determined Orville Campbell to prevail. The song was re-corded, the records sold "like hot cakes," and *A Rose And A Baby Ruth* by George Hamilton IV quickly became a national hit. In the years that followed Hamilton achieved his goal of becoming a regular on the Grand Old Opry. He is one of the top favorite country singers in Europe, particularly in Great Britain, where he is extremely popular. He is very loyal to his home state of North Carolina, and loyal to Orville Campbell, who gave him his start.

Johnny Loudermilk continued to write songs, and Orville Campbell used several more of them in the 200 records that he made for various artists on the Colonial Records label. Loudermilk also sang for a while, using the name "Johnny Dee." His voice bore great simi-larity to Gene Austin, popular singer of the 1920s, and Campbell considered bringing back an album of Gene Austin's hits sung by Johnny Dee. It was a great disappointment to many of us that he didn't. Songwriter Johnny Loudermilk continued to meet with such success, however, that Johnny Dee did not have time to sing. Loudermilk moved to Nashville and wrote a string of country hits, including *Abilene, Tobacco Road, Bad News, Break My Mind, Waterloo,* and *Sad Movies Make Me Cry.* Another of his songs, *Then You Can Tell Me Goodbye,* has been recorded, remarkably, 46 times.

Creative people have different ways of fine-tuning their artistic talents. One day in the 1950s Johnny Loudermilk turned up in my Wilmington office and asked if I knew the people in charge of the New Hanover County jail. He said a hurricane was about one day away off the coast, and when it hit shore he wanted to be in the middle of it, firmly locked in jail, for

continued

Ted Williams was in Navy Pre-Flight School in Chapel Hill when he and Orville Campbell became good friends. The Boston Red Sox outfielder was the last major leaguer to bat over .400, and he is one of America's best fishermen.

Clyde King of Goldsboro, the only North Carolinian to manage three major league baseball teams (New York Yankees, Atlanta Braves, and San Francisco Giants) holds a place of honor on Orville Campbell's hero list.

Another of Orville Campbell's Navy Pre-Flight School buddies, Otto Graham, was named the most valuable player in professional football when he was with the Cleveland Browns. Graham (right) is at the Azalea Open in Wilmington chatting with golf great Sam Snead. Snead's advice on how to learn to putt is putt for $100.

Writer-photographer Billy Arthur, at the Azalea Festival with broadcaster Ted Malone, is one of Orville Campbell's special Chapel Hill friends.

then, and only then, would he be properly inspired to write the song he was contemplating. When the hurricane missed Wilmington Johnny moved up the coast ahead of it, and made arrangements with the Carteret County Sheriff in Beaufort to occupy a jail cell there where the storm finally came ashore. Wild? Sure it was wild, but it worked for Loudermilk, who has written both music and lyrics for over 1,000 country songs—something that no one else has done. In April 1988, when Grandfather Mountain had recorded winds of 172 miles per hour, Johnny read about it in the Nashville newspaper, and let us know he wished that he had been on Grandfather's peaks.

Billy Carmichael was the friend for whom Campbell says he always had the most admiration, and always will. Campbell believes that before Carmichael died, the former UNC comptroller was the most powerful man in North Carolina. Carmichael had held a seat on the New York Stock Exchange, and he could mingle with the affluent as one of them. Yet he was popular with the most rural good-old-boy in the General Assembly when he went seeking funds for the University, leaving a calling card that read: "You Cannot Build A Vast University With A Half Vast Budget." Comptroller Carmichael worked perfectly with the president, Dr. Frank P. Graham, Campbell says, because Graham was considered liberal by many people, and Carmichael was the senior university official who provided the needed conservative balance. Graham and Carmichael, as a completely harmonious team, were able to secure both public and private funds to advance the university.

Like anyone else who believes in what he is doing, Orville Campbell always likes to have his friends listen to his new records, and hopefully then they will tell him that he has another great hit. One day Campbell walked into the University Comptroller's office and asked if Carmichael had heard his last record. Without even looking up from what he was doing Carmichael said, "I sure to goodness hope I have."

In the 1950s Clarence Stone was a powerful member of the North Carolina Senate, and headed the search committee seeking a new president for the University of North Carolina system when Gordon Gray retired. Senator Stone came to Billy Carmichael's office to advise him that the committee was in unanimous agreement that Carmichael should be the new president. Billy told the Senator that he appreciated the honor, but there was no way he could be president. Stone kept insisting. Finally Carmichael told Stone that he was a Roman Catholic. The senator leaped to his feet and said, "The hell you say!" He then left Carmichael's office, and nothing else was ever said. Times appear to have changed in North Carolina since that incident. For example, North Carolina voted for John F. Kennedy in 1960.

Orville Campbell, during part of his navy service, was in the public relations section of the Pre-Flight School at Chapel Hill, where he became friends with two of America's greatest professional athletes, Otto Graham of the Cleveland Browns football team, and Ted Williams of the Boston Red Sox baseball team. Graham, who in 1988 was athletic director at the U.S. Coast Guard Academy in New London, Conn., has visited Campbell on numerous occasions through the years, and takes pride in the fact that Orville had adopted him as a Tar Heel. Williams also stays in touch. In addition to his great string of major league batting records, he is pleased to hold the record for having batted a ball from the old Emerson field over the top of Lenoir Dining Hall at UNC. The new Davis Library now covers Emerson field so Ted Williams record will stand forever.

Robert B. House served 23 years as UNC Chancellor, longer than any other man. As a student, Orville Campbell was immediately attracted to him because House, though a learned scholar, never lost his country boy common touch. Campbell believes that all students who passed through the University while House was chancellor had fond feelings for the great teacher, who had the knack of instilling in students the belief that they were important, and that what they were doing in going to school was important.

If put to a vote of UNC's living alumni, it would probably be decided by an overwhelming margin that the most important deed of William B. Aycock's tenure as Chancellor of UNC-Chapel Hill was hiring Dean Smith as the head basketball coach. Smith, as assistant to Frank McGuire, had stepped in to help Aycock defend the University during the NCAA basketball investigation in the early 1960s. Aycock did not waver or delay in appointing him as head coach when McGuire decided to coach pro basketball in Philadelphia.

Smith was relatively unknown, so Aycock's decision then was more courageous than it might appear to be in 1988. Obviously Aycock's judgment in selecting a basketball coach has worked out just fine; the same can be said for his legal abilities, for on a number of occasions he was voted the most outstanding professor in the University of North Carolina Law School, to which he returned after serving as chancellor.

Clyde King of Goldsboro is one of North Carolina's home-grown athletes with whom Orville Campbell struck up a warm friendship. Clyde was an outstanding baseball pitcher at UNC. He later pitched for the Brooklyn Dodgers before having a career as manager of three major league teams. Orville considers King to be one of the most Christian oriented persons he has known in athletics, and says that consequently King is universally respected. Clyde King has been extremely helpful in off-season advice to the UNC Athletic Department. As an ex-pitcher who knows about sore arms, he materially aided in suggesting exercises for UNC football quarterback Mark Maye, who was plagued with arm trouble during his college career.

Billy Arthur was UNC head cheerleader, and after graduating in 1932, he took a fling at vaudeville where his diminutive size caused him to be billed as "A Yard of Fun." Billy was often the lead act to warm up the audience for such stars as Milton Berle, Eddie Cantor and

continued

Georgia Carroll Kyser holds a framed Tar Heel in the Kenan Stadium guest box as the University of North Carolina Band on the field behind her plays *Tar Heels On Hand* in tribute to her late husband Kay Kyser, who composed the popular UNC fight song when he was head cheerleader.

The scene is the United States Embassy in London, and the performer is George Hamilton IV, who was discovered and first recorded by Orville Campbell. A member of the Grand Old Opry, Hamilton was appearing before a group of British travel agents during the November 1987 London Travel Mission sponsored by the State of North Carolina and Piedmont Airlines.

Orville Campbell (right) and famous pollster Louis Harris (left) ran against each other for the editorship of *The Daily Tar Heel* when they were UNC students.

Rolfe Neill (right), publisher of the *Charlotte Observer*, invited Orville Campbell to make the induction speech which ushered Neill into the North Carolina Journalism Hall of Fame.

John D. Loudermilk is a talented young singer and song writer from Durham whom Orville Campbell discovered and launched toward a successful musical career in Nashville.

One of the great educators who was "just plain folks" was University of North Carolina Chancellor Robert B. House, who carried his "notes" to every speaking engagement. Orville Campbell was his enthusiastic admirer.

Jimmy Durante. Billy earned enough money in show business to buy the Jacksonville, N.C., newspaper, on which he carried a banner reading, "The Only Newspaper In the World That Gives A Hoot About Onslow County." When Billy sold the paper and moved to Chapel Hill, Campbell immediately recruited him as a columnist for the *Chapel Hill Newspaper.* Campbell believes Arthur has the most interesting column in the paper.

Another former head cheerleader who moved back to Chapel Hill was "The Old Professor" Kay Kyser, the most commercially successful dance band leader in the United States during the World War II era. Kyser's return to Chapel Hill was prompted by Billy Carmichael, and it was through friendship with Carmichael that Orville Campbell became good friends with Kay and Georgia Kyser. Kyser was extremely active in the national organization of the Christian Science Church, but in Chapel Hill he always remained low profile, often removing his trademark horn rim glasses to keep from being recognized on the street.

Rolfe Neill, publisher of the *Charlotte Observer,* was inducted into the N.C. Journalism Hall of Fame in April 1988, and Neill selected his former employer, Orville Campbell, to make the induction speech. Only days before Neill's newspaper had received the Pulitzer Prize for its thorough and responsible coverage of the scandal surrounding Jim Bakker and the PTL Ministry.

Also present at that Journalism Hall of Fame banquet was UNC President Emeritus Bill Friday. Neill thanked Bill Friday for educating him at the University "by setting me free without setting me adrift." Neill said that on his first day at his first newspaper job, he went to work tremendously excited, and that nearly 40 years later, he still goes to work that way. Campbell's Scottish heritage is very apparent when he admits that his fondness for Neill developed very rapidly when, as his employer years ago, he found that Neill did twice as much work for the same amount of money as everyone else.

There really seems to be no end to the list of Orville Campbell's distinguished friends. For instance, he gave another Pulitzer Prize winner, cartoonist Jeff McNelly, his first fulltime newspaper job after he graduated, and another Pulitzer winner, W. Horace Carter, was Campbell's partner in a printing business in Carrboro immediately following World War II. The Broadway musical composer, Richard Adler, is another friend. It is important not to forget Campbell's prominent father-in-law, George Watts Hill, and former UNC Chancellors Carlyle Sitterson and Christopher Fordham. And Charlie Justice, Bill Friday, Vermont Royster, Andy Griffith, and Dean Smith are covered in other chapters of this book . . . all of them friends and heroes.

Then there is another list, a much shorter one covering North Carolina's best talent scouts and hero worshipers, and at the top of it is the name Orville Campbell. *HMM*

U.S.S. NORTH CAROLINA

'The Immortal Showboat'

It all began with a brief news item that the mighty World War II battleship, U.S.S. *North Carolina*, was scheduled to be sold for scrap metal. James S. Craig, Jr. of Wilmington was horrified that the great ship would be destroyed and voiced his complaints at the local American Legion post where others urged him to do something about it.

After many discouragements, Craig managed to get his plea to Governor Luther H. Hodges that the State of North Carolina should save the ship. In the spring of 1960 the Governor appointed the U.S.S. *North Carolina* Battleship Advisory Committee. Orville Campbell of Chapel Hill was named chairman, and the authors of this book, Ed Rankin and I, were among the 15 committee members. The committee was asked to determine if it was feasible and advisable to save the ship that the U.S. Navy had scheduled to be scrapped.

After trips by committee members to Bayonne, N.J. to see the *North Carolina* in mothballs, and to Texas to view the U.S.S. *Texas* on display at San Jacinto State Park near Houston, the committee reported to Governor Hodges that it was feasible and advisable to save the ship, that the project would cost $250,000, and that the site where the ship would be seen by the most people was at Wilmington.

Governor Hodges supported the proposal but said that since he was in his last months of office, the committee should pursue the matter with incoming Governor Terry Sanford. Governor Hodges said that the $250,000 could probably be obtained from the General Assembly, but if so, relatively few people would even know that the ship was in the state.

On the other hand, if the funds were raised in a statewide campaign by public subscription, Hodges pointed out, the ship would be well advertised for 10 years to come. After hearing the governor's advice, it was apparent that every member of the committee had promotional blood in his veins, and that money would be raised by public subscription.

Governor Sanford was just as enthusiastic as Governor Hodges for saving the ship. He appointed to the Battleship Commission many of the same persons who had served on the Hodges advisory committee. One important new face was Jimmy Craig, the Wilmingtonian who had the original idea to save the ship. Governor Sanford named me chairman of the commission.

One of the most heart-warming results of the drive for funds was that many of the state's most western counties were among the first to meet their goals. It was truly a statewide campaign. Over 700,000 of the state's 1,100,000 school children paid 10 cents for advance admission tickets to the ship, and 2,400 citizens paid $100 to become Admirals in the North Carolina Navy. The goal of $250,000 was rather quickly achieved, with the final tally being $315,000. The North Carolina Press Association, the N.C. Association of Broadcasters, the Outdoor Advertising Association, the teachers and principals—everyone pitched in to publicize the drive. As Governor Hodges had predicted, the ship was "well advertised for 10 years to come."

Since many groups had tried to save other ships and failed, the U.S. Navy moved very cautiously before agreeing that North Carolina could have its namesake ship. The Navy wanted us to succeed, but it wanted to be certain the job would be done right. Governor Sanford decided to visit the White House to acquaint President John F. Kennedy with the plans for the memorial. Not only did the President show a personal interest in our ship, the Pentagon gave its active cooperation. It was smooth sailing for the U.S.S. *North Carolina* once the President's wishes were known.

On a second trip to Washington, Governor Sanford and I were joined by Senator Sam Ervin and Congressman Alton Lennon to meet with Admiral Arleigh Burke, Chief of Naval Operations. While we were waiting in Admiral Burke's outer office, an admiral on his staff, making pleasant conversation, asked, "Mr. Morton, what was your ship during the war?" I replied, "Admiral, I am just as sorry as I can be, but I was a sergeant in the U.S. Army." The admiral looked at me with absolute disdain, then looked at Governor Sanford in disbelief that he could have appointed an Army sergeant as chairman of the Battleship Commission.

Governor Sanford hastily explained that the U.S.S. *North Carolina* would be a memorial to *all* of the U.S. armed forces, and specifically for the 10,000 North Carolinians of all the services who had died in World War II. He said his appointment of an Army man was an attempt to place the memorial in its proper perspective.

No sooner had the admiral on Burke's staff

The Battleship *North Carolina* is rounding third, headed for home on the Wilmington waterfront on October 2, 1961, where she is nudged from the Cape Fear River into her freshly dredged slip by 11 tugboats. The battleship, without her own power, had needed only two large ocean-going tugs for the tow from New Jersey to the mouth of the Cape Fear River at Southport. Tricky maneuvers in the 30 miles of river upstream to Wilmington required the extra tugs to keep the ship safely in the Cape Fear channel.

One of America's wartime heroes, Admiral Arleigh Burke, was Chief of Naval Operations at the time the state received the U.S.S. *North Carolina*. Admiral Burke allowed 1,500,000 gallons of fuel oil to remain on the ship for "ballast," which the Battleship Commission sold as soon as the battlewagon reached Wilmington. The money from the oil was used to prepare the ship for public display.

A determined young member of the Wilmington Jaycees and American Legion, James S. Craig, Jr. first had the idea to save the U.S.S. *North Carolina*, and he nagged those in authority until the notion caught on. Appointed a member of the Battleship Commission, his enthusiasm for the project remained high. On this Saturday afternoon when the ship was already under tow from Bayonne, he was inspecting the dredging of soil onto the site of the parking lot for the memorial.

The following afternoon Jimmy Craig was one of five people fatally injured in a plane crash during an air show at New Hanover County Airport. Craig was a passenger in the support craft of the U.S. Air Force Thunderbirds flying team which was carrying the Golden Knights Parachute Team aloft for an exhibition jump. Jimmy Craig did not live to see the battleship in its Wilmington berth.

This photograph taken by Hugh Morton of General of the Army Douglas MacArthur on the Phillipine island of Luzon in 1945 was used by sculptor John Weaver as a guide in forming the MacArthur bust.

The original busts for the Battleship Commission created by John Weaver resulted in much favorable comment about the sculptures of Roosevelt, Nimitz, and MacArthur, but President Truman without his glasses was said not to be a good likeness. When glasses were experimentally placed on the Truman bust, the resemblance was immediately considered perfect.

President John F. Kennedy receives the first commission as Admiral in The North Carolina Navy from Governor Terry Sanford, who had to borrow a framed certificate from the office wall of White House Press Secretary Pierre Salinger when the North Carolina certificates did not arrive from the printer. When the president realized the substitution, he broke into laughter. The picture of the president and governor in the U.S.S. *North Carolina* brochure greatly facilitated the negotiations with the Navy for the ship. Other North Carolinians at the White House meeting were Conservation and Development Director Hargrove "Skipper" Bowles, U.S. Senators B. Everett Jordan and Sam J. Ervin, U.S. Commerce Secretary Luther H. Hodges, and Battleship Chairman Hugh Morton.

Lowell Thomas, the nation's best known newscaster of the radio era, is master of ceremonies at Bayonne, New Jersey for the transfer of the U.S.S. *North Carolina* from the U.S. Navy to the State of North Carolina in 1961. Left to right are Cyril Adams of Houston, Texas, the maritime engineer who designed the berthing plans for the Battleship *Texas* near Houston and the Battleship *North Carolina* at Wilmington; U.S. Secretary of Commerce and former N.C. Governor Luther H. Hodges; Governor Terry Sanford; and Thomas. General Kenneth C. Royall of Goldsboro, a personal friend of Thomas, extended North Carolina's invitation to the noted broadcaster to officiate at the transfer of the ship.

A substantial part of the $315,000 raised to establish the Battleship Memorial came from 2,400 Admirals of the North Carolina Navy, who paid $100 each to obtain their Admiral rank. The memorial was dedicated by an address by Admiral Arleigh Burke, and most of North Carolina's Admirals are on the deck of the ship.

When the battleship approached its berth, a floating restaurant, The Ark, was supposed to have been moved to another location. This did not happen so an irresistible force struck this unmoved object. In spite of valiant efforts of the hard-working tugs involved, one 40 mm gun turret on the stern of the incoming U.S.S. *North Carolina* tagged the upper structure of The Ark, inflicting minor damage. Had the 35,000 ton battleship struck the restaurant's concrete hull, the dining establishment would assuredly have sunk.

Governor Terry Sanford, a former World War II paratrooper, wears a borrowed Coast Guard cap and jacket for protection from wind and rain as he has his first view of the battleship in North Carolina waters at the mouth of the Cape Fear River off Southport.

partially recovered from the sergeant shock than Senator Sam Ervin mischievously said, "Admiral, it may interest you to know that we have 2,400 admirals in the North Carolina Navy." Even when we told him that every North Carolina admiral had to pay $100 to save the battleship, the U.S. Navy's real admiral could not hide his feelings that he had suffered a bad day.

The Battleship Commission determined at the beginning that no public money should be accepted from the national, state, or local level governments for the Battleship Memorial, and more than 25 years later that policy is still in effect. It is probably the only state project to operate independently of public funds for that length of time. Not only is the ship a memorial to the World War II war dead from the state, it is a tribute to the patriotism of the living citizens of North Carolina who supported the project with dedication and generosity.

Most similar undertakings in other states have from the outset been tax supported. The General Assembly did appropriate $450,000 as a loan to the Battleship Memorial for the installation of the elaborate Sound and Light show, but only $300,000 of that amount was used. The $300,000 was paid back from admissions almost immediately, much to the surprise of many members of the General Assembly.

The United States government still owns the U.S.S. *North Carolina*, the ship's status being described as "on permanent loan to the State of North Carolina." This means that at frequent intervals U.S. Navy inspectors check the U.S.S. *North Carolina*, and on several occasions the inspection team has found that the ship's paint job and cleanliness were as good or better than while the vessel was in service, a high tribute to Captain Frank S. Conlon, USN (Ret.), superintendent of the Battleship Memorial, and his crew.

Technically, the United States can reclaim the U.S.S. *North Carolina* when an emergency might justify such a move, but the U.S. Navy may think long and hard about that. The battleship appears to be afloat, but actually she is lodged solidly in mud. It would be a tougher job to move her out than it was to move her in, and that was not easy.

In 1969 Vice Admiral Ernest M. Eller, Director of Naval History for the United States Navy, wrote, *"North Carolina*, the first of the new battleships of World War II, has special significance to the Navy and the Nation. Her brilliant performance in gunnery in the Pacific with the fast carrier task forces played an important role in our ultimate victory. She well deserved to be enshrined."

Admiral Eller's statement, of course, speaks for itself, and the *North Carolina*'s record speaks for itself. She was in all 12 offensive naval engagements of the Pacific war, from Guadalcanal to Tokyo Bay. By comparison, the U.S.S. *Missouri* was in three of those 12 offensive naval engagements. Applying any plausible yardstick one cares to use, the U.S.S. *North Carolina* may well be the greatest battleship ever floated by the United States. We who hail from North Carolina were in luck the day it was decided to name this particular ship for our state. *HMM*

The Sound and Light show, "The Immortal Showboat," features blazing 16-inch guns and accompanying sound effects of the U.S.S. *North Carolina* in battle, and the recorded voices of President Franklin D. Roosevelt, Winston Churchill, Adolph Hitler, and President Harry S Truman. Seen each summer night from a reviewing stand beside the ship, it is the largest automated Sound and Light show in the world, and one of the most moving patriotic presentations in the United States.

"WHO'D EVER THOUGHT HE'D BE SPEAKIN' ON A BATTLESHIP?"

©*Bill Mauldin*

When famed World War II cartoonist Bill Mauldin was the Battleship Memorial's Veterans Day speaker on November 11, 1963, his characters Willie and Joe had something to say about it.

Bill Mauldin, Veterans Day speaker November 11, 1963.

Retired U.S. Navy Rear Admiral Robert B. Ellis, Superintendent of the Battleship Memorial during the major conditioning for public display, inspects one of the engine rooms with his assistant, Retired Navy Captain Brooke Jennings (left).

The members of the Battleship Commission are pictured with Governor Terry Sanford the day he announced the appointments in 1961. Shown clockwise around the Governor beginning at the left: Hugh Morton, Ed Rankin, Tom Morse, Percy Ferrebee, Jack Younts, Bill Womble, John H. Fox, G. Andrew Jones, Orville Campbell, Victor Bryant, and James S. Craig, Jr.

The U.S.S. *North Carolina* Battleship Memorial honors the more than 10,000 men and women from North Carolina in all of the United States armed services who died in World War II, and their names are carried on a honor roll aboard the ship. In some years fireworks shows have been a part of the program for Memorial Day.

WILLIAM B. UMSTEAD
Laid Down His Life as Governor

William Umstead, then a United States Senator by appointment of
Governor R. Gregg Cherry, visits with a neighbor's child and his dog.
Umstead had a special affection for children and animals. He was
born and raised on a Durham County farm. When he was nine years
old, his father gave him a trim black colt to raise and work on the farm.
The boy and his colt, Robbie, grew up together and he used her to do
his share of farm work and later earn the necessary money to pay for
his college education at the University of North Carolina at Chapel
Hill. As a reward for her faithful service, he kept and provided for the
horse until she died at the age of 33 years, and made a special trip from
Washington, D.C. to Durham to be with Robbie at her death. He was
then serving as a member of the United States House of Representatives from the Sixth North Carolina District.

William B. Umstead may be the least known governor of North Carolina in this century. His death at age 59 after only 22 months in office ended (November 7, 1954) the term of a highly qualified, intelligent and conscientious leader and public servant.

Although he became seriously ill two days after his inauguration, he strongly supported his program for "A Better Tomorrow for North Carolina," and the 1953 General Assembly approved the majority of the legislation he recommended. His major appointments to state office were able people whose performance stood the test of time. Within less than a year in office, he was faced with the sudden deaths of two United States Senators—Willis Smith and Clyde R. Hoey.

His replacement for Smith, former state senator Alton Lennon of Wilmington, was later defeated by former governor W. Kerr Scott. Sam J. Ervin, Jr., his appointment to fill Hoey's seat, won his election and served with distinction in the United States Senate for 20 years before retiring voluntarily.

On May 17, 1954 the Supreme Court of the United States made its decision on the principle of segregation in public schools, thus handing Governor Umstead the grave responsibility of dealing with one of the most complex problems ever faced in North Carolina. Luther H. Hodges, the lieutenant governor, who succeeded to office following Umstead's death, said, "He met this issue calmly and wisely. Due to his leadership and his reasonable, thoughtful approach to this decision, North Carolina kept its equilibrium during what could have been a turbulent period." (See Thomas J. Pearsall, Chapter 41.)

What manner of man was William B. Umstead? Who knew better than his former law partner, Percy Reade of Durham, who spoke eloquently to a joint session of the General Assembly of North Carolina honoring the Governor's memory, "William Umstead was a man of the finest character and ability. He was sincere, courageous, loyal, dependable, honest, just, genuine and patriotic. He worked unceasingly at whatever his hands found to do. He never sought to avoid the hard places or shift to the shoulders of others unpleasant duties. He hated sham and pretense and despised hypocrites and demagogues. He regarded men who would stoop to mislead the people for political advantage as public enemies. He would have chosen defeat at any time in preference to compromise. His public and private life was unblemished." *ELR*

Governor Umstead and General Mark Clark, President of The Citadel, enjoy talking at the Orton Mansion, Wilmington, in 1954. Both men had served their country in time of war in the U.S. Army. When the U.S. entered World War I, Umstead volunteered, took his officer training, was assigned to a machine gun battalion of the 81st "Wild Cat" division, and served overseas in combat. General Clark, a career Army officer, had a distinguished career leading U.S. forces in Europe and the Mediterranean during World War II.

The City of Wilmington, home town of Alton Lennon, gives him an enthusiastic send-off to Washington as the newly-appointed United States Senator from North Carolina. The local high school band and thousands of fellow citizens gathered to express their best wishes for the former state senator and his charming wife, Kay.

Daughter Merle Bradley plays the piano and leads her parents in song at their home in Durham. They were a happy, close-knit family, with traditional American values, living quietly, whether in Durham, Washington or Raleigh. A native of Rutherford County, and a school teacher, Merle Davis Umstead was a gracious, gentle and quiet-spoken First Lady of North Carolina. Rarely has any First Lady had to undergo more stress and emotional strain than she did when her husband suffered a heart attack within two days after taking the oath of office as governor. During the governor's hospitalization in Durham, and prolonged bed rest at the executive mansion, Mrs. Umstead maintained a warm and considerate family life for her husband and daughter while carrying on, under trying circumstances, a limited social schedule during the 1953 General Assembly session. As the Governor recovered gradually from his illness and returned to his official duties, Mrs. Umstead walked by his side. When the governor suffered a relapse of health in the next year, Mrs. Umstead and Merle Bradley were at his bedside at Watts Hospital, Durham, when he died, November 7, 1954.

Photo by June Glenn, Jr.

Governor Umstead and his daughter, Merle Bradley, officially open the mile-high swinging bridge on Grandfather Mountain in Avery County. Grady Cole (left), WBT Radio personality and commentator, and Hugh Morton, owner of Grandfather Mountain, welcome the guests of honor. A large crowd gathered to witness the brief ceremonies and cheered as the governor and his daughter crossed the bridge for the first time. A bronze plaque now marks the spot where the governor stood to make his remarks. To the left of Grady Cole can be seen Julia Taylor Morton, wife of Hugh.

THE DEATH OF A GOVERNOR

Governor William Bradley Umstead has been the only chief executive of North Carolina to die in office in this century. I served as his private secretary. Following his death, it was my sad duty to write the "sketch" of his administration in the book of addresses, letters and papers, which is published for each governor by the Council of State and the State Division of Archives and History. Here, in part, is what I wrote about the last days of a great governor and a good friend:

The year between sessions of the General Assembly is always a busy period of budget study and recommendations for the next session. So, in the summer of 1954, the Governor and Advisory Budget Commission began the intensive work on hearings, preparation and recommendations. Despite all the other major problems on hand, the governor made it clear that he expected to devote as much time as possible to every phase of the Commission's work.

On Thursday, November 4, 1954, William Umstead left his office to attend another conference of the Advisory Budget Commission. He was not well that day, although those of us in the office did not realize the seriousness of his condition. He stayed in the meeting until lunch time and then doggedly returned to the meeting following his lunch. By mid-afternoon the governor's failing strength would not permit him to remain, and reluctantly he returned to the executive mansion and to bed. After a brief examination, the doctors ordered the governor to Watts Hospital in Durham for rest and treatment. It was explained to the press that Governor Umstead had a severe cold which had failed to respond to treatment and this condition had aggravated his heart condition.

Before he left for the hospital, I had a 30-minute conference with the governor to handle a number of details, including several appointments which he wanted to announce. The governor sat up in bed, a blanket around his shoulders while we talked. He was completely exhausted, unable to overcome his physical ailments; but the determined spirit of the man shone through his clear eyes, firm voice and complete command of what he was discussing. His instructions to me were as precise and thorough as ever. We parted with a firm handshake and unspoken words of warm affection.

Following the procedure used during earlier hospitalizations, the Governor's Office began to issue medical bulletins on the governor's condition two or three times a day. On Friday, November 5,

Umstead's condition continued serious and no improvement was shown. On Saturday, November 6, the governor was reported somewhat better in the morning. Early Sunday morning, November 7, Dr. Fleming reported that the Governor had pneumonia and there was no improvement. Mrs. Umstead and daughter, Merle Bradley, were called early that morning and advised to come to the hospital. They were at the bedside when William Umstead expired quietly and suddenly at 9:10 a.m. The cause of the death was congestive heart failure.

After learning that Mrs. Umstead and Merle Bradley had been summoned to Durham, I hurried to the hospital, arriving about 10:00 a.m. It was then my sad duty to pick up the telephone at 10:15 a.m. to inform the press that the Governor of North Carolina was dead. My next telephone call was to the Lieutenant Governor of North Carolina, the Honorable Luther H. Hodges of Leaksville, to notify him officially that he was the new Governor of North Carolina.

It was a stunned and shocked North Carolina that received the news of William Umstead's death on Sunday morning, November 7. Many people heard the news while attending church. Friends of the governor, who knew his determination to complete his term of office, found it hard to believe that he was gone.

Since the state had not experienced the loss of a chief executive in the 20th century, there was no precedent for handling the ceremony of succession. The North Carolina Constitution simply specifies that the Lieutenant Governor succeeds to office upon the death of the governor. There was no precedent for a state funeral and all these details and decisions had to be worked out with the Council of State and with Mrs. Umstead and members of the Umstead family. Monday, November 8, was devoted to plans for the funeral and a motorcade was planned for state elected officials to attend the funeral in a group.

At 11:30 a.m., Tuesday, November 9, last rites were held for Governor Umstead at Trinity Methodist Church in Durham, where he had been an active member and lay leader for many years. Burial followed in the little Mount Tabor Methodist Church graveyard near Bahama. This had been the church of his ancestors. Thousands of friends from across the state attended the funeral and the graveside services. The funeral procession reached miles out into the country as it moved toward the governor's final resting place. *continued*

William Bradley Umstead (left) and Luther Hartwell Hodges view the inaugural parade in Raleigh on January 8, 1953.

At 4:00 p.m. that afternoon, Luther H. Hodges formally took his oath of office as the Governor of North Carolina. A huge crowd jammed into the Capitol's Hall of the House of Representatives to watch the brief, solemn ceremonies.

William Umstead literally laid down his life in the performance of his duties as governor. Although he was proud of his record in many high public offices, he cherished the governorship above all else and was determined, beyond description, to serve out his term of office and to complete the program he had planned for a "Better Tomorrow" in North Carolina.

This conscientious attention to duty was dramatically illustrated by one of his final acts in life.

The day after the funeral, I was approached by a lawyer who had been working for a special state commission preparing a report and recommendations on the judicial redistricting of North Carolina. He explained that the final report of this commission had been given to Governor Umstead several days before he entered the hospital for the last time, and that the report was needed immediately since it was the only complete, corrected copy in existence.

After searching the office without success, I went to the executive mansion and looked around Governor Umstead's bedroom. There was his big easy chair with a reading lamp and a small table covered with reports, journals, newspapers and other reading material. This was where he did most of his reading and studying. A careful search of all this material did not uncover the report.

The governor's maid, Margaret, was then asked if she had any idea where the report might be found. She did not remember seeing the document, and stood undecided for a moment. Then her glance fell on the worn, old-fashioned leather suitcase which the governor had taken with him to the hospital.

Moving quietly, she opened the bag carefully and began to remove the few personal articles it contained. There, at the bottom of the bag, neatly folded under a pair of pajamas, was the missing report.

Gravely ill, William Umstead had not gone to the hospital empty-handed. Conscientious always, he had carried with him this copy of a redistricting plan in which he was deeply interested because it dealt with a subject close to his heart—law and the courts. He had carried the report with him because he expected to study it at his very first opportunity.

This was typical of a brave man who struggled against greater odds and greater handicaps than any other governor in this century. He accepted his handicaps without complaint, and was willing to go every step of the way necessary to carry out the duties and responsibilities given him by the vote of the people of North Carolina. *ELR*

Author's Note: *Reprinted from* Addresses, Letters, and Papers of Governor William B. Umstead, 1953-54, *with permission of the North Carolina Division of Archives and History, Department of Cultural Resources; and with permission from the November 1970 issue of* We the People of NORTH CAROLINA, *official publication of the North Carolina Citizens for Business and Industry.*

MUSIC OF THE STARS
N.C. Country/Mountain Greats

Doc Watson of Deep Gap in Watauga County has won four Grammy Awards in the folk and country music categories. His 25 albums and many other musical accomplishments won him the North Carolina Award, the state's highest recognition, in the category of Fine Arts in 1986.

Doc Watson, world-famous musician, was at the top of a ladder, standing on the roof of a utility building, when he asked me to hand up his hammer and a piece of 2 × 4 wood. Here was a blind man doing carpentry with greater skill than I could have done it, and I have the benefit of eyesight.

This remarkable man is undaunted by any handicap. Walk along a forest trail with Doc and his devoted wife, Rosa Lee. She gives him some gentle guidance but his white cane does the rest. Observe Doc's sensitive appreciation of the beauty of the forest . . . and it is astounding.

He touches the trunk of a tree, identifies it as an oak, runs his hands along the surface of another, and correctly identifies it as a beech. Doc is in tune with his environment in a very special way. Most people with sight would not enjoy the outdoors as much as this mountain man.

Doc Watson has pursued his music with the same dedication, completely determined that his handicap will not limit what he wants to accomplish in music and performing. His blindness may limit some diversions available to other people, but it allows him to concentrate on his music with a professional competence admired the world over.

The Watsons are still trying to cope with the tragic loss of their talented son, Merle, who was killed when a tractor overturned on him in 1985. Father and son were very close. "He was not just a son who felt obligated," Doc Watson says. "He was a friend."

Merle Watson's skill on guitar provided accompaniment so perfect that three years following his death Doc Watson still was not satisfied with any other side man. Merle really did not like being a celebrity. Friends believe that it was largely at Merle's insistence that Doc and Merle resisted performing on television for many years. The Watsons already had four Grammy awards before Charles Kuralt of CBS did the first major TV feature on Doc in 1980.

The Watson family's major project in 1988 was continuing development of the "Eddy Merle Watson Garden of the Senses" at Wilkes Community College, about 20 miles from where Merle is buried at the Watson home near the Blue Ridge Parkway at Deep Gap. A benefit performance for the garden featured Chet Atkins, George Hamilton IV, Earl Scruggs, the Moody Brothers, Mac Wiseman and other top-drawer stars. Merle Watson is being remembered.

To understand how popular Lulabelle and Scotty Wiseman were with the home folks in Avery County, one needs an understanding of the politics of the region. The overworked cliche, "I'd rather vote for a yellow dog before I'd vote for a Democrat," could well have been imbedded in bronze above the door of the Avery County Courthouse.

Yet Lulabelle Wiseman, a registered Democrat, became the first woman from her district ever to be elected to the North Carolina General Assembly. She quickly won respect and affection in Raleigh, Scotty was a proud and dutiful legislative spouse, and the district had a persuasive and effective representative.

Their musical ability and charm made Lulabelle and Scotty the stars of seven full-length motion pictures that did well at the box office in the 1940s. Song writing was Scotty's love, and while he wrote serious songs like *Ballad of the Brown*

continued

Photo by Jim Morton

Merle Watson was 15 when he began playing professionally with his father. When each nation was asked to send a musical group to the 1968 Olympics in Mexico, Doc and Merle Watson were the only two musicians to represent the United States.

Mountain Light, his humorous songs were classics, such as the words to *That Good Old Mountain Dew,* and *Does Your Chewing Gum Lose Its Flavor on the Bed Post Overnight?* Members of the Country Music Hall of Fame, Lulabelle and Scotty Wiseman were lovable and talented professionals at their best.

Although a star of the Metropolitan Opera Company, the personable Norman Cordon had a valid point that he was not a "long-hair," for the top of his head was bald. Cordon's wife, the former Deane Van Landingham of Charlotte, had her family's mountain home at Linville which gave Cordon the opportunity to become friends with some colorful characters of the mountains.

At the 1947 "Singing on the Mountain," Cordon saw one of his mountain friends, known for a love of strong drink, and said, "Well, here it is past noon, and you're cold sober!" His friend smiled and confided that the sheriff had only picked up four drunks, which left three vacancies to fill in the Avery County jail. Then, and only then, was there wisdom in "going to the stump."

Johnny Cash has many North Carolina connections, and among these is an honorary degree from Gardner-Webb College for his musical accomplishments and charitable work. When Johnny Cash and his wife, June Carter Cash, performed at "Singing on the Mountain" the date happened to be June Carter's birthday. So my wife Julia quickly arranged a birthday party for her after their appearance. As Julia gathered enough food for the

Lulabelle and Scotty Wiseman were stars on the WLS Chicago Radio Barn Dance from 1932 to 1958, but Lulabelle says their lives really began when they put up their mail box at Route 2, Spruce Pine. Scotty wrote several hit country songs, the most successful being *Have I Told You Lately That I Love You.* Bascom Lamar Lunsford wrote the music and the chorus and Scotty Wiseman the verses to *That Good Old Mountain Dew,* another big hit.

Norman Cordon, star of the Metropolitan Opera Company, moved to Chapel Hill to promote interest in music in the state through the University Extension Division. The *Star Spangled Banner* never sounded better than when sung by the great basso profundo to open football games. At other programs, native Tar Heel Cordon earned applause with *Old Man River,* and at church functions *Rock of Ages* was his specialty.

party, the numbers kept growing to include the Carter Family Singers and our friends of many years, Arthur Smith and the Cracker-Jacks.

We gathered on the deck of the Morton home on Grandfather Mountain Lake for what proved to be a memorable evening of fun and good conversation. Black clothing is a trademark of Johnny Cash and his band, and Julia's memory was imprinted, in her words, with "lots of big men dressed in black."

Johnny Cash became enthralled by hummingbirds coming to the deck feeder. Rarely have the tiny birds been so bold, flying within inches of Cash's head as he sat on the deck railing. With their swift, jeweled flights, the hummingbirds put on a show for showman Cash he said he would not forget. Ten years later Rosanne Cash recalled the Grandfather Mountain party as one of the happiest family outings that the Johnny Cash family ever had.

Raymond Fairchild, who lives near the Cherokee Indian reservation at Maggie, is one-half Cherokee, proud of his Indian heritage and clearly ranks among the world's best banjo pickers. The Crowe Brothers accompany Fairchild, and now his son, Zane Fairchild, has been added on banjo and guitar. Raymond Fairchild's favorite banjo tunes are *Whoa Mule, The World Is Waiting for the Sunrise,* and *Orange Blossom Special.*

Arthur Smith of Charlotte is a man of many talents, including music. An expert musician with any string instrument, particularly guitar, fiddle and banjo, Smith is also a successful composer, record and television producer and businessman. He has learned much since World War II when he composed *Guitar Boogie,* recorded it in a Washington, D.C. studio and sold the rights for $75. He was serving in the U.S. Navy at the time. Years

continued

The ambition of most Gospel singers in U.S. is to journey to Israel, Holy Land to Christians, and sing at the River Jordan. The cast of Arthur Smith's syndicated television show did just that. Seated on the bank of the River Jordan is Arthur Smith (left) and (clockwise) from Arthur are Sister Maggie Griffin, George Hamilton IV, Brother Ralph Smith, Jackie Schuyler, Dan Ange and Dick Schuyler.

Two of North Carolina's great country music stars, Raymond Fairchild (left) and Arthur Smith, have a great time with Arthur's original instrumental composition, *Dueling Banjos.* When not on the road at other engagements, Raymond Fairchild can be heard nightly at the Maggie Valley Opry House.

later, when he was able to re-record his composition on another label, *Guitar Boogie* began to bring him income, but only after he missed out on royalties for the millions of copies of the original record that had been sold. Smith is noted for his generous donation of his time and talent for church, charitable and public service campaigns.

In 1973 Arthur Smith and his performers traveled to Israel to film their syndicated show at many locations in the Holy Land, including Nazareth, Jericho, Mt. Sinai, Jerusalem, Bethlehem, the Dead Sea and the River Jordan. I went with them to make photographs for the jackets of record albums, and was accompanied by Julia Morton and our daughter, Catherine.

As the film crew recorded the performances at various outdoor locations, military aircraft would occasionally interfere with the sound track. But war conditions were not as tense then as they appeared to be in 1988. We are glad we made our trip when we did. *HMM*

As Johnny Cash and I were walking across the Swinging Bridge, he asked, "How many flags does the wind destroy each year at Grandfather Mountain?" When I told him several, he said, "I do a recitation of a poem I wrote called *That Ragged Old Flag,* and I'd love to have the most ragged Grandfather Mountain flag you've got." Cash has it, and we are mighty pleased he asked.

'SKIPPER' BOWLES
Financier/Politico Who Made 'Dean Dome' Reality

How to capture the remarkable spirit of Hargrove "Skipper" Bowles, a North Carolinian with many talents and achievements?

Tom Lambeth, executive director of the Z. Smith Reynolds Foundation, accomplished that purpose in the euology he delivered at the funeral. Lambeth said, in part:

"If a young lawyer set up practice, Skipper wrote to friends asking them to become clients, and never told the young lawyer of what he had done. If a poor but talented young person needed a college education, Skipper helped see that the opportunity was realized. If a teenager wanted to fish in his lake, Skipper fished with him. He got excited about Carolina basketball, home-grown vegetables, and grandchildren—his and everyone else's—and his excitement made you excited, too."

Tom Lambeth

One of Bowles' good friends and political advisers, journalist John Kilgo, says, "Skipper Bowles could raise money faster than anybody I have seen in my life, and although he was a very pleasant guy, when it came time to ask you for money for his political campaign, or Terry Sanford's, or to raise money for Smith Center, he would ask you for the eyes in your head.

"He was that kind of guy. Skipper was a great salesman. He could go into a one-on-one session, or go into a room full of people and give a message, and by the time he got through he could convert people. He was a very sincere guy, and he was able to translate that to other people."

During fund-raising for the project later named for Dean Smith, Skipper Bowles and Coach Smith hit the road together to call on prospective contributors. On one of the first visits, after Smith had explained the need for the new building, the prospect, a loyal alumnus, asked Smith how much money he should contribute. John Kilgo, who related the incident after hearing it later from both Bowles and Smith, said that the coach, who does not like to solicit money, became embarrassed and said, "I think $10,000 would be a very generous contribution."

Bowles immediately stood up, excused himself and Smith, moved outside to the hallway and gave the coach a new game plan. Smith was to explain the need and Bowles would ask for money. When they returned to the office, Bowles asked the alumnus for $500,000—and got $350,000.

A naturally friendly person, Skipper Bowles had a great smile. I remember it from the first day I ever saw him in 1939 when I watched Skipper Bowles and his Orchestra play, *My Blue Heaven.* I never have been sure how much music he knew, but he was a charming front man for the band and led it well.

John Kilgo

His personal warmth and leadership helped him become successful in business, and he was on the executive committee of the board of First Union National Bank. He was a valuable member of the North Carolina General Assembly. The travel industry will ever be grateful that he initiated the personalized state license plates for autos which generate funds for the state travel and tourism division and the "Keep North Carolina Beautiful" program. When he became director of the state Department of Conservation and Development in the early 1960s, Bowles worked hard for economic development, state ports and state parks.

When Governor Terry Sanford asked me to head the U.S.S. *North Carolina* Battleship Commission, and did not reappoint me to the State Board of Conservation and Development (where I had served the previous 10 years), Skipper Bowles persuaded me to take the battleship assignment. He and Governor Sanford gave the battleship campaign all the support they promised—and more.

How did a successful man like Skipper Bowles take his defeat in the campaign for governor in 1972? He was the first Democratic nominee to lose this office in the 20th century. John Kilgo says Bowles called him several days after the defeat with this comment, "The sad thing about this is

continued

Skipper Bowles enjoyed life, and ice cream cones obviously enhanced that pleasure in this photograph Bowles said was his favorite of himself. The picture was made in Philadelphia while the UNC-Indiana game was in progress to determine the NCAA 1981 National Basketball Championship, which Indiana won that year and Carolina won in 1982.

Skipper Bowles (left) and Lieutenant Governor H.P. "Pat" Taylor, Jr., (center) are making the rounds at Democratic rallies in the summer of 1971 in preparation for a run for Governor. They fully expected to be joined in the Democratic primary by Robert Morgan (right), but Morgan chose not to file. A veteran legislator, Morgan served as Attorney General of North Carolina and as United States Senator.

The naming of Hargrove "Skipper" Bowles Hall by the Board of Trustees of the University of North Carolina was a highly deserved recognition of Skipper Bowles' leadership in raising $30 million in private funds to build the Dean E. Smith Student Activities Center. Bowles Hall, located in the Center, is used for social gatherings of the supporters who make major contributions to the University's athletic programs.

A string of trout like that is well over one person's legal limit, and Skipper Bowles knew that his brothers, John Bowles and Kelly Bowles, had helped him catch them. Skipper just wanted the fun of taking home a picture holding all of the trout the three brothers caught in Grand father Mountain Lake in May 1971.

that the people around me, my family especially, are really depressed and down. It's over as far as I'm concerned. We did everything we could to win. Now I'm going out and do new things in my life, and undertake some new challenges."

Carson Bain

One of these "new challenges" was the establishment of the Center for Alcohol Studies at UNC-Chapel Hill which Skipper Bowles helped initiate. Erskine Bowles, his son, says that his father valued this project as the most important work of his life. A great research center, it has gained international renown for its discovery that humans who have a certain chromosome or gene have a propensity to become alcoholic.

Erskine Bowles says, "They can test and determine whether a person has that chromosome. If you have the chromosome and you drink, then the probability of your becoming alcoholic is almost 100 percent. Now what they have to do is neutralize that chromosome so they can reduce the probability that someone will be alcoholic."

One of Bowles' closest friends was Carson Bain, former mayor of Greensboro. Bain and Bowles rode the bus together to Ft. Bragg to join the Army in World War II. Bain was among the thousands in Chapel Hill when the Dean E. Smith Student Activities Center was opened and Skipper Bowles came out on the floor in a wheel chair. He was terminally ill with Lou Gehrig's disease.

"I think it brought tears to everybody's eyes there," Bain said. "Skipper reminded me of the story in the Bible of Moses. He got to see the promised land, and Moses didn't. That was the highlight of his whole life, seeing that Dome open." *HMM*

133

BLUE RIDGE PARKWAY
52 Years Later: Truth About 'Missing Link'

Black Rock Cliffs is the rocky area immediately above Linn Cove Viaduct. The controversial "high route" for the Blue Ridge Parkway at Grandfather Mountain would have run the roadway above Black Rock Cliffs. The battle for the "high route" raged from 1954 until it was abandoned in 1966, much to the relief of those interested in preserving the natural beauty.

To say that my family has cooperated with the Blue Ridge Parkway would almost be an understatement, because long before ground was broken in 1935 my grandfather, Hugh MacRae, was serving on boards and in delegations to Washington calling for the National Park-to-Park Highway, one of the names used before the name of the Blue Ridge Parkway was adopted.

MacRae had contacts with President Franklin D. Roosevelt, primarily through Josephus Daniels of *The News & Observer,* Raleigh, who was Secretary of the Navy in World War I when FDR was Assistant Navy Secretary. Another of MacRae's acquaintances was Secretary of Interior Harold Ickes, whose department would ultimately administer the Parkway. MacRae had worked closely with Ickes in the development of the Interior Department's project of Penderlea, which was modeled after my grandfather's highly successful farm development at Castle Hayne near Wilmington.

The Linn Cove Viaduct on the Blue Ridge Parkway won nine national awards for its beauty and design, even before it had been opened for traffic. It allows the Parkway to tiptoe through fragile and spectacular scenery without doing harm to the environment.

Meanwhile, Virginia was hard at work under the leadership of U.S. Senator Harry F. Byrd, who was that state's leading political counterpart to Josephus Daniels in North Carolina. Working closely together, the supporters convinced President Roosevelt and Secretary Ickes that the Parkway was worthwhile.

In 1939, our family's company, the Linville Improvement Company, sold an eight-mile stretch of right-of-way to the state for the modest sum of $25,000. This provided a corridor for the Parkway with an average of 125 acres per mile, or 1,000 feet wide, the entire length of our property. The southern four miles were used almost immediately to begin the Parkway's section from Pineola across Grandmother Mountain to Beacon Heights, while World War II delayed use of the northern four miles of right-of-way that ran along the eastern slope of Grandfather Mountain.

In 1944, while World War II was still in progress, my father, Julian W. Morton, and grandfather Hugh MacRae, granted an option to Harland P. Kelsey, for the purchase of all of Grandfather Mountain. Kelsey was a "front man" for the National Park Service, and the price was ridiculously low—$150,000 plus a $15,000 commission for Kelsey.

Even after two extensions of the option, Kelsey was not able to raise the money, and in a last desperate effort to do so he told the *Charlotte News* that "villainous woodsmen" would desecrate Grandfather Mountain unless he was able to save it. The embarrassment caused by that news article so infuriated Hugh MacRae and other members of the family that Kelsey was not given any further extensions of the option.

While Kelsey's unwise and exaggerated statement had ended that episode, the fact that he had held the option may have contributed to the National Park Service beginning, in 1954, a 12-year battle to locate the Blue Ridge Parkway high on the side of Grandfather Mountain following the so-called "high route." It would appear that while Kelsey held the option to buy the mountain, officials within the National Park Service began to consider the property as an expected acquisition to do with as they wanted, so they began making new plans without having title to the mountain.

Even when Kelsey failed to raise the money for purchase, Parkway Superintendent Sam Weems and National Park Service Director Conrad Wirth continued their plans for the "high route" across Grandfather Mountain, although 15 years earlier our family had pro-

continued

At the time Alaska became the 49th state, J. Ed Broyhill (right), furniture manufacturer and head of North Carolina's Republican Party, brought Secretary of Interior Fred Seaton (left) and Congressman Charles R. Jonas to visit Grandfather Mountain, and Jonas did the honors to raise for the first time Grandfather's new 49-star flag.

Gordon Gray

When the crowd of reporters and photographers dispersed and the official cavalcade passed by, the Grandfather Mountain link was completed. All 470 miles of Blue Ridge Parkway opened for traffic on September 11, 1987.

vided along the "low route" all the Parkway right-of-way that was authorized by state and federal law.

To accommodate the requested "high route," the state condemned additional land and we protested to Chairman A.H. Graham of the North Carolina Highway and Public Works Commission. In our presence, Chairman Graham called into his office Chief Locating Engineer R. Getty Browning and said, "Mr. Browning, Mr. Morton tells me that you condemned several hundred acres of his land on Grandfather Mountain, and he found out about it in the newspaper. Why didn't you notify him?" Graham was obviously annoyed when Browning replied that he knew I would not like the decision to condemn and so he did not communicate with me. The chairman promptly arranged for a hearing before the State Highway Commission for the National Park Service and me.

Almost immediately I received an invitation from WRAL-TV, Raleigh, to debate the Grandfather Mountain right-of-way controversy with National Park Service Director Wirth. The program was scheduled for the night before the State Highway Commission hearing in Raleigh. Later I was notified that Wirth was bringing his engineer, and it was suggested that I bring my engineer or lawyer to even up the sides in the debate. I had neither engineer nor lawyer. So I invited my friend Arthur Smith, a talented musician-composer, to join me that night.

Wirth obviously did not know Arthur Smith when I introduced them, and was unaware that he performed daily in nearly every television market in the southeastern U.S., including WRAL-TV. The Park Director and his engineer spoke first on the program, making a routine statement that did not sell the need for a "high route." I made a brief statement and then Arthur Smith, in his slow Southern drawl, said, "When a man like Hugh Morton owns a mountain and loves it like he does, it don't seem right for a big bureaucrat to come down here from Washington and take it away from him."

The telephone switchboard at WRAL-TV lit up with support for our position and it was soon obvious that Conrad Wirth had lost the debate. The public hearing the next morning was a breeze. The State Highway Commission voted to return the illegally condemned land.

While the controversy delayed the Grandfather Mountain link, it did not delay the construction of the Parkway at other locations, and money was transferred to the Cherokee and Asheville links while the settlement of the Grandfather right-of-way was being resolved.

The "high vs low" route at Grandfather Mountain was not the only controversy on the Parkway. During the Eisenhower administration, the National Park Service decided to impose a toll on the Blue Ridge Parkway. The proposal was actively opposed by North Carolina officials and the state tourism industry, pointing out the plan was harmful and unworkable. However, 30 toll collection booths were constructed and prepared for use, in spite of protests

continued

At a meeting in Washington in 1963, Governor Terry Sanford tells Secretary of Interior Stewart Udall (left) and National Park Service Director Conrad Wirth (right) that the State of North Carolina will have no part of the so-called "high route" for the Parkway at Grandfather Mountain.

U.S. Representative Robert L. Doughton's northwestern North Carolina district was bisected by the Parkway, and as chairman of the powerful House Ways and Means Committee he made sure the Parkway budget was not neglected during his time in Congress.

Rep. Roy Taylor served as chairman of the National Parks Sub-Committee of the U.S. Congress, which was helpful in completion of the Parkway.

William Penn Mott, Director of the National Park Service, and Mrs. Elizabeth Dole, U.S. Secretary of Transportation, were the principal speakers for the dedication and opening of the Blue Ridge Parkway at Grandfather Mountain on September 11, 1987. Mrs. Dole is a native of Salisbury.

from the entire North Carolina Congressional delegation and vigorous editorial criticism from state newspapers.

Meanwhile, Governor Luther H. Hodges, who opposed the tolls, happened to be meeting with UNC President Gordon Gray regarding other business that Gray was to discuss in an appointment with President Eisenhower. Hodges suggested that Gray explain briefly the proposed Parkway toll problem to the president. Gray took advantage of the opportunity with President Eisenhower in the Oval Office and carried out his assignment so well that the Chief Executive immediately placed a call to Secretary of Interior McKay.

Gray heard this conversation, "Mr. Secretary, I do not know how you got into this business of a toll on the Blue Ridge Parkway, but I want you to get out of it the soonest and best way you can." The National Park Service did not learn until months later how North Carolina reached the President on the eve of the toll imposition. Its frustration at not being able to impose the tolls did nothing to move the Grandfather Mountain dispute nearer to solution.

Soon after Governor Terry Sanford came into office, Conrad Wirth and Sam Weems launched another push for the "high route," but Sanford was well informed on the controversy and recommended a compromise "middle route" to Secretary of Interior Stewart Udall and Wirth. The governor firmly rejected the "high route," and expressed the belief that "Morton and everybody" would cooperate with the "middle route."

Events moved along and a resolution was found. Udall fired Conrad Wirth, and Sam Weems was loaned as a consultant to Australia to help set up a national park system there. Under new leadership in the National Park Service and Blue Ridge Parkway, and by the time that Governor Dan K. Moore took office in 1965, an agreement was reached expeditiously on the "middle route." Ground was broken by Governor Moore and others on October 27, 1968.

Public approval of the "middle route," site of the beautiful Linn Cove Viaduct, has been overwhelmingly favorable. The Blue Ridge Parkway has experienced a dramatic increase in visitation. The comment of Phillip Hanes of Winston-Salem on the final link is typical, "Not only does it not deface the prettiest part of the mountain, it makes a fantastic scenic contribution of its own to the area."

Statements like that were music to my ears after years of contention. Perhaps the best tribute came in a statement by Gary Everhardt, a North Carolina native who has served as Director of the National Park Service, and who was Superintendent of the Blue Ridge Parkway in 1988. Clearly the stormy story had come to a happy ending when Everhardt said:

"Traveling the Grandfather Mountain segment of the Parkway, I find it difficult to believe that there might have been a better alignment. The road and its environment not only are compatible, they are complementary, making the drive truly a pleasure." *HMM*

Harland P. Kelsey of East Boxford, Mass., obtained an option to buy Grandfather Mountain for the National Park Service in 1944, but he was unable to raise the purchase price.

Sam P. Weems

Gary Everhardt

Governor Dan K. Moore and National Park Service Deputy Director Hawthon Bill head a happy throng for the groundbreaking of the final Parkway link on October 22, 1968, not realizing it would take nearly 19 years to complete. Others pictured are Senator Sam J. Ervin, Congressman James T. Broyhill, Parkway Superintendent Granville Liles, and Parkway Association President Ronald Ligon.

(Photo credit unavailable)

Through the years Grandfather Mountain cooperated with every reasonable request of the National Park Service, and Senator Sam J. Ervin, Jr., witnessed Granville Liles (left), Superintendent of the Parkway, and me exchanging deeds to straighten the Parkway boundary at Julian Price Park on Grandfather Mountain's northeast slope.

Franklin D. Roosevelt, Jr., (right), Virginia Governor Charles Robb (left), and National Park Service Director William Penn Mott attend the 50th Anniversary of the Parkway at Cumberland Knob, on September 11, 1985, which was a good warm-up for the celebration of the opening of the whole Parkway at Grandfather Mountain two years later.

The Linn Cove Viaduct is a masterpiece of design and construction.

The contracts for the design and construction of the Linn Cove Viaduct were awarded during the Carter administration, and former President Jimmy Carter was pleased to receive a color photograph of the completed structure to be included in the archives of the Jimmy Carter Presidential Library in Atlanta.

Hugh Morton answered the door at his home on Grandfather Mountain Lake one day to find Governor Hodges standing there with a trout fly embedded in his cheek. "How about cutting this thing out for me, Hugh?" Hodges asked. Afraid that his "doctoring" might become infected, Morton promptly hustled the governor to the nearest hospital where a local physician handled the removal. The photo was made in the hospital waiting room. The fishing companion that day, who accidentally hooked the governor instead of a trout, was Jack Behrman, who later was the first Luther H. Hodges Professor of Business Ethics in the School of Business at UNC-Chapel Hill.

LUTHER H. HODGES
'The Lionhearted' Governor, Commerce Secretary

When Luther Hartwell Hodges became governor in 1954, he was the first businessman to occupy the office in nearly 70 years. There had been 14 lawyers and two farmers since Thomas M. Holt, an Alamance County textile manufacturer, was chief executive in 1893.

Reaching the governor's office was another step forward in the saga of a tenant farmer's son, very poor in material things but rich in spirit, character and courage, whose ability, intelligence, ambition and hard work brought him great success in business and industry.

Yet he never forgot that his success was made possible by the freedom and opportunity offered by America's democratic way of life. At age 52, the peak of his business career, he retired from business to devote the rest of his life to public service.

During a history-making six-year term, Governor Hodges had a solid record of achievements in effective, responsible government. A man of ideas and action, deeply concerned about the economic problems facing the state, he traveled thousands of miles each year and made hundreds of speeches to develop a statewide spirit of enthusiasm and support for economic development and growth.

What did he achieve? Here are a few examples:

—Provided such vigorous, constructive leadership that North Carolina responded with tremendous growth and new vitality. Before he left office the state was hailed as the No. 1 industrial and agricultural leader in the southeast.

—Gave the state a revitalized industrial development program that resulted in North Carolina establishing more than $1 billion of new and expanded industry. He sought only sound growth from reputable, diversified industries looking for economic opportunity. There were no state or local handouts.

—Gave his leadership, time, thought and boundless enthusiasm to the Research Triangle Park concept. Without his early and determined support, this unique North Carolina project, involving three great universities, may not have survived.

—Succeeded in getting increased legislative appropriations for public schools, higher education (especially faculty salaries), mental hospitals, schools for mentally retarded and a revitalized correctional program for juvenile delinquents.

—Improved and tightened up operations of state government, including a new Department of Administration to coordinate and consolidate all fiscal and planning operations, and a Board of Higher Education to provide better coordination and results from state-owned colleges.

—Helped develop a state-wide system of vocational education centers to train youths and adults in new industrial skills. They were so successful that they proved to be the forerunner of the state community college system which was established in 1963.

—Inspired North Carolinians from all walks of life to contribute their time and money to many worthwhile public projects, including the North Carolina Museum of Art and various study commissions dealing with basic government problems.

One of the most perceptive comments about Hodges came later from a Republican governor, James E. Holshouser, at ceremonies marking the establishment of a Distinguished Professorship in Business Ethics at UNC-Chapel Hill in Hodges' memory:

"My most vivid memory of Luther H. Hodges was that of a man always on the go, always flying off to another part of the country or another part of the world in relentless pursuit of economic development for North Carolina, for more and better jobs for North Carolina. Hodges was truly a giant in North Carolina's history. He was known as the 'Businessman Governor' and this was a fitting description.

"He believed in the American dream because he saw that dream come true in his own life. He believed in the work ethic because he made it work for himself. He believed in American free enterprise because he saw from his own experience what it meant to our nation and to our people.

"He believed in the value of education, and he believed in North Carolina's institutions of higher education. Governor Hodges throughout his career was a stickler for ethical business practices. In this day and time I don't have to tell you how much our institutions are being questioned. And how important it is that we prove to the people of this country and to the world that the leaders of American business, as well as our other important institutions, are governed and guided by high ethical principles.

"This professorship will provide the highest quality instruction in business ethics for generations of men and women who will take their places in the business community of this state and nation." *ELR*

A vigorous and active man, with a sturdy body radiating energy and drive, Luther Hodges loved sports and the outdoors. Here he displays his day's string of rainbow trout caught at Grandfather Mountain Lake where he had built a mountain retreat. Note the tattered sweater, a favorite garment used to cut the chill of early morning fishing in Avery County. Hodges played varsity basketball and baseball at UNC-Chapel Hill, and followed all Tar Heel sports for the rest of his life. Soon after graduating, he lost a front tooth while playing for the Leaksville YMCA team in an exhibition basketball game against the UNC White Phantoms. Play stopped long enough for him to retrieve the tooth and the game went on. The Carolina player who delivered the elbow to Hodges' mouth was Billy Carmichael, star forward and later university controller.

This is an unretouched photograph, taken in the late 1950s, of Luther Hodges' birthplace—a tenant farmer's cabin located in Pittsylvania County, Virginia, just a few miles north of the North Carolina line. He was born March 9, 1898, the next to the youngest of nine children. Times were hard for this farm family and when the price of tobacco fell to five cents a pound, John Hodges moved his family to the textile town of Spray, North Carolina, where he went to work in the textile mills. Eight of his children, at one time or another, also worked in the mills. Hugh Morton says that Martha Hodges was not happy with this picture and objected to its public use but was overruled by the governor. "But it did not look that bad when Luther was living there," she protested vainly.

Presidential candidate John F. Kennedy chats with Governor Hodges who later became his Secretary of Commerce. Kennedy needed a respected conservative who could help sell him and his administration to business and industry. Kennedy did not want to be known as anti-business and sought to minimize in public any conflict with business. Although originally a Lyndon Johnson supporter in 1960, Hodges was attracted to JFK and became an effective campaigner for him in the south and among business people. Kennedy's appointment of Hodges, announced only a week after the election, pleased textile leaders, many of whom believed JFK to be an unrestrained "free trader." With his usual vigor and enthusiasm, Hodges brought new life to the staid Commerce department and was successful in helping Kennedy deal with business and industry. The new secretary enjoyed pointing out "I am the only cabinet member who was born in the 19th century." Following Kennedy's assassination, Hodges continued to serve in the Lyndon Johnson cabinet.

The inauguration of a governor in North Carolina is far more than a ceremonial event every four years. In addition to meeting constitutional and traditional requirements, it is a gathering of the political, governmental, business, agricultural and educational leaders of the state to witness the beginning of a new administration in Raleigh. Luther H. Hodges, dressed in formal wear, speaks from the stage of the Raleigh Memorial Auditorium to a joint session of the General Assembly of North Carolina, following his inauguration, February 6, 1957. The stage is crowded with many notables, including Lt. Governor L.E. Barnhardt, Speaker of the House J.K. Doughton, members of the Council of State, members of the North Carolina Supreme Court, the North Carolina Congressional delegation and state Democratic party leaders.

LESSONS TO BE LEARNED

What lessons can be learned from Luther H. Hodges, businessman, governor of North Carolina, secretary of Commerce under two presidents, and president of Rotary International? Why was he so successful? Here are some answers:

THE VALUE OF TIME

Early in life he gained a basic respect of the value of time and the use of it by other people. Punctuality ranked high with him, along with honesty, discipline and hard work. He considered tardiness a discourtesy. In the governor's office, his schedule consisted primarily of 15-minute appointments, no personal business was conducted in the office, no coffee break for him, a light lunch and it was back to the office for more of his fast-paced schedule. The letters he wrote were as brief as possible and his phone conversations the same.

THE VALUE OF ORGANIZATION

His work, whatever it was, was always a challenge and a joy. He had learned long ago the value of being organized to achieve the best results with his time and efforts. A skilled professional manager, he knew how to select staff, delegate responsibilities and expect results. He did his homework and expected others to do the same. He detested red tape but was a prodigious reader of essential mail, reports and other information which followed him to the executive mansion each night in a large wooden box. Early the next morning the box returned to the staff with his dictation discs, cryptic notes, comments and directions. Everything going to or from him was dated (and with the hour, if important).

THE JOY OF PERSONAL CONTACT

A lifelong salesman, he enjoyed travel and working directly with people. In 1955, for example, he traveled 44,927 miles by the following means: automobile, airplane, train, helicopter, ship and motor grader (the only transport available during a hurricane at the coast). On one brief, hectic trip to New York City, he scheduled and had 19 different interviews with news media. And he loved it all— the swift movement, the challenge of new opportunities, motivating people—and seeing results.

THE APPEAL OF PUBLIC SERVICE

A lifelong Rotarian, he believed in the Rotary motto, "Service Above Self," and used its unselfish appeal to recruit top people for appointments and jobs in state government. His open, unabashed love for his state brought positive responses from within and without North Carolina. He could be very convincing to a leading business person with this appeal, "You have done well in North Carolina and you need to repay your debt to your state by helping my administration do something worthwhile for others less fortunate."

continued

When Luther Hodges needed a new director for the State Department of Conservation and Development, he convinced William P. Saunders (left), a retired textile executive and a friend of Hodges since student days at Chapel Hill, to join his administration. A quiet-spoken, well-organized and intensely loyal man, Saunders played a vital role in North Carolina's efforts to create new economic development, both from existing industry and new businesses. At one point in the difficult, early days of the Research Triangle Park project, Saunders advanced his own money to help keep the project alive. He understood and shared Hodges' deep love for North Carolina. Saunders served four terms in the state senate, 24 years as a UNC trustee and received an appointive position from each governor from Ehringhaus in 1933 through Moore in 1967.

Martha Blakeney Hodges, dancing with her husband at the Pirates Festival, Nags Head, was a friendly, gracious and intelligent First Lady of North Carolina. Long accustomed to being the wife of a successful business and civic leader, Martha Hodges understood her dynamic husband, his priorities and his ambitious program for North Carolina. The executive mansion operated smoothly and effectively under her firm and watchful guidance. She quickly adjusted to the rigorous schedule and requirements of First Lady, including frequent travel with the governor. A wife, mother of three children and grandmother of nine grandchildren, Martha Hodges was as much at home in Raleigh as she was in her home town of Monroe, where she grew up, in Leaksville, where she taught school and married, and in New York City, where she was the busy wife of a textile executive until he took early retirement. The Hodges had been married 47 years when a tragic fire at their retirement home in Chapel Hill caused Martha Hodges' death on June 27, 1969. Luther Hodges suffered from smoke inhalation and minor injuries but survived.

President Dwight D. Eisenhower chats with Governor Hodges and other members of a Governors Conference committee during a tense visit to the White House in 1957. While serving as chairman of the Southern Governors Conference meeting at Sea Island, Georgia, Hodges found himself propelled into the middle of the Little Rock school crisis. Arkansas Governor Orville Faubus called out the National Guard to curb violence and block integration at Central High School, and the President ordered Army paratroopers to Little Rock to take control of the school property. Hodges and a small committee were sent to Washington by the Southern Governors Conference to urge quick resolution of the federal-state confrontation, and to urge withdrawal of the paratroopers. The president stood firm, Faubus backed down and the committee's efforts, politely received by Eisenhower, were in vain. Hodges later wrote that "the whole painful and damaging experience of Little Rock made me thankful that we North Carolinians were anxious to work out our own problems resulting from the anti-segregation decision in an orderly and peaceful manner, and in such a way that the federal government would have no cause to send paratroopers to our state."

THE VALUE OF HUMOR

A keen sense of humor was one of his greatest assets. He never forgot his humble beginnings, how he struggled to succeed and realized the danger of taking himself too seriously. Even his enemies conceded that he was the greatest salesman the state had ever had. A natural showman, he was also a talented storyteller who used funny experiences, often his own, to illustrate his remarks or to lighten the mood of the audience. On the day he became governor, he jauntily stuck a white carnation in his buttonhole and he wore a fresh carnation every day as a kind of badge until the day he left office. Newspaper cartoonists dubbed him "Luther the Lionhearted" and he loved it. To promote the virtues of North Carolina textile products, he once posed for a *Life* magazine photographer in his underwear, and another time he demonstrated the washable nature of a suit by getting into a shower fully dressed. Martha Hodges was not amused by such behavior—but she understood her salesman husband. *ELR*

An extraordinary ambassador of good will for North Carolina, Governor Hodges presents Queen Elizabeth II a small statute of Sir Walter Raleigh during half-time ceremonies at the North Carolina—Maryland football game at College Park. He also had a brief chat with Prince Phillip. An inveterate world traveler, Hodges made an extensive tour of the Soviet Union with eight other U.S. governors to study Soviet life and government. The booklet he wrote after the trip, "A Governor Sees the Soviet," was praised by the U.S. State Department as one of the most objective reports it had received from an American visitor.

Since Hodges became governor in November 1954 due to the death of Governor William B. Umstead, he was the first incumbent in the 20th century to be able to seek nomination for the next full, four-year term. Governors were then limited by the state constitution to one four-year term. By 1956, when he filed for the full term, the dynamic Hodges was such a strong and popular chief executive that he was elected without too much difficulty in the Democratic primary and fall election. To run his campaign while he continued his unrelenting pace as governor, he named a small group of friends and associates who met with him on a regular basis at the executive mansion. Shown (clockwise) with Hodges at the head of the table are Hugh Morton, Paul A. Johnston, Ed Rankin, Mutt Burton, John Harden, Harold Makepeace (campaign chairman), Ben Trotter and Al Resch. The campaign committee raised about $30,000. After the election, there was enough money left to return about 25 percent to contributors—at Hodges' insistence.

In North Carolina, personal friendships, business relationships and school ties are often important ingredients for success in politics and government. B. Everett Jordan (left) and Luther H. Hodges were friends, business associates, political allies and successful men who enjoyed being movers, shakers and achievers. Jordan gets credit for convincing Hodges to offer for lieutenant governor, and thereby launching his remarkable career in elective office. Shown here at the 50th anniversary celebration of the City of Greensboro in 1958, little did they realize that Hodges, as governor, would later appoint Jordan to the United States Senate . . . and then join him in Washington as President Kennedy's Secretary of Commerce. A consummate politician, Jordan gave Hodges invaluable advice and assistance in carrying out the governor's complex responsibilities as titular head of the state Democratic party. Before Hodges ran for lieutenant governor, he was a successful textile executive and civic leader . . . but was a novice on the North Carolina political scene.

The Little Rock school crisis, with its dramatic federal-state confrontation, drew sharp and critical attention of national news media to southern states struggling to create integrated schools. In a televised interview with Governor Hodges, who was serving as chairman of the Southern Governors Conference at the time, Dave Garroway of NBC News seemed at times to lecture, rather than question, the governor on North Carolina's approach to school integration. Hodges did his best to explain the state's moderate efforts, adding that "the key to the situation is to bring about better understanding between the races . . . and I have worked hard to accomplish that goal." Then looking directly at the newsman, the governor asked, "Now, Mr. Garroway, what are you doing to bring about better understanding between the races?" Caught unaware, Garroway flushed and was so obviously at a loss for words that the interview ended abruptly with a cut to a commercial.

The North Carolina Trade and Industry Mission in 1959 told the state's story of economic opportunity to 1,600 European business and industrial leaders. This photo was made at Raleigh-Durham airport as Governor Hodges and 68 North Carolina business leaders prepared to depart for a trip which covered 10 major European cities in 14 days. The business volunteers paid their own expenses, followed a carefully planned and gruelling work schedule, and made many valuable contacts seeking new business, new industrial plants and more ocean traffic for state ports in North Carolina. It may have been the first such intensive trade mission to Europe by a U.S. state, and proved to be the model for later North Carolina missions that followed.

President Edward Fogle of Union Carbide Chemical Company (standing) shows Governor Hodges an architect's drawing of the new laboratory his company planned to build in the Research Triangle Park. This announcement, made during Hodges' last year in office, was further evidence of the success of the triangle concept which utilizes the faculties and research facilities of North Carolina State University at Raleigh, Duke University at Durham, and the University of North Carolina at Chapel Hill. Hodges later wrote that the Research Triangle Park "was a result of hard work and dedication of many people. It is certainly to the credit of our business, industrial and educational leaders that efforts to promote and develop the Research Triangle met with their enthusiastic cooperation and encouragement. They saw the economic need of the state and realized early that the Research Triangle could be a means of leading not only the area but all of North Carolina into a future of industrial development."

For a man who had little political experience before he became an elected state official, Luther Hodges quickly gained national political recognition as governor of North Carolina. Here he speaks to the 1956 Democratic National Convention in Chicago where he endorsed the nomination of Adlai Stevenson for president. Sam Rayburn (left), Speaker of the United States House of Representatives, kept a firm grip on convention proceedings as the presiding officer. In 1952, as the Democratic nominee for lieutenant governor Hodges had so little influence with state party leaders that he was not even selected as a delegate or alternate to the national Democratic convention in Chicago. Through the assistance of B. Everett Jordan, a close friend, Hodges obtained a badge to the convention floor and was able to attend the convention as an observer.

Photo by Charlie Kelly

Luther Hodges was successful in attracting many able, talented people to join his administration in various positions of responsibility. Paul A. Johnston (left) joined his staff in 1954 as a legal assistant after serving as a staff member at the Institute of Government at Chapei Hill. He was instrumental in assisting the governor in many crucial problems, including the Pearsall Plan (see Ch. 41). Hodges, the businessman governor, and Johnston, the astute young lawyer, became close friends for the rest of their lives. Johnston served as first director of the North Carolina Department of Administration, as senior deputy to Secretary of Commerce Luther Hodges, and then became the successful owner and chairman/CEO of Johnston Industries of New York and London, a textile firm. A resident of Chapel Hill, Johnston endowed two professorships to the School of Law (Albert Coates and Henry Brandis) and the Gladys Coates professorship in the Institute of Government.

Colonel Robert W. Madry, mayor of Chapel Hill and director of the UNC News Bureau, is seated center, holding court with the North Carolina sportswriters covering UNC's Sugar Bowl game in New Orleans with Oklahoma on New Year's Day in 1949. Left to right: Furman Bisher, *Charlotte News;* Hugh Germino, *Durham Sun;* Frank Spencer, *Winston-Salem Journal;* Wilton Garrison, *Charlotte Observer;* Smith Barrier, *Greensboro News;* Earle Hellen, *Greensboro Record;* Dick Herbert, *The News and Observer,* Raleigh; and Jack Horner, *Durham Herald.*

SPORTSWRITERS/ SPORTSCASTERS
They Cover the Games

It is easy to start a lively debate about the quality of athletic competition—for better or worse—in the Atlantic Coast Conference, and in the independent colleges in the area. In recent years the consensus appears to be that the region's athletes, especially when academic requirements are included, are a cut above those in many other regions of the U.S.

There is also reason to believe that the sportswriting and sportscasting in the area compare most favorably with the best the nation has to offer—and there is evidence to support this point of view.

Fifty years ago I took my first sports picture for one of the fine sports editors in the state, Burke Davis of the *Charlotte News.* I was young and inexperienced, while Burke Davis was a pro who knew exactly what pictures would pep up the sports page of an evening newspaper. Davis went with me for my first Big Four pre-season football roundup at Duke, North Carolina, Wake Forest, and N.C. State.

If I happened to pose three or four players or coaches in a rather spread-out arrangement, over my shoulder I would hear Burke Davis say, "The closer they are together, the bigger they will be in the paper." The sports personalities being photographed, upon overhearing a

The dean of the Atlantic Coast Conference basketball writers, Smith Barrier, discusses the game with John Wooden, one of America's premiere basketball coaches. Wooden was at the ACC Tournament in Atlanta in March 1983 to present the John Wooden National College Player of the Year Award to Virginia's Ralph Sampson.

remark like that, would then stampede to see how closely they could squeeze together. Davis left sportswriting to do political and feature writing for the *Greensboro Daily News,* before finally becoming one of the nation's most celebrated authors of books on the Civil War.

The mechanics of sports coverage are dramatically different today than they were 40 years ago when the colorful, rotund mayor of Chapel Hill, Robert W. Madry, was director of the University News Bureau. It is fun today to speculate how Madry would deal with word processors, television, wirephoto transmission, game coverage by satellite, and so on. Photo coverage of sports underwent startling changes as the result of better cameras and lenses, too, and the comparison of films 50 years ago with the films today is difficult to comprehend.

For example, in high school I made sports pictures with a fine grain film with a speed of 10, but in 1988 Eastman Kodak sent me some test rolls of film with a fine grain that was rated at a speed of 3200. Also, color film was virtually unheard of 50 years ago, but today the use of color film in sports photography is commonplace. General coverage of sports has certainly been enhanced, and information on sports quickly reaches many more millions of people.

Jake Wade at the *Charlotte Observer* and Frank Spencer at the *Winston-Salem Journal,* afterward soon joined by Dick Herbert of *The News and Observer,* Raleigh, and John Derr and Smith Barrier at the *Greensboro Daily News,* were the pillars of sportswriting in North Carolina when I began taking sports pictures for them in the late 1930s and early 1940s. Their newspapers provided budgets which were large enough to allow travel to the sports events of major interest to their readers, and so they were able personally to interview sports figures that readers of smaller papers had to learn about from the wire services.

After serving in World War II, John Derr became head of CBS Sports. Derr's specialty was broadcasting the Masters and other major golfing events, but he is also in the record book for announcing a horse race that was the first live color television broadcast outside a television studio. By the time Smith Barrier and Dick Herbert were enjoying retirement in the 1980s, they were writing books, and they had become oracles to whom other sports enthusiasts went

continued

Glenn E. (Ted) Mann (left) was the sports information director for Duke University for 46 years, and he was so loved and respected that he was inducted into the N.C. Sports Hall of Fame. Others inducted then were football star Red O'Quinn of Wake Forest fame, basketball great David Thompson of N.C. State, and stock car racer and car builder Junior Johnson. Mann served for nine years as president of the professional baseball Carolina League.

Four of the winners of the Sportswriter and Sportscaster of the Year awards started by Salisbury restaurant owner Pete DiMizio were, clockwise from upper left: Charlie Harville, *WFMY-TV*, Greensboro; Dick Herbert, *The News and Observer*, Raleigh; Jim Reid, *WPTF Radio*, Raleigh; and Bob Quincy, *Charlotte News.*

Jake Wade became a legend in North Carolina as the sports editor of the *Charlotte Observer.* After retiring from the newspaper, he was sports information director at UNC-Chapel Hill in the Charlie Justice years. Jim Reid of WPTF Radio, Raleigh, is interviewing Wade (right) about the Carolina team.

for information. In 1988 Herbert and Barrier were both in the first group of sportswriters to be elected to the United States Basketball Writers Association Hall of Fame, an especially high tribute when it is considered that both are from the North Carolina area.

In the early days, the primary clients for my sports pictures were Burke Davis and Furman Bisher at the *Charlotte News,* but an unfortunate incident in the 1941 basketball season suddenly made my pictures more widely in demand. A photographic freelancer at another North Carolina university sent pictures to the *Charlotte Observer,* representing them to be from the second Wake Forest—North Carolina game that year when actually they had been made at the first game between the two schools earlier in the season.

I was the new kid on the block, and when pictures I had taken at the second game appeared in the rival *Charlotte News* showing the teams in different uniforms than the shots appearing in the *Charlotte Observer,* it was my pictures that were suspect. Ultimately Jake Wade, sports editor of the *Observer,* discovered that a Wake Forest player shown in the *Observer* had influenza during the second game and had not played. Jake then wrote the most enraged sports column that I can remember, apologized to his readers for having been deceived, and vowed never to purchase another picture from the photographer who had missed the second game.

Ray Reeve of WRAL-based Tobacco Sports Network in Raleigh was the first of the radio sportscasters to push for the rights to cover basketball games in the North Carolina area. His efforts were slow to meet success because of the fear of college athletic directors that live radio coverage would impede ticket sales. A Duke—North Carolina game might be a sellout, but many other games were not, and interesting experiments were tried as the athletic directors felt their way along, tinkering with progress.

For his first basketball games, Reeve was not allowed to cover the first half, and was only allowed to record the second half for re-broadcast later. In due time the college officials came to the conclusion that Reeve's broadcasts were increasing interest, and not hurting ticket sales, yet similar agony was experienced later with the arrival of television. For example, Public Television Channel 4 in Chapel Hill was permitted to carry certain athletic events on video only, and viewers had to tune in on radio to commercial stations if they wanted to hear a play-by-play commentary with the WUNC-TV video.

Add Penfield, while still a student at Duke, shared the radio play-by-play duties with Lee Kirby of WBT Radio, Charlotte, on the Atlantic Football network coverage of Duke football that began in 1938, while Woody Woodhouse of WDNC Radio, Durham, provided the color commentary. Bob Harris handles the Duke Sports Network now. Soon the other Big Four

For 30 years the Atlantic Coast Sportswriters Association invited the head football coaches of the Atlantic Coast Conference to an annual golf outing in the Linville area. The constant turnover in coaches has given the sportswriters new friends to golf with and write about. None of the coaches gathered at Linville 20 years ago in 1969 holds his same job today. The 1969 group, front row, left to right: Roy Lester, Maryland; Cal Stoll, Wake Forest; Bill Murray, Duke; Earle Edwards, N.C. State; and Paul Dietzel, South Carolina. Back row, left to right: Bill Dooley, North Carolina; George Blackburn, Virginia; Frank Howard, Clemson; and Tom Harp, Duke.

At the NCAA basketball finals in New Orleans in 1982, Woody Durham, "The Voice of the Tar Heels" (right), and associate Jim Heavener (left) ask N.C. State Basketball Coach Jim Valvano and former UNC Coach Frank McGuire for halftime comments on the championship game between UNC and Georgetown.

schools saw wisdom in developing networks of area radio stations, because it helped alumni loyalty, ticket sales, school spirit, and football and basketball recruiting.

Bill Jackson and Wally Ausley of the anchor station WPTF, Raleigh, launched the Wolfpack Radio network for N.C. State, and after Jackson died, Gary Dornburg joined Ausley at the mike. Ray Reeve, aided by the color commentary of Bill Currie, formed the early Carolina Sports Network for UNC, and after Reeve's death, the UNC games were broadcast by Bill Currie and Jack Callahan, with most recent UNC coverage handled by Woody Durham and Jim Heavener.

Gene Overby of WSJS Radio, Winston-Salem, has been the key announcer for the Wake Forest Demon Deacon sports broadcasters. The colleges have now taken an "if you can't lick 'em, join 'em" attitude about radio and television coverage that they feared at first, and many of the head football and basketball coaches now have their own weekly television shows during the seasons.

Furman Bisher moved from the *Charlotte News* to the *Atlanta Journal,* where he continued his outstanding sports coverage, and I had the pleasure of making the induction comments when he was presented to the UNC Journalism Hall of Fame. A host of great sportswriters followed Jake Wade at the *Charlotte Observer,* including Wilton Garrison, Whitey Kelley, Bob Quincy, Ronald Green, Tom Higgins, and Leonard Laye.

North Carolina newspapers are fortunate to have had many talented and top-flight sportswriters. They include Bob Terrell, Larry Pope and Doug Mead, *Asheville Citizen;* Horace Billings, *Salisbury Post;* Billy Hunter, *Burlington Times-News;* Jerry Hooks, *Wilmington Star-News;* Joe Tiede, Bruce Phillips, Caulton Tudor and A.J. Carr, *News & Observer—Raleigh Times;* Jack Horner, Hugh Germino, Art Chansky, Frank Dascenzo and Keith Drum, *Durham Herald-Sun;* Irwin Smallwood, Larry Keech, Wilt Browning and Gary McCanne, *Greensboro Daily News;* Lenox Rawlings and Mary Garver, *Winston-Salem Journal;* Ken Alyta and Reece Hart, *The Associated Press.*

Even the smaller newspapers like to send their own writers to any bowl game or Final Four in which a North Carolina area team is a participant, making it possible for reporters like Howard Ward of the *Fayetteville Observer-Times* and Jim Pettit of the *High Point Enterprise* to attend such events.

Smith Barrier was told by NCAA officials that the sports press corps of the North Carolina area invariably generates more requests for championship credentials than do writers from any part of the nation, a clear indication of the region's intense interest in sports and the need for talented, dedicated sportswriters. *HMM*

No blood was shed as the Tigers met the Cougar during the Atlantic Coast Sportswriters picnic at Grandfather Mountain. Clemson Tiger Football Coach Danny Ford (left) and his university's Sports Information Director Bob Bradley prudently decided to be gentle with Rajah, Grandfather Mountain's Cougar (Panther or Mountain Lion).

Mayor Wayne Corpening reads the proclamation designating October 5, 1985 as Howard Cosell Day in Winston-Salem. The well-known ABC Network sportscaster seemed moved that the North Carolina city took pride in the fact that he is a native son.

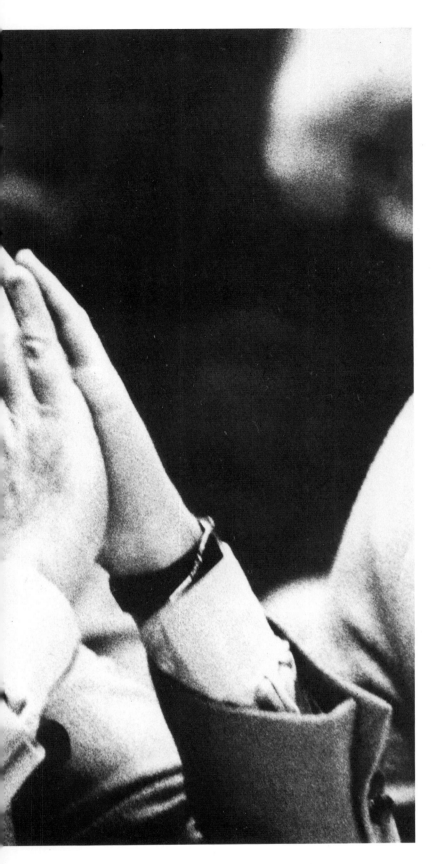

One of the nation's most widely read sportswriters is Curry Kirkpatrick, a UNC alumnus. Kirkpatrick's sports beat takes him frequently to all of the ACC campuses. Jim Lampley of CBS Sports is also an alumnus of UNC.

Bill Currie, known as the "Mouth of the South" during his days broadcasting UNC football and basketball games, was always ready to be the center of a gag photograph. Toasting Currie in the background are two of his fellow sportscasters, Ray Reeve (left) and Jim Reid.

THOMAS H. DAVIS/
PIEDMONT AIRLINES
Last Living Founder of Major U.S. Airline

These aviation industry leaders, T.H. Davis (right) and William G. McGee, have spent their working lives building Piedmont Airlines from ground zero to a major air transport company. They are shown at Piedmont Plaza, the headquarters complex in Winston-Salem. Davis is founder, former chairman of the board, chief executive officer and treasurer. McGee was chairman, president and chief executive officer.

A Winston-Salem youngster who loved to build model planes and earned his pilot's license before receiving his driver's license is the only living founder of a major U.S. airline.

He is Thomas H. (Tom) Davis, and the small, fixed-base operation he bought 40 years ago in his home town became Piedmont Airlines. A pilot for over 50 years, he says with a quick smile, "I'm still fascinated with airplanes and flying."

His early fascination with aviation led him to Camel City Flying Service where he learned to fly in 1934 while in high school. Later he not only earned an instructor's rating but learned how to sell aircraft as well as fly them. After completing college, he joined Camel City as a salesman and in his first year sold over 100 airplanes—more than any competitor in the U.S. He bought the company in 1940 and changed the name to Piedmont Aviation, Inc.

During World War II, the company operated flight training schools at Winston-Salem and Greensboro for U.S. and Central and South American pilots.

In 1948, beginning with two used DC-3 aircraft, Tom Davis built a home-grown, "local service" airline into the seventh largest air carrier in the United States. The sturdy DC-3s have been replaced with an all-jet operation of over 200 aircraft that is nationwide, trans-continental and international.

Piedmont's first year as a scheduled air carrier had less than $250,000 in revenues. In 1988, revenues are expected to exceed $3 billion and the airline will transport 37 million passengers. Piedmont's financial performance is exceptional. It has lost money in only three of its 40 years and has more years of profitable operations than any other airline, with the exception of Northwest.

Tom Davis is quick to share credit with others who have helped achieve these remarkable results. "Good people are the reason for our success," he says with pride. "I think Piedmont has a higher level of seniority among our supervisory people and throughout our organization than most of our competitors. Our people are dedicated, efficient, steady and hard workers."

William G. McGee, the fourth employee hired by Davis and Piedmont chairman, president and CEO, explains that, "Our people are driven by the service-oriented philosophy which Tom Davis instilled from the very beginning. That philosophy is a hallmark of this company and has given us a competitive edge."

Deregulation of commercial air carriers was a major breakthrough for Piedmont. When it came, Piedmont was ready, willing and able with plans for route extensions. As a "local service," connecting airline for many years, Piedmont knew it had enough traffic in its own system to support the "hub" concept of service. Roanoke and Bristol/Johnson City/Kingsport proved the value of hub operations as far back as 1955 and helped Piedmont to become an industry leader in providing this type of service. Since deregulation in 1978, the "homegrown" airline has also established hubs at Charlotte, Baltimore/Washington, Dayton, and Syracuse and has inaugurated service to 60 new destinations in 22 states as well as Ottawa, Montreal, Nassau and London.

Winston-Salem and North Carolina have always been supportive and enthusiastic about Piedmont Airlines and its future, Davis points out. With close ties to Wachovia Bank & Trust Co., its legendary president, Robert M. Hanes, and those who followed him, Piedmont is noted for sound financial management. Tom Davis is the son of Egbert L. Davis, who was a top corporate official with R.J. Reynolds Tobacco Co., and sold the first freight car load of Camel cigarettes for Mr. Reynolds.

What impact has Piedmont's success had on North Carolina? "The birth of Piedmont was one of the most important things that happened to continued

A sleek Piedmont Airlines jet makes a low level pass over downtown Winston-Salem, the piedmont North Carolina city where the airline was born. Piedmont President Bill McGee arranged for the special flight so that Hugh Morton could shoot this beautiful and memorable photo from a smaller plane at a higher altitude. The Piedmont name, the only original one left of the early "local service" companies, will be lost because Piedmont Aviation is in the process of merging with US Air. Winston-Salem will not lose, however, the existing airline administrative and maintenance facilities.

Two of the first Douglas DC-3 aircraft put in service by Piedmont are shown at a Wilmington hangar. Known as the original American airliner, the DC-3 era began in 1936 when it sold to commercial airlines for $100,000. The standard version provided 21 seats, seven rows of three, with pilots and one flight attendant. There were 330 in domestic service when World War II began, and at the war's end 11,000 had been built. As major airlines bought larger aircraft after the war, "local service" airlines were born with the availability of the sturdy, dependable DC-3. At one time Piedmont had a fleet of 24 of these planes serving its system.

While searching through his huge photo collection, Hugh Morton found this picture of General of the Army George Marshall and Ted Malone, national radio star. And behind them, enjoying a piece of chicken, is young Tom Davis, founder and president of Piedmont Airlines. The photo was made during the festivities at the 1949 Azalea Festival in Wilmington, one of the many North Carolina cities served by North Carolina's only home-based airline.

North Carolina in the past 40 years," McGee emphasized. "The economic development resulting from Piedmont's service would astound you. Virtually every city we serve in North Carolina has come to us with pleas for help in attracting new industry and business. Air transportation is vital to any business. Piedmont has made hundreds of presentations for these cities and the state. One of the major factors in the economic development of North Carolina has been the air transportation system that was brought about by the vision of Tom Davis and others at Piedmont."

At Piedmont's 40th anniversary celebration, the North Carolina Travel Council presented a resolution of appreciation to Tom Davis calling Piedmont the "best corporate friend of the North Carolina travel industry during its entire 40 years of operation."

What of the future of Piedmont Airlines as a part of USAir Group, Inc.? Tom Davis and Bill McGee are optimists. How else could they have built the seventh largest air carrier in the U.S. from the Camel City Flying Service?

"The legacy of this company in North Carolina is never going to die," McGee said. "The name may change but the 22,000 people of Piedmont are not going away, and the way they do business—the excellent service levels—are going to be there in spite of what some people may say."   *ELR*

Piedmont, the home-grown airline, is accustomed to meeting local needs and problems, often on short notice. When Azalea Queen Janet Leigh cancelled at the last moment, festival officials did not panic. They convinced Cathy Downs, Hollywood actress and wife of pro golfer Joe Kirkwood, Jr. who was in Wilmington playing in the Azalea Open golf tournament, to fill the role. To make it look official, and to provide news media with the necessary arrival excitement, Piedmont Airlines quickly agreed to fly Cathy Downs from Wilmington to Fayetteville and back so she could make the Queen's arrival in style and on schedule. Just another good deed by Piedmont—and Cathy Downs.

Photo by Jean Cunningham

This photo, innocently made, records one of Winston-Salem's most history-making pranks. It was cleverly planned by Joe King, the famous artist who is also famous for his practical jokes, with the help of Piedmont President Tom Davis, Congressman Thurmond Chatham and others. The photo shows Mayor Marshall Kurfees (holding his hat) welcoming an "Arabian Sultan" and his 12 "wives" (leaving 80 at home because he was traveling light) at the Smith Reynolds airport in 1952. The "Sultan" and entourage were supposed to be enroute to South America but Chatham said he had prevailed upon the "Sultan" to speak briefly at a fund-raising event for the Arts Council. All local people in disguise, they had been flown from Greensboro to Winston-Salem by Piedmont but were supposed to be arriving from Washington, D.C. Following a parade through downtown Winston-Salem with a band leading the way, the "Sultan" spoke to a packed house and several of his "harem wives" performed a provocative dance before a wild, staged melee broke out and the hoax was revealed. Most of the audience roared with laughter, a few were not amused but the Arts Council raised a record $26,000. What was the theme of the Arts Ball? Why, Arabian Nights, of course.

TERRY SANFORD
Governor, Educator, U.S. Senator

Terry Sanford (left) looks forward to being Governor and retiring Governor Luther H. Hodges looks forward to being U.S. Secretary of Commerce as they arrived for Sanford's inaugural ceremony at the Raleigh Municipal Auditorium in January 1961.

Margaret Rose and Terry Sanford await the arrival of U.S. Senator John F. Kennedy at the Greenville airport during the Kennedy presidential campaign in October 1960. Congressman L.H. Fountain, Governor Luther H. Hodges, and Congressman Harold Cooley are in the background.

Photo by Betsy Sanford

Jacqueline Kennedy receives a check for $250,000 from Governor Terry Sanford and Kennedy Library N.C. Chairman Hugh Morton for the state's contribution to the Presidential Library. Mrs. Kennedy remarked that the Tar Heel contribution was the largest given by any state except Massachusetts, where the library is located.

"I don't think there is any doubt, watching Terry through the years, his years in the governorship were his highlight," says Bert Bennett, Sanford campaign manager, close friend, and advisor.

Bennett adds, "he would have liked to be governor twice, or more."

Terry Sanford held several other jobs and did them well, in national politics, at Duke University, and as U.S. Senator, Bennett says, but "nothing has touched him like that governorship."

"The day-to-day thrill and the challenge; he never got it out of his system once he left for Duke, for he is a born public servant that loves it more so than anybody," Bennett believes.

Julian Scheer, *Charlotte News* political writer during Sanford's term as governor, says "most people say he has unusual political and other skills, but I skip over those to the essence, and that essence is wisdom. Terry Sanford has exceptional maturity and wisdom. He's the guy to go to for advice."

Terry Sanford has been governor, president of Duke University, and currently is United States Senator—three major careers—and any of them could stand alone as a significant lifetime accomplishment.

While the full story of Terry Sanford's service in the U.S. Senate is yet to unfold, the records of his first two careers as governor, and as Duke University president, are well-known and outstanding.

After receiving the Democratic nomination for governor, Sanford had to make difficult decisions that most people like to avoid, but he thrived on them. The first decision was to endorse John F. Kennedy for president.

In Los Angeles, Sanford boldly escorted the boyish Jack Kennedy into a breakfast meeting of North Carolina delegates at the 1960 Democratic National Convention, knowing that in the room were Governor Luther H. Hodges, Senator Sam J. Ervin, Senator B. Everett Jordan, and North Carolina's Democratic congressmen, all solidly in the corner of Lyndon B. Johnson for president.

Kennedy wasted no time telling his story and asking for North Carolina's support. He was pleased to have the backing of Sanford, and said, "Your next governor is the kind of a Democrat I want to be associated with in North Carolina and the nation."

Civil rights sit-ins and other thorny matters came before Sanford as governor. He dealt with them fairly and decisively, and was ostensibly unruffled. The truly controversial issue was the food tax, the political ghost that haunted him until he finally turned it around to his benefit in his race for the U.S. Senate in 1986, more than 20 years later.

The food tax was, of course, the essential element of the ambitious Sanford program to bring "quality education" to the North Carolina public schools—the crowning achievement which gave Sanford his reputation as the "Education Governor." While many of the state's citizens agreed with the governor's program to push for education, not many would have agreed to submit themselves to the flak he was forced to take to accomplish it. Everyone was aware of the controversial food tax.

continued

Due to early support of John F. Kennedy's bid for president in 1960, Terry Sanford was chosen by Kennedy to be one of four national leaders to make an official nomination speech at the Democratic National Convention in Los Angeles.

Terry Sanford for President was the main message, but David Erdman wanted Marian Erdman in Bridgeton, N.C., to know he would be home following the Democratic Convention in Miami in 1972. The North Carolina delegation let the nation know it was proud of Duke University President Terry Sanford, although George McGovern received the presidential nomination.

At an Honorary Tar Heel meeting in 1963, I went fishing for blues off Oregon Inlet with Governor Sanford, Bill Sharpe and Tom Alexander. Sanford and the rest of us were burned rosy red, so on the way back to the Carolinian we stopped by a Nags Head convenience store to buy sunburn lotion. The governor, wearing a baseball cap, dark glasses, and a flashy Hawaiian sportshirt, placed the order for the sunburn lotion.

The young lady behind the counter said: "That'll be one dollar, please, and three cents for Terry."

The governor slowly pushed back his cap, removed his dark glasses, and solemnly said, "I *am* Terry."

There was silence, a long silence, and then everybody, the embarrassed sales clerk behind the counter included, burst out laughing.

Terry Sanford's predecessor at Duke had been in poor health, and had difficulties in coping with a lengthy student uprising. The campus was without a president for many months, and the student unrest was still at a boil when Sanford arrived. Within hours the ex-paratrooper, ex-FBI agent restored order, and the students learned they had a

continued

Shown in a Democratic display of unity (left to right) are: U.S. Senator Tom Eagleton, U.S. Senator Hubert Humphrey, Congresswoman Shirley Chisholm, U.S. Senator George McGovern, U.S. Senator Henry Jackson, U.S. Senator Edmund Muskie, and Duke University President Terry Sanford, following the nomination of McGovern for President at the 1972 convention in Miami. McGovern was soundly defeated by Richard Nixon in the general election in November.

Terry Sanford, with left hand on the Bible held by his wife, Margaret Rose, takes the oath as U.S. Senator from his longtime friend, Federal Judge Dickson Phillips. The crowd of several hundred Sanford friends necessitated holding the ceremony on the Capitol steps rather than in the Senate chamber.

Terry Sanford's U.S. Senate colleagues, John Glenn of Ohio and Dale Bumpers (right) of Arkansas, join in the "Tribute to Terry Sanford" in the Hotel Sir Walter, Raleigh, in February 1988. The affair virtually retired Sanford's 1986 U.S. Senate campaign debt.

new friend and leader, willing to listen and to work with them. They called him "Uncle Terry," and it was a term of respect and endearment. True, they can at times be rowdy at athletic contests, but as a group the Duke students functioned well within the system during Sanford's 16 years there.

The location of Richard M. Nixon Presidential Library seems to be the major setback Sanford suffered at Duke. Sanford wanted the Duke Law School graduate's papers, not out of interest in glorifying the shamed president, but because he felt Nixon's documents were essential to historians studying Eisenhower, Kennedy, the McCarthy episode, the opening of China, and countless other significant matters. Unfortunately, the possibility of the Duke location was raised by Nixon's lawyer in the summertime when faculty members, who felt they should be consulted, were not on campus. The resulting battle for campus turf removed the project from Duke's agenda.

Mary Duke Biddle Trent Semans, chairman of the Duke Endowment, says, "During the Sanford years some sort of magic created just the right climate for a new Duke spirit. There has been a sense of vitality on the campus. Students are open in their enthusiasm for Duke and want to tell the world about it. The campus exudes energy and is an exciting place to be."

Commenting on other Sanford assets, past chairman of the Duke trustees J. Alex McMahon says, "When the presidential search committee in 1969 submitted Terry Sanford's name to the board of trustees, it did so with great expectations for the vision and leadership he would bring to Duke. Not only did he exceed those expectations, he added unexpected strengths in fund-raising and resource reallocation that converted the visions to reality."

Another chairman of the Duke trustees, Charles B. Wade, Jr., says of Sanford, "Innovation has been his strong suit: Do it because it is right and good—not because it is easy and safe. . . . I believe history already 'says' he has been a great president of Duke University."

As governor, Terry Sanford founded the North Carolina School of the Arts, The Governor's School For The Gifted, The North Carolina Advancement School, and the Learning Institute of North Carolina. He reduced the state prison population with a more successful means of prison administration and rehabilitation. He was the first southern governor to insist on employment without regard to race, creed, or color.

Sanford advanced the Research Triangle Park begun by his predecessor, Governor Luther H. Hodges. He established the state's system of community colleges and technical institutes. He increased the budgets for public schools by 50 percent and for colleges and universities by 70 percent. Those who are aware of an even partial list of his good deeds were pleased, but not surprised, when a study of the 50 states by Harvard University ranked Terry Sanford as one of the 10 best governors in the nation in this century.

So we are down to the remaining question: How will Terry Sanford be as United States Senator? The beginning looks extremely good, and his track record assures he will be excellent. *HMM*

The highlight of the retirement party for Terry and Margaret Rose Sanford at Duke University was the presentation of their official Duke portrait. Praise was heaped upon the Sanfords for the effectiveness of their service at Duke.

Graduate of UNC Terry Sanford, following his years as president of Duke University, was invited "home" to Chapel Hill by Chancellor Christopher Fordham to be University Day speaker October 12, 1987.

The May-June 1985 issue of *Duke Magazine* reveals that Terry Sanford and Bert Bennett, his longtime friend and political ally, were not in harmony over Sanford's bid for the Democratic presidential nomination in 1972. That year Bennett was pushing Jim Hunt for lieutenant governor, and Governor Bob Scott had made an early commitment to Edmund Muskie for president. The resulting disarray let George Wallace win the N.C. primary, and in Sanford's words, "I didn't get home support."

MEADOWLARK LEMON
U.S. Ambassador of Good-Will

These young Wilmington autograph seekers are happy because they accomplished their mission. They have Meadowlark Lemon's autograph. The unexpected bonus was to have their pictures made with him, too.

Everybody in the audience is smiling, and that is what counts with Meadowlark Lemon, whose goal is to bring pleasure to the whole world. Persons in the stands often are consulted by Meadowlark to determine whether the referee made a correct call.

An Official White House Photo

Meadowlark Lemon and his wife, Lorelei, (right) greet President Ronald Reagan in the receiving line at the White House dinner honoring Russia's head of state Mikhail Gorbachev (left) during the December 1987 summit. Meadowlark Lemon says that being included in the relatively small guest list for the dinner was extremely meaningful, and "it was an experience to see history in the making." *Newsweek* referred to those invited to the dinner as "movers and shakers."

Leaders in the community, both black and white, worked tirelessly following the death of Martin Luther King to mediate Wilmington's racial unrest, with only minor success. Then Meadowlark Lemon came to town to literally and figuratively "make it a new ball game." Meadowlark Lemon made personal appearances at nearly every school in New Hanover County, and racial tensions that had appeared hopeless were virtually resolved overnight.

Meadowlark Lemon of Wilmington may have created more good will for the United States of America than any other American citizen. That statement covers a lot of territory, but so has Meadowlark, first as the star of the Harlem Globetrotters, and later with his own group, Meadowlark Lemon and the Stars. "The Clown Prince of Basketball" has actually visited 90 nations in person during these performances, and has been seen on television in many more.

Leaders of great nations may be popular in half the world and unpopular in the other half, but Meadowlark's popularity knows no political boundary lines. This is a great source of delight to Lemon, who simply enjoys making people happy. Neither he nor anyone else will know how many millions of joyful fans make up his loyal following.

Every American, irrespective of his or her politics, can probably cite instances when our government has not been altogether smart, and it is therefore gratifying when Washington demonstrates the brilliance that it did in inviting Meadowlark Lemon and his wife to be among the Americans to greet Mikhail Gorbachev at the White House state dinner during the December 1987 summit meetings.

Meadowlark's approach to life may even be the key to arms reduction. It is: love everybody, regardless of their nationality, race, or creed. This may not be the whole solution to a very complex problem, but most people will agree it is a step in the right direction.

One thing is certain—the Meadowlark Lemon approach worked at the local level in Meadowlark's home town of Wilmington, where Tom Jervay, editor and publisher of the black-oriented *Wilmington Journal* refers to him not as "The Clown Prince of Basketball," but as the "Clown Apostle of Interracial Good Will." Jervay, whose newspaper office was one of several places bombed or burned in the spring of 1971 during a period of racial violence, remembers that his son, Tom Jervay, Jr., and former Wilmington Jaycee Ed Godwin telephoned from the *Journal* office to Lemon, whose Globetrotters team was playing in Charleston, S.C., at the time, to invite the basketball star to help Wilmington. Godwin arranged for a private plane to bring Lemon to the troubled city.

Editor Jervay says, "Meadowlark really cooled things down here when we needed him." Looking back on the strife in Wilmington which he helped defuse, Meadowlark says he would do it again, but that he will never have to, because things like that happen due to ignorance on the part of both whites and blacks, and "all of us have grown."

Happily, the Meadowlark Lemon sphere of influence is not local. Invariably he has been in the Top 10 of the world's most loved and recognizable personalities in the elite "Performance Q Poll," and was ranked fourth overall behind the late John Wayne, Alan Alda, and Bob Hope in the similarly important "TV-Q Poll" which is based not only on popularity, but also credibility.

One of the most enthusiastic welcomes ever given a returning home town son was given Meadowlark Lemon when he returned for Meadowlark Lemon Day in Wilmington. The sign in front of the Hilton Hotel spoke for the whole city.

Even Nikita Krushchev, who had revealed to the world his plans to "bury" the United States, greeted Meadowlark at Red Square in Moscow. The Royal Family of England, the Queen of Luxembourg, Pope Paul and Pope John have been among the fans who have cheered the Lemon basketball buffoonery.

At Williston High School in Wilmington, Lemon was an All-State end in football, and in a brief baseball career there he hit a homer his first time at bat. Earl Jackson, an instructor at the Wilmington Boys Club, taught Meadowlark the basketball hook shot, and through the years Jackson remains Lemon's best home town friend, with the two staying closely in touch.

E.A. Corbin, the basketball coach at Williston, knew Abe Saperstein, owner of the Harlem Globetrotters, and it was through that connection that Meadowlark Lemon was given his first chance to play with the Globetrotters. While the team performed in Raleigh he substituted six minutes for the legendary Goose Tatum. From that point on it was assured that Meadowlark would inherit the title "Clown Prince."

How does Lemon rank basketball players in 1988? He says in 1986 Larry Bird was the best, and Magic Johnson in 1987. The 1988 best player in the world, Meadowlark Lemon says, is his fellow townsman Michael Jordan. *HMM*

DAN K. MOORE
'Mountain Man' Governor, Supreme Court Justice

Daniel Killian Moore was mountain born and bred—and quietly proud of it. He was named for two of the families, the Killians and the Moores, who had shared in the settlement and building of western North Carolina. He was a descendant of the first white man—William Moore—to settle west of the French Broad River. The governor's father, Fred Moore, when appointed to the Superior Court bench, was the youngest such judge in the history of the state. This was a record that stood until Governor Moore's administration. Moore was only the third governor in the past century to come from the mountains of North Carolina. The others were Zebulon Baird Vance (1862-65 and 1877-79) and Locke Craig (1913-1917).

Governor and Mrs. Moore stand proudly beside the magnificent silver service which they returned to the U.S.S. *North Carolina* after the great battleship was berthed at Wilmington as a state historic attraction. A gift of the State of North Carolina, first presented by Governor and Mrs. Broughton, the wardroom silver had been aboard the ship during World War II. It was returned to the state following decommissioning of the ship and was used at the executive mansion in Raleigh.

As governor, Dan K. Moore sought to stir our sense of purpose, our inherent vitality, our creativity and our pride in our state and people. His total development approach involved people, institutions and groups from all parts of North Carolina. He recognized that the quality of life requires far more than governmental services, important as they are. So he sought to encourage and stimulate improvement in the lives of people by every means possible.

As spokesman for the people of North Carolina, his calm and unpretentious voice spoke firmly and clearly in behalf of public schools, community colleges, higher education, health, welfare, highways, equal job opportunities, housing, economic development, conservation, orderly planning, the administration of justice—to mention a few of the issues and concerns.

He sought in his quiet, effective way to lead North Carolina forward toward a better, more productive and more creative approach in all these essential parts of life. Dan Moore made significant contributions in most of these efforts, and was always quick to share credit with others. He served 1965-69.

Any governor who provides strong leadership attracts criticism as well as support. Dan Moore had his share of both. He also had his share of crises—the Speaker Ban law, the reapportionment of the General Assembly and realignment of congressional districts, night riders and civil disorders, the "one university debate," and racial unrest—to mention a few.

Moore displayed a remarkable ability to absorb quietly and calmly the most scathing and unjustified criticisms. One of the bitterest attacks came from his own beloved alma mater, UNC-Chapel Hill, during the Speaker Ban battle, a controversy which he inherited from the previous administration. Perhaps the governor recalled the admonition credited to Professor Albert Coates in teaching UNC law students that a public official must "suffer fools gladly." If so, Dan Moore learned his lesson well.

Jeanelle Coulter Moore, the First Lady, was a great asset to the governor. She fulfilled her role with boundless energy, a warm personality and a captivating exuberance of spirit and charm. This was in decided contrast to her earlier reservations expressed when Moore discussed with her whether or not to run for governor. *continued*

In 1964, the primary race for the Democratic nomination for governor earlier appeared to be a contest between L. Richardson Preyer (left) who had the strong support of Governor Terry Sanford, and I. Beverly Lake (center), who had opposed Sanford for governor four years earlier. Dan Moore came out of the west to enter the race, unknown to many, and with no state-wide organization and no campaign funds. When this photograph was made on the City Hall steps, Wilmington, during the Azalea Festival, Moore was definitely the dark horse candidate. However, to the surprise of many political observers, Moore ran a strong second to Preyer in the first primary (May 30) and became the Democratic party nominee in the second primary, with the support of Lake, who had been eliminated in the first primary. Nominee Moore was successful in uniting Democrats to defeat the Republican candidate, Robert Gavin, in November.

She recalls, "I did not want Dan to run for governor. We were pleasantly situated. Both of our children were happily married. We had come to a stage and condition in our lives where we enjoyed each other in a relaxed and secure atmosphere."

But when the decision was made to run, Jeanelle Moore became an enthusiastic, effective and tireless campaigner. And when her husband was elected, she became a gracious First Lady who kept the executive mansion humming with activities, including formation of the Executive Mansion Fine Arts Commission.

Any review of Dan Moore's record as chief executive should include these contributions of his leadership:

—His strong sense of responsibility to serve all the people of North Carolina as fairly, objectively as possible, and without fear or favor. Rarely has any governor completed his term of office with his personal popularity undiminished.

—His strong adherence to the rule of law at all times, his judicial temperament and his ability to act swiftly yet dispassionately in times of grave trouble.

—His ability to improve the general management of state government, North Carolina's largest enterprise, and to require full utilization of every available resource.

—His insistence on planning—short and long—in every aspect of government services, especially in public schools, higher education, highways and economic development.

—His success in gaining public support of his $300 million highway bond program to provide needed financing for better, safer highway transportation. Legislators were impressed with his generous proposal that $60 million of the bonds would be spent by the following administration.

—His keen understanding and support for the essential value of economic development in its fullest, most productive form. He knew the value and meaning of a job, a paycheck and a stake in life.

—His compassion for the very young, the very old, the handicapped and ill, the imprisoned and the troubled. He was never too tired, never too busy, never too occupied with the many duties of his office to lend a hand to those in need. *ELR*

Dan Moore knew much more about fishing than cameras but he readily agreed to pose with Bob Garland, an Honorary Tar Heel and former photographer for the *Saturday Evening Post*. As a youngster, Moore roamed the mountains around the Jackson County community of Webster where he lived, and enjoyed fishing, hunting and the outdoor life. He spent a great deal of time with his brother, William Enloe, who had rheumatic fever which was to claim his life. The two boys would sit on the porch and shoot at cans with a 22-calibre rifle.

When Dan Moore announced for governor, Joseph Branch liked what he saw and knew about this soft-spoken, unpretentious man. A well-known lawyer and veteran eastern North Carolina legislator, Branch agreed to be Moore's state campaign manager. It was a happy choice for both men. They became devoted friends in the heat of the political battle with Preyer and Lake. As the first primary approached, Moore's chances for nomination appeared bleak. Branch recalls that on one late night drive back to Raleigh from a disappointing political rally in eastern North Carolina, Moore asked, "Joe, is there any honorable way I can get out of this race?" Branch replied, "Dan, I know how you feel . . . but it's too late." Governor Moore later appointed Branch to the State Supreme Court where he served with distinction and ended his judicial career as Chief Justice. Moore later joined Branch on the Supreme Court, by virtue of an appointment by Governor Robert Scott, and served nearly 10 years before his retirement.

Governor Dan Moore understood the importance of keeping in touch with the North Carolina Congressional delegation in Washington. He is shown at a meeting of employer association executives with several members of the delegation at the Capitol. Seated (left to right) are Rep. Roy A. Taylor, Rep. Charles F. Jonas, the Governor, Senator Sam Ervin, Jr., and Senator B. Everett Jordan. Standing are R. Thurman Taylor, Gastonia; Tom Walker, Raleigh; Harry W. Clarke, Asheville; Ed Rankin, Raleigh; E.R. Vaught, Morganton; Rep. Basil Whitener; Rep. James T. Broyhill; and Edward J. Dowd, Charlotte.

This remarkable photographic study of three North Carolina governors—Dan Moore, Terry Sanford, and Luther H. Hodges—was made while Moore was governor. They were attending a gathering of the Honorary Tar Heels, a talented group of writers, editors and photographers representing national news media, whose loyalty and support to North Carolina benefitted each governor's administration and the state.

Governor Lester Maddox of Georgia pours coffee for an amused Dan Moore at a meeting of the Southern Governors Conference. Well known as a former restaurant owner, Maddox delighted in demonstrating his skills with food service. Moore's term during the mid-60s was a challenging time for the south and the nation. President Lyndon B. Johnson and his Great Society programs were impacting all state governments and budgets, while the growing conflict in Vietnam was creating increasing strife and division. Debate and controversy over public school integration continued throughout the southern states.

N.C. PUBLICISTS
Bill Sharpe and Other Good Press Agents

North Carolina's first official publicity agent was Bill Sharpe, hard at work at his typewriter.

Aycock Brown, "The Barker of the Banks," did more to publicize the North Carolina coast than did any other individual. The message posted on the window shade above Aycock's desk reads: "A Neat Desk Is A Sign Of A Sick Mind."

There is some uncertainty about the year that the late great author and humorist, Irving S. Cobb, made his famous statement, "All North Carolina needs is a press agent." It was probably in the 1920s or early 1930s. There is certainty, however, that in 1937 William P. Sharpe became North Carolina's first official press agent, and those who knew Bill Sharpe well are certain that no state will ever have a better one. Bill Sharpe was a master, and many of his promotional approaches in those early years are still being practiced today.

Bill Sharpe was an extremely interesting writer. He had a knack for rooting out the folksy sort of stories that he knew to be fleeting, stories that had to be written and/or photographed then, or not at all. Thankfully his several books, as well as the many issues of *State* magazine that he edited, are in the better public libraries, and they will be forever a source of reference material that can be called upon.

Virtually every publisher of a weekly or daily newspaper in the state, and all the principal editors and writers, were known to Bill Sharpe. It was from these people whom he visited and corresponded with frequently that he got wind of the people, places, and events that, if reported, would place North Carolina in a favorable national light. While some of these leads went out as Bill's own stories from the State News Bureau, by far his most meaningful work was placing good story ideas in the hungry hands of *Saturday Evening Post, Look, Life, National Geographic,* the wire services, and a dozen of the nation's big city newspapers. Bill knew that these huge organizations had large staffs looking for interesting things to cover, and that if a staff person took the time and expense to come to North Carolina to do a story, that staff writer or photographer would return to his office with a determination to see that the story was published. Bill's theory was that it is better to plant a story idea and have it published than try to do it all yourself and have it never see print.

One of Bill Sharpe's fine qualities that made him so well suited to be North Carolina's press agent was his attitude about answering mail. Bill had the notion that all correspondence should be answered the day it came, even if the answer was just a brief postcard to say that a longer reply would follow later. Sharpe was also a friendly, witty person who could make friends instantly with anybody. Writers and photographers from all over the nation who knew him quickly came to love him, and they would go to great lengths to use material that they knew would help him and North Carolina.

During World War II Sharpe left the job as head of the State News Bureau for a period, and that position was given to Charles J. Parker. While Parker lacked some of the personal charm and charisma that had served Sharpe so well, Parker was a hard worker, and did an effective job as state press agent. He was elected president of the National Association of Travel Organizations during the term of Luther Hodges, which helped focus the attention of the tourism industry nationwide on North Carolina. There was some overlap, but essentially Bill Sharpe served under Governors Hoey, Broughton and Cherry, and Charlie Parker headed the state's publicity and advertising during the terms of Governors Kerr Scott, Umstead and Hodges. *continued*

Richard S. Tufts, President of Pinehurst, Inc., a member of the North Carolina Board of Conservation and Development, was instrumental in organizing North Carolina's advertising program for tourism and industrial development.

Harold Martin, an Honorary Tar Heel and staff member of the *Saturday Evening Post*, wrote a fictional piece about a mountain rifle contest that involved the governor and two of his friends, and an artist for the *Post* illustrated the article. The story perfectly described as its central characters, left to right, Tom Alexander, Bill Sharpe, and Governor R. Gregg Cherry. At a meeting of the Honorary Tar Heels they re-enacted the artist's scene at Alexander's Cataloochee Ranch in Haywood County.

Bill Sharpe (back row left) was not a photographer, but he helped organize the Carolinas Press Photographers Association in 1938. Many of the members of the association gave valuable assistance to Sharpe in publicizing North Carolina. Seated, left to right: Tom Franklin, *The Charlotte News;* Jim Wommack, *Winston-Salem Journal;* Carol Martin, *Greensboro Daily News;* and Frank Jones, *Winston-Salem Journal.* Among those identified in the back row, left to right: Sharpe; Duke Sanchez of Charlotte; Bugs Barringer of Charlotte, later Rocky Mount; and on far right, Jake Houston, *Charlotte Observer.*

One of the early appointments as Honorary Tar Heel went to Joseph Costa, staff photographer of the *New York Daily News*, and first president and founder of the National Press Photographers Association. Joe Costa performed many acts of friendship for North Carolina.

Bill Sharpe persuaded Governor Cherry to appoint an informal but extremely effective group of national media friends of North Carolina to be known as Honorary Tar Heels. They were loyal to the state, liked to mingle with governors, and had a tremendously favorable impact on the travel and tourism programs during the administrations of Governors Cherry, Kerr Scott, Umstead, Hodges, Sanford, and Moore. A few Honorary Tar Heels were still around in 1988, and it was amazing how the loyalty originally instilled by Bill Sharpe lingers. At least one yearly meeting of the Tar Heels was held in the mountains, frequently at Tom Alexander's Cataloochee Ranch near Waynesville. The most often used coastal location was the Carolinian Hotel at Nags Head run by Lucille Purser (later married to J. Emmett Winslow), assisted by Weyland Sermons, her brother, Lima Oneto, her sister, and Lima's husband, Julian Oneto, all gracious hosts. Care was taken to select as Honorary Tar Heels persons who would be congenial with each other, and those who did not try to attend meetings were eventually dropped from the roster. While the majority of the meetings were at Cataloochee Ranch or Nags Head, others were held at Morehead City, Wrightsville Beach, Pinehurst, Raleigh, Linville, Winston-Salem, Asheville, New York, Philadelphia, and Washington, D.C.

The three members of the Board of Conservation and Development who were probably the most influential in helping Bill Sharpe launch the state tourism program in the beginning were Coleman Roberts of the Carolina Motor Club, Josh Horne of the *Rocky Mount Evening Telegram,* and Richard S. Tufts of Pinehurst, Inc. The director of the Conservation and Development Department, R. Bruce Etheridge of Manteo, known as the "Duke of Dare," was also supportive.

John G. Hemmer was North Carolina's first official state photographer, hired by Bill Sharpe. Hemmer (right) is shown with television personality Brother Ralph Smith at a press photographers program honoring Hemmer's work.

Sharpe realized early that an expert staff photographer was essential to his program. He was impressed with John G. Hemmer who was a photographer for the *New York Daily News* and had been the first president of the New York Press Photographers' Association. During the pre-TV years of intensely competitive photo-journalism, Hemmer had drawn assignments such as covering Charles A. Lindbergh's takeoff from the Long Island airport for his epic first crossing of the Atlantic. (Weather delayed the Lindbergh flight for 2 or 3 days, and because the young aviator had sunk his last penny into preparing the *Spirit of St. Louis* for the flight, Johnny Hemmer passed the hat among the writers and photographers present to buy sandwiches and coffee for Lindbergh to take on the trip). North Carolina simply didn't have the pay scale to bring Hemmer south, but Sharpe was finally able to hire him for the six summertime months each year while Richard Tufts hired him to work for Pinehurst the other six months. This arrangement gave both the state and Pinehurst the services of an expert cameraman that neither could otherwise afford. Hemmer had scores of contacts with writers and photographers on national publications that were helpful to North Carolina, and

continued

John Parris, columnist for the *Asheville Citizen-Times*, is the author of six books on the North Carolina mountains that have been a great resource in publicizing interesting facts about the state.

Photo by John G. Hemmer

This group picture made during a meeting of the Honorary Tar Heels at Linville placed the Tar Heels born and bred in the back row and the Honorary kind in front. The front row (left to right): Don Short, travel editor; Don Tracy, author; Ollie Atkins, *Saturday Evening Post* photographer and later White House photographer for President Eisenhower; Bill Perry, U.S. Senate Press Gallery; Sam Weems, superintendent of the Blue Ridge Parkway; Paul Harmon, *Washington Post;* and Robin F. Garland, Eastman Kodak. Tar Heels in the back row are, left to right: John Pottle, Lynn Nisbet, John Harden, Ed Rankin, Bill Sharpe, Charlie Parker, and Hugh Morton.

When Bill Sharpe retired from the public relations staff of Carolina Power & Light Company to become editor of *State* magazine, a party was given by his friends, most of whom had played a role in creating the state advertising program that Sharpe once headed. Sharpe is on friends' shoulders, and others (left to right) include Carl Goerch, R. Bruce Etheridge, Joe Lowes, Lynn Nisbet, John G. Hemmer, Norwood "Red" Pope, Carl Sink, Josh Horne, John Harden, and Bob Thompson.

Charles Heatherly (right) served as N.C. Director of Travel and Tourism 1981 through 1986 during much of Governor Hunt's administration and two years under Governor Martin. He was succeeded by Hugh Morton, Jr. Heatherly received the Travel Council of North Carolina's first Bill Sharpe Award for his skilled and dedicated service in promoting the state.

he was of invaluable assistance to Sharpe and Parker during the years he worked for the state while playing a major role in putting Pinehurst on the map as the "Golf Capital of the World."

When Dan K. Moore took office as governor in 1965 he appointed Bill F. Hensley as the head of travel and tourism for the state. Hensley ran an effective program, and one of his most important accomplishments was the beginning of the system of Welcome Centers at the major highway entrances to the state. Seven of the centers were approved in the six years he was in the tourism director's office. Hensley also kept the Honorary Tar Heels an active group.

The state promotional program had its ups and downs through the years, and on occasion the advertising firm that had handled the candidate's political campaign wound up with the state advertising account after the new governor was in office. Situations of that kind found the advertising agency living in an environment of favor, often minimizing the incentive for the agency to give the taxpayer full value for its services. To protect the program, the Travel Council of North Carolina makes a concerted effort to monitor and combat such possibilities for corruption, and hopefully state policies are in place that will assure that the program will always be squeaky clean.

Charles Heatherly became Director of Travel and Tourism during the Hunt administration, and he saw as one of his main objectives the creation of a statewide awareness of the value of the tourism industry. The budget for advertising the state was doubled during Heatherly's six years, and North Carolina's tourism income leaped from $2.5 billion to $5 billion in the corresponding period. Heatherly gave leadership to volunteer travel trade missions to major travel markets, a new award-winning state travel film was produced and widely distributed, and he actively assisted in the campaign to save Cape Hatteras Lighthouse. Heatherly's office did much to support America's 400th Anniversary program, including facilitating the sponsorship by Piedmont Airlines of the Charles Kuralt-Loonis McGlohon album, *North Carolina Is My Home*. The Travel Council of North Carolina's first Bill Sharpe Award was given to Heatherly in recognition of his outstanding service to the travel industry.

In March 1987 Hugh Morton, Jr., who ran his own public relations firm in Greensboro, was named Tourism Director by the Martin administration, to the pleasant surprise of Morton's parents and others. Morton followed through with much of the program initiated by Charles Heatherly, including travel missions which featured performances of the McGlohon-Kuralt *North Carolina Is My Home* album. One such mission was to London, jointly sponsored by the state and Piedmont Airlines, and all of the missions were considered highly successful. When the natural disaster known as "Red Tide" struck the North Carolina coast in late summer of 1987, Morton, in cooperation with the travel industry, the North Carolina Association of Broadcasters, the North Carolina Press Association, and others, organized with Governor Martin's blessing the "North Carolina, First In Fish" campaign to restore public confidence in the safety of consuming the state's seafood. That same season North Carolina joined with Virginia in celebrating the long-awaited opening of the 470-mile long Blue Ridge Parkway. The two states jointly had produced a Parkway film which went into widespread distribution, and National Park Service officials reported Parkway visitation increased by 40 percent in spring 1988. *HMM*

Hugh Morton, Junior (left) had his promotional skills put to an early test when he and Governor Jim Martin called on sports celebrities and other well known North Carolinians to tape television spots and pose for newspaper ads designed to combat the bad effect of the Red Tide disaster on the seafood and tourism industries. The public service ads received good play in the papers and on radio and television.

Bill F. Hensley of Charlotte, formerly the Director of Travel and Tourism under Governor Dan K. Moore, is shown during the Governor's Travel Conference.

UNC PRESIDENTS
Leaders of First State University

THE PRESIDENTS

In the past 50 years, UNC has had outstanding leadership in its four presidents: Frank Porter Graham, Gordon Gray, William Friday and C.D. Spangler. William D. Carmichael served as acting president in the transition period between Graham and Gray. J. Harris Purks served as acting president in the period between Gray and Friday.

It was nearly 200 years ago when the University of North Carolina opened its doors at Chapel Hill on January 15, 1795. North Carolina's first constitution required that "... all useful learning shall be duly encouraged and promoted in one or more Universities."

In the eloquent words of Albert Coates, this first state university "... has been a magic Gulf Stream flowing in an ever-widening current through the lives of people in the cities, the counties and the state of North Carolina and beyond—tempering the customs, traditions and habits of the people it serves and lifting them to higher levels of living wherever it has gone."

The first expansion of the University of North Carolina came in 1931 when North Carolina State College of Agriculture and Engineering (now North Carolina State University) and North Carolina College for Women (now UNC-Greensboro) at Greensboro were combined with the Chapel Hill campus in what was called the Consolidated University of North Carolina.

Following World War II, public higher education began rapid expansion and growth with the flood of returning veterans. Dr. Arnold K. King, who spent 60 years of his life in association with UNC, describes the many changes in his excellent book, *The Multicampus University of North Carolina Comes of Age, 1956-1986.* It details the planning, growth and development of public senior institutions from the three campuses of the Consolidated University to the 16 campuses of the University of North Carolina with its own Board of Governors.

The huge multicampus university, with locations in every region of the state, offers diverse educational programs and enrolls 125,000 students. The UNC system, according to Dr. Clark Kerr, "has become one of the two or three best models for the nation as a whole, and perhaps the best of them all."

The 16 constituent institutions are: The University of North Carolina at Asheville, the University of North Carolina at Chapel Hill, the University of North Carolina at Charlotte, the University of North Carolina at Greensboro, the University of North Carolina at Wilmington, North Carolina State University, Appalachian State University, Western Carolina University, East Carolina University, North Carolina Agricultural and Technical University, North Carolina Central University, Winston-Salem State University, Fayetteville State University, Elizabeth City State University, Pembroke State University and the North Carolina School of the Arts. *ELR*

William Friday, UNC President (1956-86), pauses during a walk across campus in Chapel Hill on a spring day for a photographic study made against the background of pink dogwoods in bloom. Well aware of the potential for conflict between the offices of system president and Chapel Hill chancellor, one of Friday's first acts as president was to move the system office off campus to another location. Over nearly four decades of public responsibility, Friday moved from the youngest president of a major university to the second-longest tenured among major educational administrators. During his tenure Friday served with distinction under seven governors of North Carolina—Luther Hodges to James Martin. Under his wise and intelligent leadership, the UNC system of higher education grew, flourished and became a model for other states to follow.

An ovation greets Ida and William Friday after they received the university's highest award, the University Medal. Shown with them is their daughter, Betsy. Commenting on his service as president of the University of North Carolina in an October 1985 interview in *North Carolina* magazine, Friday said, "For all these years I have had the best job in North Carolina because, if you stay with it, you can do a lot more to influence worthwhile development than any governor or senator or legislator. Besides, I've worked with the brightest and most talented people in this state. Put these circumstances together, it's really not work; it's a privilege. I owe much to many people. I would not have been able to make this pilgrimage if it had not been for the helpfulness and love of our daughters, Frances, Mary and Betsy, and the wonderful companionship I have enjoyed with my wife, Ida, for 43 years."

Dr. Frank Graham escorts Mrs. Eleanor Roosevelt across the campus with Louis Harris (right), a student leader and later a noted pollster and political analyst, and Ridley Whitaker (left), another student leader. The wife of President Franklin Roosevelt was in Chapel Hill for a speech to students and faculty. Dr. Frank and Mrs. Roosevelt were both deeply concerned with human values. William Aycock, former chancellor and law professor, in a University Day address (1986) described the man in these words, "His keen mind, strength of character and purity of spirit had a wholesome influence throughout the campus—an influence which continued unabated after he became the first president of the consolidated university system. The recognition of his leadership extended beyond the state and region to the national scene." Graham later served in the United States Senate by appointment of Governor W. Kerr Scott, and also served 19 years with the United Nations as a senior mediator and diplomat.

With the Old Well in the background, Dr. Frank Graham poses in his South Building office for a photo made for use in a student publication. The former history professor always had time for students, individually or in groups. As a fledgling reporter for *The Daily Tar Heel,* I timidly made my first visit to the president's office. "I'll do my best to keep you informed, Ed," he said. "If my office door is open, and no one is with me, just come on in." True to his word, he later gave me the announcement about plans to build Woollen Gymnasium as a replacement of the old Tin Can.

Frank Porter Graham, UNC President (1931-1950), takes aim during a game of horseshoes in the backyard of the president's home, Chapel Hill. Dr. Frank, as he was known to most people, had invited Hugh Morton, then a freshman, to his home for a Sunday afternoon visit. Morton was the grandson of Hugh MacRae, a long-time friend of Graham. When Dr. Frank suggested they pitch horseshoes, Morton readily agreed and asked permission to make this photograph. It is Morton's most requested picture of Dr. Graham. William Friday noted that Graham loved people and "more than anyone else, he established that the boundaries of the University were indeed coterminous with the boundaries of the state . . . he defined what is meant by the public service obligation of a public university."

President John F. Kennedy addresses an audience of 30,000 people assembled in Kenan Stadium at Chapel Hill for University Day on October 12, 1961. The president received an honorary degree as part of the ceremonies. Shown (left to right) are U.S. Secretary of Commerce Luther H. Hodges, former governor of North Carolina, Governor Terry Sanford; Chancellor John Caldwell, North Carolina State University; President William Friday, University of North Carolina; and the President. It was 25 months before President Kennedy met his tragic death in Dallas.

C. Dixon Spangler, Jr., wearing the Great Seal of the University of North Carolina, assumes the presidency in a colorful and impressive ceremony in Chapel Hill on October 17, 1986. President Emeritus William Friday, who had retired after 30 years in the office, offers congratulations. In his remarks, Spangler outlined a broad educational agenda for UNC and concluded, "What we are trying to do, after all, is something we North Carolinians believe we are good at: inspiring our citizens to become the best that they can be. Our mission for the future may have a familiar ring: to make the weak students strong and the strong students great." Since assuming office, the former Charlotte business leader has been tested by campus trustees, faculty members, chancellors and legislators. An intelligent, direct and forthright person, Dick Spangler has received high marks for his performance and leadership to date.

John Motley Morehead (left), 1891 UNC graduate, industrialist, diplomat and philanthropist, chats with Dr. Frank Graham, former UNC president, at a UNC alumni dinner in New York City. A generous supporter of his alma mater, Morehead gave the university its bell tower, planetarium and the Morehead Award program. Since 1945 the Morehead foundation has been responsible for 1,694 alumni who were Morehead Scholars. Morehead patterned the program after the Rhodes Scholarships at England's Oxford University. Twelve Morehead Scholars have won Rhodes Scholarships. The Morehead Foundation has contributed $60 million in disbursements on behalf of UNC-Chapel Hill. This may have been the last photograph made of John Motley Morehead. Following the alumni dinner in December 1964, the UNC benefactor returned to his home in Rye, N.Y., where he died January 7, 1965 at age 94.

Private support has played a significant role in the growth and development of the University of North Carolina at Chapel Hill. Two of its prominent benefactors are shown during a visit at the Carolina Inn. Friends of many years, they are well-known business and community leaders of the Chapel Hill/Durham area. Frank H. Kenan (left), with the help of President Emeritus William Friday, was responsible for the development of the Kenan Center and The Frank Hawkins Kenan Institute of Private Enterprise. The Kenan family, through a charitable trust, has provided Kenan professorships, the football stadium and a chemistry fund. George Watts Hill, whose many public-spirited activities include being a founder of the Research Triangle Park, gave $3.5 million to the Alumni Center. His father, John Sprunt Hill, gave the university two of its best-known buildings—Hill Hall and Carolina Inn.

Enjoying a basketball game at Dean Smith Student Activity Center, Chapel Hill, are five notables in higher education, government and philanthrophy. They are (left to right) UNC President Emeritus William Friday, Frank H. Kenan of the William R. Kenan Charitable Trust, Chancellor C. Fordham, III of UNC-Chapel Hill, Governor James Martin and UNC President C. Dixon Spangler, Jr.

State Magazine named Gordon Gray, UNC President (1950-55), as
"North Carolinian of the Year" and this photographic study, made at
the president's home, Chapel Hill, was later used on the magazine
cover. After 19 years of Dr. Frank Graham's distinctly personal approach to administration, Gray brought experienced and talented
management to the operation of the consolidated university. A shy, re-
served man, Gray set high standards for himself and all aspects of
university activity and life. Racial integration in education was a crucial problem that he faced with intelligence and courage. He also
strongly supported the efforts of Governor Luther H. Hodges and others to create the Research Triangle Park involving the University of
North Carolina at Chapel Hill, North Carolina State University at
Raleigh and Duke University at Durham.

Gordon Gray welcomes President Harry S Truman at the Winston-
Salem airport when the chief executive arrived for the ground-
breaking ceremonies of the new Wake Forest College (now Univer-
sity) campus in Winston-Salem. In addition to his years in business
and higher education, Gray had a distinguished career in the federal
government. This included service as Secretary of the Army, Assistant
Secretary of Defense and as a member of the Foreign Intelligence
Advisory Board under Presidents Kennedy, Johnson, Nixon and
Ford. Gray also was chairman emeritus of the National Trust for
Historic Preservation.

JOE HARTLEY/'THE SINGING'

A Mountain Man's Legacy

The hand-lettered sign facing the highway at the edge of the singing grounds Joe Hartley believed was the principal advertising for "Singing On The Mountain."

There was no big organization behind it, no chamber of commerce. It began very modestly, and completely spontaneously. A small mountain church, the Linville Methodist Church, decided to have a Sunday school picnic at MacRae Meadows at the base of Grandfather Mountain on the fourth Sunday of June in 1925, and they invited a few friends from other churches to join them. Not one person in the 150 who were there that day had the slightest idea that what they were doing was the beginning of "Singing On The Mountain," now the largest annual religious singing convention in the mountains of the south, nationally known and regularly attended by people from almost every state in the nation.

Jack Cook of Linville led the gospel songs at the first "singing," and the main preaching was by Reverend Will Cook of Mount Vernon Baptist Church in Watauga County. There were other religious talks, not really sermons, by Joe L. Hartley, Lloyd Suddreth, and Preacher Shelby E. Gragg, a colorful mountain minister whose flowing white beard made him a favorite subject for the photographers who covered "Singing On The Mountain" in later years. Everyone present was so pleased with the success of the first one, it was voted that the gathering should be held the next year. Joe L. Hartley was duly elected chairman and Jack Cook as secretary.

By then it was beginning to be called "Singing On The Mountain," and it continued on a rather limited scale, picking up a few more people each year. Those who had attended the first one in 1925 had come in wagons or walked. By the 1930's cars and trucks were beginning to appear, and it was natural that attendance would increase. Word of mouth was the principal advertising, there was no admission, and Chairman Hartley adopted from the Bible the slogan, "Whosoever Will May Come." The event was held every year on the fourth Sunday in June without interruption, with the years of the early forties seeing much time devoted to prayers for the safe return of hundreds of mountain boys in service during World War II.

In the late forties, with the war ended and mountain tourism on the upswing, the "sing" crowds increased, and it reached a sort of milestone as a mature and established event in 1947 when a North Carolina governor, the Honorable J. Melville Broughton, who was running for the U.S. Senate, gave the principal address. Broughton, a prominent Baptist, was a fine orator who delivered an appropriate Christian message. He did not dash in and rush back out by helicopter, of course, because there was none. He stayed around a few days to enjoy the mountains, and even hiked up Beacon Heights for a picnic, and a view of the Brown Mountain lights.

Other Tar Heel governors followed in later years, including W. Kerr Scott, Luther H. Hodges, Terry Sanford, and James E. Holshouser, Jr., and a distinguished South Carolina governor, Robert McNair, also was principal speaker at the "sing." Jimmy Davis, one of the nation's finest country singers, sang at "Singing On The Mountain"

following his retirement from being governor of Louisiana.

Amazingly, those who attend the "Singing On The Mountain" have readily accepted the traditional, sometimes almost amateur, gospel singers along with some of America's most polished big-time performers, and have always shown a deep appreciation of both. There is no reasonable way to compare old-timers like Bascom Lamar Lunsford or Dr. Ike Greer and his dulcimer with the Nashville-based bands of Roy Clark or Johnny Cash, yet folks who come to the "sing" love them all, old-timers as well as top country stars. The same courtesy is accorded those who come to preach. Billy Graham and Oral Roberts were made to feel completely at home in the Grandfather singing grounds with bygone era mountain ministers like Shelby E. Gragg and Alphonzo Buchanan.

While people came from everywhere to chairman Hartley's singing, though principally from the Carolinas, Tennessee, and Virginia, the boundary of his personal horizons never seemed to extend beyond North Carolina. In 1948 when Hartley introduced Metropolitan Opera star Norman Cordon to sing *Rock of Ages,* he said, "Ladies and gentlemen, it is my pleasure to introduce to you Professor Norman Cordon, who has pleased the Yankees with his singing in New England, and who has sung all over the universe, from the Atlantic Ocean to the Tennessee line!"

As warden of Grandfather Mountain, Joe Hartley was in charge of maintaining the extensive system of hiking trails. There one day he was on the mountain, two or more miles from the paved highway, working with his laboring assistant Tom Owens to clear encroaching rhododendron from the trail. Hartley many times had counseled Owens to take a greater interest in religion, so an interesting situation developed when gospel singing suddenly filled the air. Owens fell to his knees and said, "Uncle Joe, listen, the Lord's a coming. I can hear the angels a singing." Hartley was gratified to see Tom Owens humble, but he had to laugh about it, too. He knew that his longtime friend, Reverend Alphonzo Buchanan, must have found a handful of people to preach to on the highway, and to begin his service the speaker on top of Buchanan's car was carrying its religious recording full blast.

Around 1950, soon after Joe Hartley's expanded Sunday school picnic had reached the mellow age of 25 years, a big boost came in the form of Arthur Smith and the Cracker-Jacks, a group of polished radio and television performers who attended the Grandfather Mountain gospel sing each year for the next 30 years. Hartley soon gave Arthur Smith the designation of Music Master for the annual event, because Smith played a major role in inviting outstanding musical groups in addition to his band.

The 30-year roster of Smith's own expert musicians was a true collection of stars, including Sonny Smith, Brother Ralph Smith, Roy Lear, Tommy Faile, Don Reno, George Hamilton IV, Wayne Haas, Don Ange, Sister Maggie Griffin,

continued

Bascom Lamar Lunsford, "Minstrel of the Appalachians" (left) and George Pegram played gospel tunes for Joe Hartley on their banjos. On a less sacred occasion, Lunsford and Scotty Wiseman composed the all-time favorite, *That Good Old Mountain Dew.*

Colorful mountain preacher Alphonzo Buchanan of Hawk, with his own loudspeaker atop his car, was prepared to deliver the gospel to anyone who would listen, be it three or three hundred. He was one of Joe Hartley's best friends.

At the early "sings" people came by the carloads and truckloads and parked next to a large boulder, which was used as a speaker's stage.

Joe Hartley's home on Moore Mountain was heated by a fireplace in the living room and a wood stove in the kitchen, so on a chilly day in November 1965 his dogs decided it was warmer in the sun outside the house.

Roy Acuff, "The King of Country Music," came to the 1975 "Singing On The Mountain" as guest of his friends, Lulabelle and Scotty Wiseman, prominent country music stars themselves.

Sometimes politics injected itself into who would be principal speaker at the "sing," and Chairman Hartley, a lifelong Democrat, was caught in the middle. One year the problem was mediated by Hartley having two speakers—Lieutenant Governor H.P. "Pat" Taylor (white suit on left), the Democrat, and U.S. Federal District Judge Johnson J. Hayes, a prominent Republican, at the microphone.

Reverend Oral Roberts (right) invited country music superstar Roy Clark to appear on his hour-long 1976 television special that originated at "Singing On The Mountain." The production was directed by Jerry Lewis, and was aired by 450 television stations.

and Dick and Jackie Schuyler. Arthur Smith discontinued his popular syndicated television program and disbanded the group following the death of Ralph Smith in December 1982. A new generation of Smiths then became singing fixtures, the group including Arthur's son Clay and Ralph's sons Tim and Roddey. The Smith family had a significant beneficial impact on "Singing On The Mountain" for well over 30 years. A second generation of Hartleys took over, too, with Joe Lee Hartley and Robert Hartley becoming co-chairmen upon the death of their remarkable father.

All of his life Joe Hartley devoted his time to rugged outdoor labor, and when any of his children, grandchildren or other friends ended up with desk jobs he considered them to be somewhat lazy, or afraid of work. He felt the only real career was his kind of hard work in his garden raising strawberries and other produce to sell to the "summer people." Also included was the kind of work it took to fight forest fires or hike 20 miles in his job as warden of Grandfather Mountain. Time and again he was heard to say, "the house cat always dies first," and almost all of us in Joe Hartley's eyes were house cats.

At age 94, Hartley was a passenger in a truck which was struck broadside on his side of the cab at a highway intersection in Linville. It was his first trip to a hospital in his lifetime, and hospital attendants could not get him to give up his old brown felt hat because he was ready to leave the moment he got there. Hartley came away proud and somewhat boastful with what appeared to be simply a broken arm. He said, "You've never seen another man like me, and you never will. I'd of probably made 150 years if I hadn't broke my arm." His logic in that statement, of course, was that his broken arm was preventing his customary amount of exercise, so he wouldn't live to be 150.

In the same conversation, Joe Hartley said, "The Almighty didn't make but one mistake. He didn't make a man who would last 200 years." Regrettably, Hartley lasted only one more year. He died at 95 from an intestinal blockage which doctors believe may have been brought on by the truck accident. *HMM*

When they were both in their eighties, Joe Hartley traveled to Wilmington to see my grandfather, Hugh MacRae, for their last visit together. Hugh MacRae founded the resort of Linville beginning in 1885. Hartley was waiting tables at the Green Park Inn in Blowing Rock in 1891 when MacRae gave him a job on the construction crew for the Yonahlossee Road (now US 221), which MacRae built as a stage coach road to connect Linville with Blowing Rock and the outside world.

For more than 30 years Arthur Smith served as Music Master at the "sing," performing with his own group of talented musicians. He also invited famous friends like Billy Graham and Johnny Cash to be participants.

The 50th "Singing On The Mountain" in 1974 was a big one featuring Johnny Cash and Bob Hope, either of whom would have filled the MacRae Meadows grounds with people and cars. The highways were jammed, and Hope quipped that he had to jump from car rooftop to car rooftop to arrive on time.

On his trip to Wilmington to see Hugh MacRae, Joe Hartley rode to Wrightsville Beach for his first glimpse of the ocean. He tasted water at the edge of the surf and said, "It is salty, isn't it!" He saw a 40-lb. drum caught at a fishing pier, and told Hugh MacRae, "I saw a fish as big as a boy."

Singing On The Mountain
Chorus to song composed by Arthur Smith

Singing on the Mountain, come sing with me,
Singing on the Mountain, come sing with me,
I've been down in the valley, and I'm so glad to be,
Singing on the Mountain.

ROBERT W. SCOTT
Governor, President of Community College System

A thoughtful Bob Scott sits under a replica of the University medal just before he received the prestigious award from the Board of Governors of the University of North Carolina in 1987. In its tribute to him, the board praised his leadership for the restructuring of the system of state-supported higher education, despite "vociferous opposition from nearly every newspaper in the state and opposition from most of the higher educational community as well." The board said "this state and its students enjoy today a system that is the envy of the country. One need only look at other states to understand the rarity and significance of his achievements."

Democrat and Republican hopefuls gather at the candidates forum held by the North Carolina Press Association in Chapel Hill in 1968. Shown (left to right) are Reginald A. Hawkins of Charlotte, J. Melville Broughton, Jr. of Raleigh, Robert W. Scott of Haw River, John L. Stickley of Charlotte, and James C. Gardner of Rocky Mount. Scott eliminated Broughton and Hawkins in the Democratic primary and defeated Gardner, the Republican nominee, in the fall election.

At age 39, Robert Walter Scott was the youngest governor in more than a century and received the largest vote—821,232—this state had ever given a candidate for governor.

As the son of a former governor, Bob Scott was expected to have been carefully groomed for the post. "I did not learn politics at my father's knee," Bob Scott says. "The truth of the matter is that my father said that one in the family is enough. He told me to operate the farm and the family business and that he would handle the political business.

"Again, the truth is that he handled both. I was fresh out of college, and even though I thought I knew it all he knew better and consequently gave me strong advice on farming matters."

When Scott was governor-elect, Governor Dan K. Moore helped him with the transition of administrations and assured him "there is no training ground for governors." And the young chief executive soon found out how true those words turned out to be. As a former lieutenant governor, he knew the basic structure of state government and how the General Assembly enacted laws.

"But there is no preparation for the sheer magnitude of the responsibilities and overwhelming pressure of time as the governor strives to balance all his duties," Scott noted.

The untested young man proved to be a quick study. By the end of his term, (1969-73), Bob Scott had—among many achievements—helped frame North Carolina's future though comprehensive planning, and won approval for the complete reorganization of state government and the restructuring and reform of public higher education. His term was also known as "The Years of Local Government" when the General Assembly allowed sweeping changes in home rule for local governments. In recognition of his leadership, the North Carolina League of Municipalities named Scott as its first lifetime honorary member.

In 1983 Scott became the president of the North Carolina Community College system, which was begun in 1963. "I have never done anything in my life professionally that gives me as much fulfillment as what I'm doing now . . . even as governor," he says.

"This job allows me to concentrate in an area I like very much—education. My field is administration and it has come from experience, not formal training. I like my positive role in providing education for people and communities, making a substantial, fundamental and essential contribution to the economic growth of North Carolina."

Scott has appointed a Commission on the Future of the Community College System to study and explore the needs for the next decade or so. He believes that the North Carolina system is at the right place at the right time but that it must anticipate and prepare for what the future may hold. There are 58 institutions in the system.

People are coming from an economy which didn't exist when the colleges were founded. The profile of students is different. The average age is 30. Over half those enrolled are women—and more and more are single parents with children. Most are working full time so night classes enroll about as many as day classes.

Most important, he says, we must "remain true to our mission—train people for jobs and a better future." *ELR*

If Terry Sanford had been successful in winning the Democratic nomination for president, Margaret Rose Sanford (second from left) might have become the First Lady of the U.S. A former First Lady of North Carolina, Mrs. Sanford was seated beside the current First Lady Jessie Rae Scott at the 1972 Democratic national convention in Miami. The men are former governor Luther H. Hodges (left) and Governor Bob Scott.

HOW ELECTIVE POLITICS CHANGED SCOTT'S LIFE

Planning for the future was a hallmark of his administration. But former Governor Bob Scott readily admits that advance planning had no part in how he entered elective politics.

When he was growing up Bob Scott rarely went with his father to political activities. "I regret it not because I didn't learn as much politics as I could," he says, "but because I missed the father-son association. There were never any problems between us but we were rarely together. We never went to ball games together, fishing together, those kinds of things. Consequently, I realize now I missed a lot."

At least a year before he announced for lieutenant governor, if anyone had told him that he would be active in politics he "would have laughed out loud." So what happened to change his life so drastically?

After his father's death in 1958, Bob Scott and the family continued the annual dove hunt for political leaders across the state at the family farm. After the day's hunt, the guests gathered for supper on the grounds and there was always talk of politics and candidates.

In 1963 the dove hunt discussion focused on the coming contest for governor between L. Richardson Preyer, Dr. Beverly Lake and Dan K. Moore. The Scott supporters and so-called "Branch Head Boys" were not entirely satisfied with any of the candidates. Political writers who attended the hunt reported this talk and mentioned that perhaps young Bob Scott "looks like a comer."

Bob Scott admits that the newspaper attention "went to my head" and he decided to travel around the state and make his own appraisal of the governor's race. He found a reservoir of good will left over from W. Kerr Scott but that it wasn't entirely transferrable to the son. Other Scott supporters suggested "it's too late to raise the money . . . you are a little bit too young . . . and you haven't paid your dues yet."

By this time Scott's travels and activities had attracted press attention. After intensive meetings with Ben Roney and Roy Wilder, political allies of W. Kerr Scott, and others, Bob Scott called a news conference to announce "I have made the decision that I will not be a candidate for the office of governor. To those of my friends who have expressed support for me, I simply say 'keep the faith.' "

With that statement made, Scott turned, walked out of the room and refused to answer any further questions. He continued discussions with his advisers and soon thereafter decided that the office of lieutenant governor offered him the best opportunity for winning the Democratic primary of 1964.

And so began the political career of Robert Walter Scott. *ELR*

In his last year as governor, Bob Scott went to the 1972 Democratic national convention in Miami firmly committed to supporting Terry Sanford for president of the United States. Earlier he had endorsed Senator Edmund Muskie. Scott is shown in the middle of the North Carolina delegation as it stages an enthusiastic demonstration for the former governor of North Carolina.

Governor Scott, a husky young man with boundless energy, enjoyed traveling across North Carolina and meeting its people. Here he chats with young people at a youth project in Watauga County. As a farmer and dairyman, he enjoyed getting out of the office and talking with people in small towns and rural areas about their work and the outlook for the future. Like his father, former governor Kerr Scott, he had the ability to mix and mingle with average people and learned a great deal from their opinions and suggestions.

The snow carnival queen, Pat Mozingo, of Seven Devils, welcomes Governor Scott on a visit to the popular ski resort in western North Carolina.

Bob Scott, a left-handed golfer, leans into a fairway shot during a round of golf in the Greater Greensboro Pro-Am tournament. His golf bag follows him at a respectful distance on a state-of-the-art robot caddy.

N.C. AZALEA FESTIVAL
A Pioneer, Regional Celebration at Wilmington

Ronald Reagan is holding my camera in a tourist pose at Orton Plantation in April 1959, and with him is actress Debra Paget, that year's Azalea Queen. Reagan came to the festival courtesy of the General Electric Company to be master of ceremonies of the Azalea Coronation Pageant. At the time the future governor of California and future president of the United States was sponsored by G.E. to make patriotic, motivational speeches around the nation.

In 1948 Jacqueline White, RKO motion picture actress, was crowned Queen Azalea I. None of the forty queens since has surpassed her gracious charm. She is shown with Carl Goerch, Raleigh radio personality and publisher of *State Magazine*, who was master of ceremonies at the coronation ball at Wrightsville Beach.

W. Houston Moore, M.D., was the wonderful old gentleman in Wilmington who had the idea for starting the Azalea Festival. With help of the local Rotary Club, he had been a leader in beautification of Greenfield Lake, a 300-acre Cypress pond on the south side of Wilmington in an area previously used principally as a trash dump. Azaleas and other flowering shrubs had been planted at Greenfield during the Depression years and World War II, and by the time the war ended in 1945, Greenfield was transformed into one of the most beautiful municipal parks in America.

The J. Lawrence Sprunt family had done a magnificent work in developing the gardens at Orton Plantation, and the W.C. Corbett family had purchased the Airlie Gardens part of the Walters property, another outstanding garden in the Wilmington area. Dr. Moore wanted these three gardens to be the centerpieces for an Azalea Festival, but he was not completely sure how to go about it.

In 1947 Dr. Moore invited Wilmington's major civic clubs to send one or two representatives each to an organizational meeting that would form an Azalea Festival Committee, and I was there as the representative of the Wilmington Jaycees. At the first meeting tentative plans were made to hold the first Festival in April 1948 to coincide with the expected peak bloom of the dogwoods and azaleas.

When the second meeting was held, I was away on business in Washington and returned to town to learn that I was elected president of the first Azalea Festival. I tried to decline, but W. Houston Moore was a very persuasive gentleman. With pledges of support from most of the leadership of Wilmington, particularly from my boyhood friend Rye Page, Jr., at the *Wilmington Star-News*, it was full speed ahead.

Rather than become embroiled in the politics of selecting a local girl as queen, the committee voted to try for an actress from Hollywood, if a suitable one could be found. We wrote to more than a dozen studios, and the only person responding was Linn Unkeffer, publicity director for RKO Radio Pictures. Once he understood that the committee wanted a young lady who would match the beauty and charm of the azaleas, Unkeffer came up with the perfect queen in actress Jacqueline White.

After we carefully explained that we were not conducting a beauty contest, the mothers of six attractive young Wilmington ladies permitted their daughters to serve as Queen Jacqueline's court. Bill Burns of Wilmington was a friend of Ted Malone, who had a daily program coast-to-coast on the ABC Radio Network, and Malone agreed to originate his show

continued

Debra Paget is happy about having just been crowned 1959 Azalea Queen by Governor Luther H. Hodges. Teenage Princess Nancy Stovall and the master of ceremonies, Ronald Reagan, look on.

from the Azalea Festival.

When the curtain rose on the first Azalea Festival, everything fell into place. The weather was ideal, the flowers were perfect, the Queen and her court were beautiful, and there were 11 floats in the Azalea Parade instead of an expected three. What was more, Ted Malone, who has such a gentle and soothing way with words, brought tears to the eyes of hundreds who stood in front of the Community Center to hear him tell the nation that Wilmington had the most wonderful springtime observance on earth. Dr. W. Houston Moore, the instigator of it all, was "floating on air."

The first Azalea Festival was a low budget, largely volunteer effort, with the committee determined to show a profit on the first one so the next year there could be a second one. After modest expenses, the 1948 Festival cleared $5,000, to the pleasant surprise of everyone. There were many presidents to follow who did not achieve that satisfaction, but by then the event was so well established that everyone knew it could continue, whether there was a profit or not.

At the time the Wilmington celebration began, there was a competing Azalea Festival in Charleston, S.C., but with a different twist. Charleston strategists, we were told, were scheduling that event in the middle of winter, before the flowers were in bloom, believing that there would be visitors to the festival activities who would come back a second time when word was spread that the flowers were in bloom. In spite of the Charleston theory, Wilmington did not waver in its determination to make its festival coincide with the flowers. In a few years, to our surprise, the Charleston Azalea Festival disbanded. This reinforced the belief that the peak bloom of the flowers should always be the cornerstone of the Wilmington celebration.

We believe that every North Carolina governor holding office since the Azalea Festival began has attended at least one Azalea Festival, but Governor Luther Hodges probably won the sweepstakes by attending every Azalea Festival during the six years he was governor. The festival was Hodges' kind of fun, but more than that, it enabled him to have valuable contacts with visiting industrialists, national celebrities, and newsmen who could help him accomplish his objectives for the state.

Hodges and I were close friends by reason of my service as his state campaign publicity manager when he ran for governor, and I was witness to an intense but harmonious discussion between Hodges and Ronald Reagan at a Cape Fear Country Club reception during the

continued

Vivacious Polly Bergen, an accomplished film actress, was on every U.S. television screen advertising Pepsi Cola in 1956 when her sponsor agreed she would be excellent as North Carolina's Azalea Queen IX.

1959 Festival. The conversation with Reagan was devoted to a favorite Hodges theme, the obligation of all businessmen to render public service, and Reagan appeared to be taking every word to heart. Since that time I have often wondered how much influence Governor Hodges' thoughts may have had later in Reagan's decision to run for governor in California, and in his decision to run for president. The two seemed to be in absolute agreement on the matter of public service, so my speculation may not be far-fetched.

Kenneth Sprunt, host to Reagan and other Azalea Festival celebrities at a party at Orton Plantation, recalls, "Reagan's seriousness was somewhat of a damper on the festive occasion of a daytime party in Orton gardens, but he was a delightful and welcomed guest."

Reasonably early in the life of the festival a concerted effort was given to making it a truly statewide event. The name was changed officially to The North Carolina Azalea Festival At Wilmington, and the sponsoring group was granted an incorporation charter in Raleigh. It became traditional for the May Queens of leading North Carolina colleges and universities to be invited to be members of the Azalea Queen's Court.

In 1958 swimming star Esther Williams was Azalea Queen, and the Duke University May Queen in her Court was a pretty young lady from Salisbury, Mary Elizabeth Hanford. Miss Hanford is the present Liddy Dole, former U.S. Secretary of Transportation, the wife of Robert Dole, U.S. Senate Republican leader.

When the festival was started in 1948, by actual count there were more than one million individual azalea plants within Airlie, Orton, and Greenfield Gardens, various city plazas and public parks. Campaigns were conducted to encourage every property owner to plant azaleas, response was tremendous, and there is no way to know what a thorough plant census would show today. It would be fun to learn the answer, but quite a burden to make the count.

Over the years the committee learned what went over with Azalea Festival audiences and what did not. George Jessel, master of ceremonies at the 1957 coronation of native Tar Heel Hollywood star Kathryn Grayson, went over like a lead balloon with his nightclub brand of humor that made local personalities and institutions the victims of every joke. The modern hotels now in the Wilmington area had not been built in 1957, so festival celebrities were housed in the Cape Fear Hotel, then Wilmington's finest. Jessel really targeted the Cape Fear Hotel, mentioning among other things that he had found George Washington's initials on the men's room wall. He was not a hit.

The Wilmington area churches insisted, and rightfully so, that the Azalea Festival should never coincide with Easter, which meant that depending on when Easter occurred, the festival might miss the peak bloom of the flowers in some years, but that did not happen often. A further scheduling complication involved trying to dovetail with the dates of the Azalea Open Golf Tournament, a separate organization which had its own problems trying to fit into the schedule of the PGA.

Prior to the start of the Azalea Festival in 1948, the tourism season in the Wilmington area began around June 1 and ran through Labor Day. The Azalea Festival gave the area another attraction in addition to the Atlantic Ocean, and it kicked off the tourism season two months earlier than previously. Probably the greatest value of the Azalea Festival, however, was that the whole region learned to work together. No event in the state has been more successful over a comparable period. *HMM*

Of Wilmington's many famous sons, one of the most popular with sports fans is Sonny Jurgenson, who quarterbacked the Washington Redskins following his football career at New Hanover High and Duke. With him are Emmett Kelly, Jr., Snow Queen Pat Mozingo, and actor Ed Platt of the "I Spy" television series.

Mary Elizabeth Hanford
Duke University May Queen

Actress Kathryn Grayson, noted for her lovely voice, was known in her home town of Winston-Salem as Zelma Kathryn Hedrick. She was crowned Azalea Queen X by Metropolitan Opera star Lauritz Melchior, with comic George Jessel standing by. Miss Grayson was a star of the movie *Show Boat* with another beautiful North Carolinian, Ava Gardner of Smithfield.

Doak Walker (left), SMU football great, in 1950 crowns Gregg Sherwood Azalea Queen III, having been handed the crown by Charlie Justice, who had crowned actress Martha Hyer the year before. Young Peter Davis is the crown bearer.

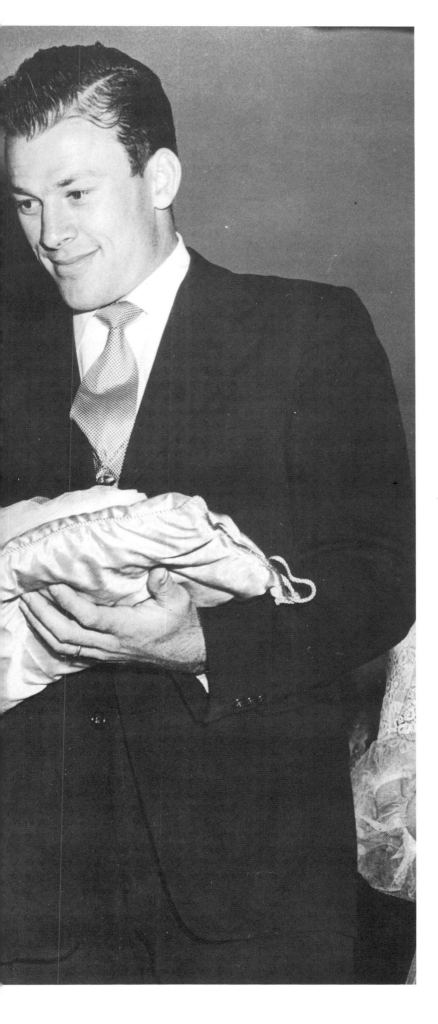

Arnold Palmer (left) was still a student at Wake Forest in 1954 when he won the top amateur trophy in the Azalea Open. Actress Anita Colby made the presentation, with winning professional Bob Toski looking on. In August 1954 Palmer won the U.S. Amateur Golf Tournament, then turned pro.

George Davis, Attorney General of the Confederacy, stands in a bed of azaleas at Third and Market across from the Cornwallis House in Wilmington, where the facetiously disrespectful said he pointed the way to the liquor store. His daughter, my Aunt Cary MacRae, was none too happy about that sort of talk, nor would she have been pleased to see a young gentleman perched on Uncle George's arm to view the Azalea Festival parade.

DEAN SMITH
Coach, Teacher, Role Model

Dean Smith, head basketball coach, at UNC-Chapel Hill, was the subject of the conversation, and doing the talking was former UNC President Bill Friday, who said, "Bill Aycock was the motivating force and the genius who found him, and we put him in there. Some people did not want him, because they didn't think he was experienced enough. What you have witnessed here is a man becoming a legend in his own time, and he has earned it. It's a spectacular career that he has put together, and what he has done for inter-collegiate basketball is just incredible.

"Right now, for example, he has nine boys playing in the NBA every night, which is unheard of by any other coach. What is so important about him is that he sticks by the rules. He teaches self discipline, he teaches organization, he teaches team play, and he teaches respect for academic excellence. He is a real leader, and he deserves the designation which is accorded him by everybody as this country's greatest basketball coach."

More than a few people, and particularly opposing coaches, have sought to pinpoint the one thing that might be the secret of Dean Smith's success. The insiders, which include former players, the coaching staff, and other close friends can probably agree that his regard for his players may be the key to it. To define that philosophy briefly, Smith himself says, "If I recruit a player, I feel an obligation to guide him the best that I can, like I do my own children."

Bobby Jones, one of Dean Smith's All-America players who went on to outstanding accomplishment in the NBA, substantiates the unique bond between Smith and the players by recalling, "I've always respected him for being the great coach, really a genius as far as knowing basketball and the game in general. He motivates through the kind of person he is. He doesn't have to scream and holler, he just tells you what needs to be done, and you know he is the kind of person who wants you to play at your best.

"After I graduated I got to know him a little bit better as a person, and as I look back now I can see really he loves his players, not just because they are basketball players, but because they are special people. I really appreciate the fact that he has kept up with me. He's kept up with all the guys who have made it in pro athletics and have done well, but more than that he has kept up with those guys who really haven't made it into the pros and have just taken a regular job, or who have maybe had some struggles in their lives and some problems. He is concerned about people, and he seeks to make the world a better place."

The Raleigh *News & Observer*'s sports editor Joe Tiede is intrigued by another attribute of the Dean Smith program. He comments, "The most amazing aspect of his regime is the consistency. There are a lot of good programs in the country when you think of Louisville, Indiana, Georgetown, and Kentucky. There are a lot of other very reputable, strong programs, but I do not know of one that has ever been as consistent over as long a period as Dean Smith's program at North Carolina. They may lose two first round picks to graduation one season, and the next year there may be a slight decline, but it's never much. They are always in contention, they're always in the rankings. Their record in the ACC in the last 20 years is so far ahead of anybody else's in a league known for its competitiveness, it's remarkable. I do not know how he has done it. You'd think that sooner or later he would have an off season, he'd lose a couple of people he couldn't replace and it's going to be an ordinary team, but it just hasn't happened."

In the basketball coaching profession possibly the most prestigious character reference Dean Smith could receive is one spoken from the heart by UCLA's sainted Coach Emeritus John Wooden, who says, "If I failed to recognize Dean Smith as one of the all-time fine coaches of the game, I would probably be out of my mind. He certainly is, but I am fond of Dean for even more than his basketball coaching ability. I think he does a great deal for the young men under his supervision other than just basketball. Dean recognizes why youngsters are in the university. Their only reason for being there is to get an education. He understands that, and puts that ahead of basketball. Every coach in the country should do that. One of the things of which I am most proud is that practically all of my players got their degrees, and are doing well in their chosen professions. I know that is true of Dean's." *continued*

What may be the finest basketball facility in the nation is called by most people the Dean Dome, but officially it is the Dean E. Smith Student Activities Center. It was a few months short of completion when Coach Smith hiked to the rafters for this picture.

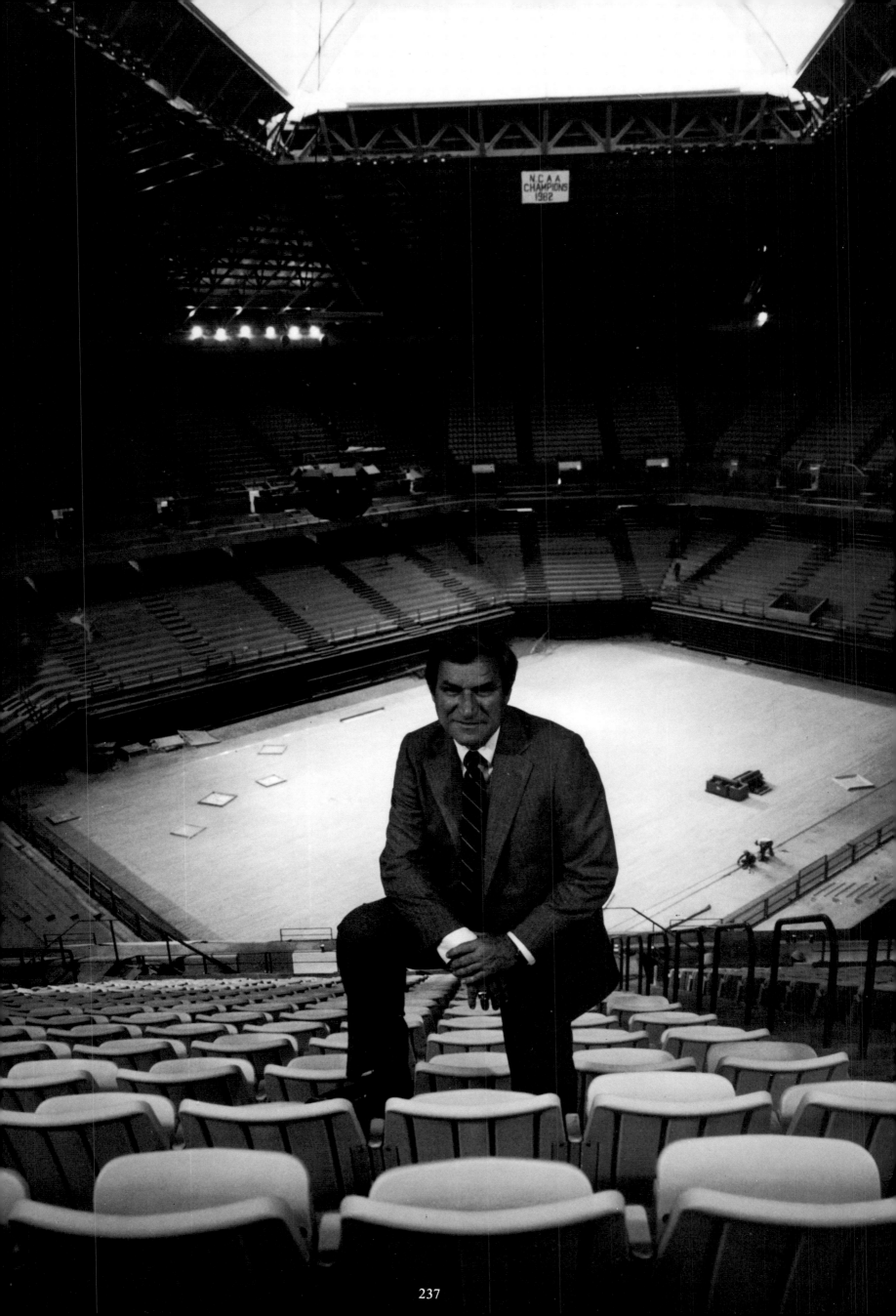

Dean Smith was rather inconspicuous on the sidelines in Reynolds Coliseum, scouting his next ACC tournament opponent. Smith had just been appointed head basketball coach at UNC-Chapel Hill by Chancellor Bill Aycock, while some alumni had wanted a committee to pick a top name coach to replace Frank McGuire.

Dean Smith greeted the opposing coach before the game with, "Hi, Jim, that certainly is a handsome yellow jacket you are wearing." Coach Valvano replied, "Do you really like it, Dean? I like it, too. It fits me, and look at the label, it's tailored by a top company. You know, Dean, I never wear a jacket again if I lose a game while wearing it. You would not want me to get rid of this jacket, would you, Dean?" The conversation was at the 1982 ACC Tournament. North Carolina won, and advanced to become 1982 NCAA National Champion. Valvano's opportunity to keep his jacket came the next year. His 1983 NC State team won the ACC, and the NCAA National Championship.

The North Carolina—Virginia game in Chapel Hill in February 1986 was tense, and at one point Dean Smith and assistant coach Bill Guthridge dashed onto the court to prevent the Carolina bench from emptying into an impending brawl. A well-intentioned but foolish 1988 NCAA rule forbids coaches from doing this.

Dean Smith's wife, Linnea, is a medical doctor and psychiatrist, and their charming daughters are Kristen and Kelly.

Coach Dean Smith and assistant coach Larry Brown cut down their first ACC Championship net in 1967. During his first year as head coach in 1962 Smith won 8 games and lost 9, but he was well established by 1967, the beginning year of winning three successive ACC championships.

Dean Smith coached the United States Basketball Team to victory in the 1976 Olympics in Canada, and his gold medal smile was captured by cartoonist John Branch to be made into a poster. Coach Smith signed hundreds of the posters for admirers.

Moments before in March 1982 at New Orleans the North Carolina team won the NCAA National Championship but only the net around James Worthy's neck is an indication of it. Everyone is exhausted, except Sports Information Director Rick Brewer, who is checking his watch to be sure his heroes are interviewed in time to make the morning papers.

Just as Coach Wooden emphasized scholastics in his praise of Dean Smith, so did the *Charlotte Observer* in its editorial of February 13, 1987, the week Smith had his 600th win. The editorial read, in part:

"With the possible exception of Joe Paterno, the football coach at Penn State, we are hard pressed to think of another coach in Dean Smith's class. His players really *are* student-athletes. Most of them do obtain not only their degrees, but a college education. And although they attend class regularly, it may well be that they learn even more on the court under the tutelage of Coach Smith—lessons in competition, sportsmanship, teamwork and unselfishness that will make them better human beings, no matter where they go when their playing days are over."

Rumors abounded during winter 1988 that All-America sophomore J.R. Reid would turn pro in the 1988 spring draft, although Reid and his parents emphatically denied it. In a news conference in Seattle prior to the NCAA Final Eight game between North Carolina and Arizona, Dean Smith made it clear that he and J.R. had work to do before Reid would command top dollar in the NBA. "J.R. will be best when he is about 27 years old. I do not have time to list all the things he needs to do to improve, but he knows them."

The discussion of Reid's future did serve as a reminder of the respective early departures of James Worthy and Michael Jordan, however, both having left a year early on advice from Coach Smith. While UNC students and alumni selfishly would have relished the services of Worthy and Jordan for another year, most agreed Dean Smith's priorities were correct when he put players first and strength of the following years' Carolina teams second.

Coach Smith may sound defensive, but nevertheless resolute, when he explains, "The school is fortunate to have had Michael Jordan and James Worthy here. We'd have done better if they had stayed a year extra, but they got their degrees, and that's what they came to school for. I don't think I was hurting the school. I obviously encouraged them to go, and I'm absolutely right. The next year I said, 'Where are you, Michael? Where are you, James?' when we were losing, but I honestly think that off the court I have to give them my advice of what is best for them. When we get on the court, they do what I think is best for the team."

continued

Coach John Wooden of UCLA and Coach Dean Smith of UNC-Chapel Hill established basketball programs at their respective universities which have been admired and copied by other schools. Their emphasis on scholastic accomplishment as well as athletic prowess made their teams outstanding.

Golf takes second place only to basketball as Dean Smith's favorite sport, and the favorite foursome over the years has been, left to right: Dr. Earl Somers, Dean Smith, Simon Terrell, and Dr. Christopher Fordham.

The conflict between academics and athletics is often noted, so it was a real switch when Dr. Richard Phillips (right) of the School of Education at UNC-Chapel Hill took the lead in establishing the Dean E. Smith Academic Scholarship. Coach Smith presents the $4,000 check for the first scholarship to Kimberly Ann Stewart of Durham. Robert Eubanks, UNC Trustees Chairman, and Moyer Smith of the UNC Educational Foundation, lend their approval.

Al McGuire

Mark Wicker

Al McGuire, NBC-TV's basketball analyst who coached at Belmont Abbey College in North Carolina before going to Marquette University to win the NCAA National Championship against the Tar Heels, believes he has seen every major basketball arena in the nation, and Dean Smith Center comes out best. McGuire says, "There is no comparison. It is the true amateur building in the country. It is state of the art that all future on-campus buildings involving basketball will be modeled after into the next century. Any architect will definitely visit Chapel Hill three or fours years before he breaks ground on his building."

Mark Wicker, a former sportswriter for the *Chapel Hill Newspaper* and the *Winston-Salem Journal*, who moved to the *Orange County Register* in California, was delighted that UNC was sent west for NCAA tournament games in spring 1988. When some sportswriters predicted that Carolina would be devastated by Loyola-Marymount in their game in Salt Lake City, Wicker knew first hand that North Carolina had the best coach around sitting on her bench. Interviewed by Jim Heavener on the UNC network, Wicker remained true to his upbringing by saying, "Dean Smith did not just fall off a turnip truck. He is the most successful coach of the last 20 years in college basketball." The contest with Loyola-Marymount did turn out to be devastation, but it was Carolina doing the devastating by scoring the greatest number of points ever scored in a NCAA playoff game. North Carolina won 123 to 97, and the Tar Heel 79 percent field goal percentage set yet another record for the NCAA tournament.

For our parting tip on winning at basketball, we bring you in Dean Smith's own words, "Rebounding is the most important thing. If you get one shot, and the other team gets two, guess which team is going to win." *HMM*

JAMES E. HOLSHOUSER, Jr.
Watauga Legislator is First GOP Governor

James E. Holshouser, Jr., the first Republican Governor of North Carolina to be elected in the 20th century, and the First Lady, Patricia Hollingsworth Holshouser. The young lawyer from Boone had served in the House of Representatives in the 1963, 1965 and 1969 sessions, providing valuable experience which served him well in carrying out his gubernatorial responsibilities and working with a General Assembly controlled by Democrats. Born in Asheville, Pat Holshouser is a graduate of Appalachian State University and visited more than 80 counties during her husband's campaign. She was an active and charming First Lady.

It is a stormy night in Avery County when Governor Holshouser greets President Gerald Ford who was late in arriving, due to inclement weather, for a Republican campaign appearance. It was actually the first visit by a president to Avery County. During Holshouser's term as governor, national events had great impact on North Carolina and its economy. The Republican president, Richard M. Nixon, resigned. The war in Vietnam came to an inglorious end, and the OPEC oil embargo caused an energy crisis in North Carolina and the nation.

As the first Republican governor elected in the 20th century, James Eubert Holshouser's first legislative message held great historical significance. Speaking to the 1973 General Assembly, dominated by Democrats and led by Lieutenant Governor James B. Hunt and Speaker of the House James E. Ramsey, both Democrats, the youthful (38) chief executive opened with these words:

"The present situation is unique in our lifetimes. The state could be hurt by it. I am convinced it will not be. I'm convinced because I know so many of you already, and I know what kind of men and women you are. I know that when the chips are down, you'll put North Carolina and our people first. I think you know me well enough to know I'll do the same."

Holshouser did fairly well with his program in the 1973 General Assembly, had more problems with the 1975 session, but the long-standing relationship between Governor and General Assembly was changed forever. For over 70 years the Democrat-controlled legislature had dealt only with a chief executive of the same party. The balance of power, never static, which exists between the legislative and the executive branches of government, began a slow but inevitable shift to the legislative.

Some legislative leaders dispute this point of view, and describe the recent growth of staff and other activities as needed legislative initiatives reflecting broad support from the districts they represent.

The former Watauga County legislator proved to be a hard-working, effective and popular governor. Here are some of his achievements:

—Gained expansion of the state kindergarten program, increasing the number of five-year-olds in schools from 3,427 to over 80,000 and imposing a legal limit on class size.

—Gave strong and effective support to the im-

plementation of the reorganized university system of higher education. In his legislative message in January 1973, he said, in part, ". . . our history books may well say that the most lasting result of the 1973 Legislature was your determination to protect the concept of our new university system. This new system was carefully molded in 1971 by a General Assembly which set aside all secondary considerations in its finest hour of statesmanship. I urge you to defend the new university system and its Board of Governors, and prove to the people of North Carolina that we will stand behind the commitment we made here in 1971."

—Made efficiency in government a hallmark of his administration. The Governor's Efficiency Study Commission, which he appointed, attracted business support in money and talent, resulting in state savings estimated at $80 million.

—His support for state parks resulted in the purchase of more land for park use than the purchases of all previous administrations put together.

—Worked hard to base highway planning and construction on "real need," not politics. Gave the interstate highways the state support needed to assure their completion.

—Established area health education centers and rural health centers across the state. Many small or rural communities were assisted in locating physicians and other health care personnel.

—Opened a People's Office and made People's Day visits around the state because "I really care and want every citizen to have the opportunity to talk face to face with the governor if he has a problem with state government."

In his final telecast as governor (for which he paid $10,000 of his own money), Holshouser closed with these words:

". . . all I hope for is that you'll remember me as a governor who cares about you, and that this governor is a man you can trust." *ELR*

First GOP Governor in 20th Century

In an interview with Jim Holshouser, who lives and practices law in Southern Pines, the former governor spoke of several topics of interest from a current perspective:

Getting Started. "It is almost impossible to describe how difficult it was to put together a staff and cabinet as the first Republican governor. There were so few experienced people to choose from. That is one reason why Gene Anderson (his assistant and political adviser) was so important to me. He knew issues, people, how the General Assembly worked and had experience in state politics."

Checks and Balances. "The opportunity for the governor to serve two terms was needed, but we should have limited the terms of the Speaker of the House. We are paying a high price for this. Legislative fiscal research was intended to be primarily post audit, but it appears to have become a second Budget Division. The growth of the legislative services staff can allow a small clique in the General Assembly to run the legislature. This is very unhealthy. I never thought the Advisory Budget Commission was constitutional but it worked."

North Carolina Assets. "Most North Carolinians do not know what a good state we have to live in . . . to have the variety of our regions, the down-home friendliness and outgoing interest in your neighbors. Two things in North Carolina are most important: The University of North Carolina system of higher education and the Research Triangle Park. I think they set us apart from the rest of the south. The founders of both have never received proper credit for what they achieved. C.D. Spangler (UNC president) is the right man for the job at the right time. He has settled down and will bring a business background to help the University be the force that it can be in helping bring about more economic development and growth."

The Future. "Our future will involve so much change that it will catapult us into the new century. Planning is vital, especially in the Piedmont and along the I-85 corridor. We must protect I-85 from too much growth. We must avoid the urban glut and sprawl which results from lack of planning. North Carolina is becoming more international and less provincial. We were never considered a national leader, but the opportunity is there for our state, with proper economic development, to be a leader."

Joan Van Ark, television and motion picture actress, is crowned as the Azalea Queen by Governor Holshouser in 1973. Like all governors, Holshouser was expected to crown queens, cut ribbons, participate in dedicatory ceremonies, and represent his office at innumerable public and private events. A naturally friendly person, Jim Holshouser handled these many appearances with warmth and personal charm.

Governors of North Carolina travel widely and often meet and associate with famous people. Governor Holshouser (left) chats with General William Westmoreland, Terry Sanford and Bob Hope. All were attending the "Singing on the Mountain" in Avery County where Johnny Cash also appeared. Westmoreland was host to Hope. Sanford, who was president of Duke University, came over from his home at nearby Hound Ears.

At an annual meeting of the Travel Council of North Carolina, Governor Holshouser presents the G. Lynn Nisbet Award to Cliff C. Cameron of First Union National Bank in recognition of the bank's outstanding promotion of the state's travel industry. At left is William A.V. Cecil of Biltmore House and Gardens, Asheville. Cameron now serves as a senior cabinet official with Governor James G. Martin.

Whenever a governor plays golf, the foursome is usually arranged so the governor stands a good chance of winning. This is what happened when Jim Holshouser was given his fellow Republican Billy Joe Patton of Morganton (right) as his partner for a match at Grandfather Country Club. Patton, an amateur champion golfer, gained national prominence by taking the legendary pro Ben Hogan to the wire at the famed Masters tournament in Augusta.

A VISIT TO THE OLD KENTUCKY HOME

While a student at Chapel Hill, Hugh Morton was given the assignment by a student publication to make photographs of Tom Wolfe's mother, Julia, in Asheville. The famous novelist had been dead about two years, and as every reader of *Look Homeward Angel* knows, Wolfe's treatment of his mother in the book was not kind. She had not welcomed the news media attention which resulted. When Morton appeared at the "Old Kentucky Home" and asked to make photographs, he was summarily dismissed by Mrs. Wolfe. The next day he returned, was given a more promising audience and his entreaties gained her permission to make these two pictures. She also rode out to the cemetery to show Morton where her son was buried but she did not get out of the car. Morton's recollections of Julia Wolfe: "She was obviously proud of her son, proud of the success his works enjoyed . . . but she had mixed feelings about what he had written about her. Perhaps she didn't know whether to laugh or cry." *ELR*

'NOW, GENTLEMEN . . . ONE LAST QUESTION'

A noted humorist and well-known practical joker, Carl Goerch was also a political reporter and commentator for WPTF Radio, Raleigh. During sessions of the General Assembly, he would frequently invite various members of the House and Senate to the studio for chats about the legislative day. At one such broadcast, with the legislators gathered around a table facing Goerch and with their backs to the control room clock, he paused long enough to let his program time expire. Then he said: "Now, gentlemen, one last question . . . are there as many S.O.B.s in this session as there were in the last?" Believing that WPTF's 50,000 watts would transmit their answers to thousands of voters, the honorables were in such obvious distress that Goerch had mercy and broke out in peals of laughter. His victims joined in moments later— when they realized they were *not* on the air. *ELR*

John Harden, the proud father of twins, poses with the boys, Holmes Plexico and Mark Michael Harden. A third son, Jonathan, joined the family later. Harden was married earlier to the late Jo Holt Harden and there are two children, Glenn Abbott Springer-Miller and Jack.

JOHN W. HARDEN
PR Pioneer, Noted Communicator

It was the first Christmas after John Harden was employed by President J. Spencer Love to begin a public relations department at Burlington Mills (now Burlington Industries). Harden sent a small gift of Burlington socks, with his business card, to a list of corporate friends in Greensboro, including the managing editor of the afternoon newspaper.

The next day, the managing editor, a crusty old-timer, called to say that he could not accept the gift and implied that the socks could be considered a bribe, seeking his favorable treatment of Bur-Mil news. Harden, who had known the managing editor for years, was not offended.

"The gift is really in lieu of a Christmas card," Harden explained, "but if I thought I could buy your favor for six pairs of socks I wouldn't want you."

The editor chuckled and admitted, "you've got a point there, John . . . and I'll keep the socks." And so the new corporate public relations program passed an early credibility test with local news media.

Harden pioneered in establishing the major corporate public relations department in 1948 with great success, and I worked there as his assistant for four years. Ten years later he left the company to pioneer in organizing John Harden Associates, believed to be the first full-service public relations consulting firm in North Carolina. JHA later added offices in Raleigh and Charlotte. I opened the Raleigh office and served as vice president and manager for four years.

During his 27 years as a PR consultant, Harden represented a vast array of corporate, non-profit and civic organizations, helping them tell their stories to their many publics. He would often say, "in its simplest form, public relations is doing good and getting credit for it." A skilled professional, Harden could quickly organize the first North Carolina trade mission to Europe which was led by Governor Luther H. Hodges accompanied by 68 business leader volunteers, or direct a successful state-wide bond election for the support of public schools and mental hospitals.

The recognition of John Harden as "father of professional public relations in North Carolina" and as the first member of the North Carolina Public Relations Hall of Fame is well deserved. However, it should be noted that his long and active life of 81 years also encompassed many other achievements. These included journalism (21 years as editor and reporter), literature (author of two popular books on North Carolina folklore), politics and government (trusted adviser to four governors), historian (author of four histories: two corporate, one county and one on North Carolina highways), and public service (countless boards and committees at city, county and state levels, all serving the common good).

And a final, and little known, dimension. He served as an interpreter of North Carolina in the written and spoken word. For over 40 years he knew and worked closely with writers, artists, photographers, commentators, historians, archivists and others in the field of literature and communications who were interested in North Carolina or North Carolina topics. John Harden's deep love, knowledge and understanding of North Carolina were shared freely with many creative people—and there is really no way to measure the value of such sharing. *ELR*

John and Sarah Plexico Harden, shown on their honeymoon at Grandfather Mountain, read the plaque which marks the spot where Governor William B. Umstead stood while dedicating the Mile High Swinging Bridge in 1952. The Hardens later purchased a vacation home at Grandfather Mountain Lake and spent many happy years there.

The Harden twins, Holmes and Mark, prance across the Mile High Swinging Bridge at Grandfather Mountain on an outing with their father, John. Both boys and their younger brother, Jonathan, spent many summers at the Linville resort, including work at the attraction when they were old enough to be employed.

John Parris, prolific author of books on the North Carolina mountains and mountain people, points out a distant peak to Governor Dan K. Moore, another mountain man, and to John Harden, Ed Rankin and Jerry Elliott. Harden served by appointment of Governor Moore on the State Board of Conservation and Development and was chairman of the committee on advertising and tourism. Rankin was Moore's Director of the Department of Administration, and Elliott was a member of the governor's staff.

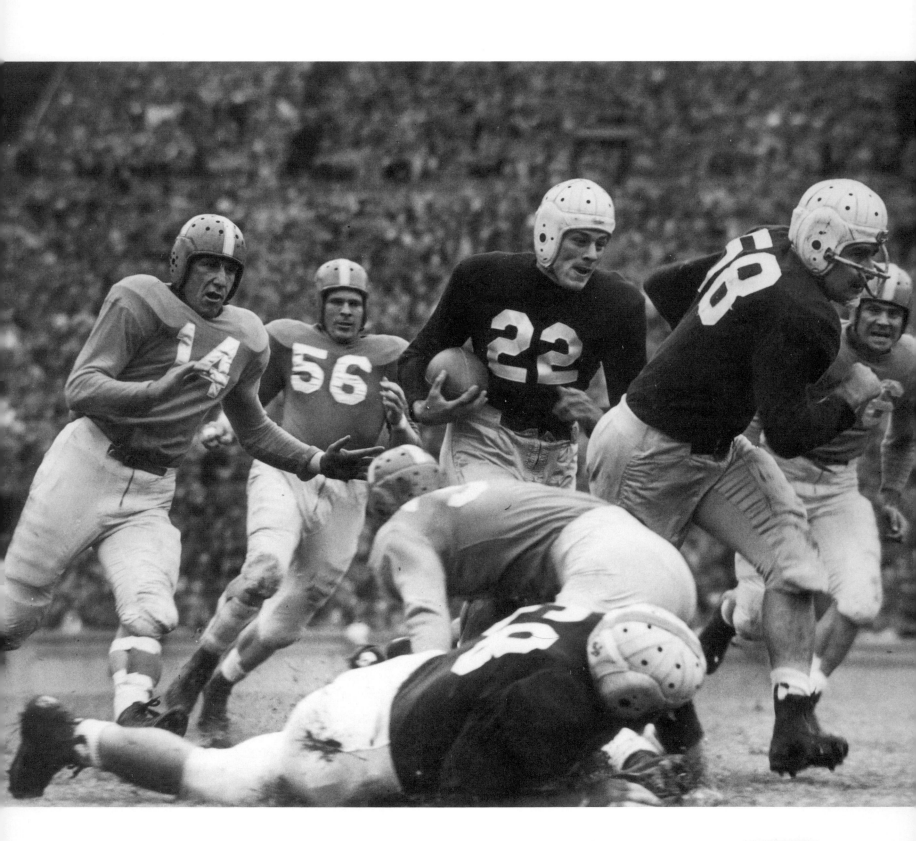

Charlie Justice carefully follows the interference supplied by Carolina tackle Heywood Fowle (58) for a good gain against Tennessee in Kenan Stadium. In his high school days at Asheville, Charlie was inclined to break into the open and go it alone, but his teammates from pro football that he played with in the Navy taught him to take advantage of his good blockers.

In November 1948 C.D. Spangler, Jr., president of the University of North Carolina, was an 11th grade student at Woodberry Forest School. Recalling that time he says, "I saw Charlie Justice devastate the University of Virginia football team in Scott Stadium in Charlottesville, and his jersey was ripped in one of his great runs. I persuaded a North Carolina cheerleader to retrieve the torn jersey for me after Justice came to the sidelines for a new one. The jersey I obtained is now back in Chapel Hill where it belongs, and it is one of my most prized possessions."

CHARLES JUSTICE
Legendary Athlete and Humanitarian

"Charlie Justice was the greatest athlete I saw perform in our generation, and I include all sports," says William Friday, President Emeritus of the University of North Carolina. Quickly Friday adds, "The Charlie Justice I know best, however, is the civic leader, the great humanitarian, the great giver of himself. I have never seen anybody that did as much as he has done in causes from the Heart Association to Crippled Children to Christmas Seals to the university itself. Here is a fellow who has undergone three major surgical procedures and lived a very full and vigorous life, and the other side of him is that his personal life has been exemplary. He doesn't smoke, he doesn't drink, he doesn't gamble. He inspires young people everywhere by being himself, and that makes him such a symbol. He is a great, great American."

When Bill Friday speaks, it is the voice of a highly respected educator, yet when sports people talk about Charlie Justice, they say much the same thing, even if they say it differently. Woody Durham, the radio voice of the UNC Tar Heels, says, "In all my associations in sports over the years, I have never known a person to wear the mantle of fame any better than Charlie Justice has. His story to me is one of the most amazing stories in all of sports when you think about the fact that it was 40 years ago when he achieved the stardom that he did, and today his name is still magic. Nationally people talk about Babe Ruth, and I almost have to put Charlie Justice in that same category, because when people in North Carolina talk about Justice, they do it in terms of reverence."

Charlie Justice has always been modest and humble, but an event that he considers a turning point in his life took place in the summer of 1948 which assured that he will retain that humility until his dying day. Charlie recalls that North Carolina had a tragic polio epidemic that summer and the disease struck an outstanding fullback from Rocky Mount High School. The boy had been recruited by many coaches, and had decided to attend Duke. He was paralyzed from the neck down, kept alive under an oxygen tent in Duke Hospital on a rocking bed constantly in motion. The young man told his parents that he wanted to see Charlie Justice, but the doctors were uncertain whether Charlie should risk exposing himself to the dread disease, and they advised against it. Charlie nevertheless insisted, and wearing a surgical mask, he was allowed into the stricken player's room for 30 seconds.

Charlie says, "I looked down on him in that tent and he looked up at me, and the biggest smile came across his face. I said right then I will never refuse to see somebody in that condition who wants to see me, and I haven't. I will never forget that. It did me more good than it did him." That incident, more than any other, is the reason that Charlie Justice has unselfishly lent his good name to every conceivable cause to aid the infirm and unfortunate in the 40 years since.

Advice from an older brother that still sticks in Charlie's memory is "know you are good, believe you are good, but don't tell anybody, because they will find out." That philosophy was Charlie's blessing when he was drafted into the Navy in 1943 and sent to the Bainbridge Naval Base in Maryland. Had Charlie Justice not believed in himself and had great will and determination, the 18-year-old high school star would never have been a member of the Bainbridge football team made up of college All-Americans and professional all-stars, who were two deep at every position.

Justice, known only as "Hey Kid" to his coach, was small and without a pro or college football reputation, so he was sent to the back of the line five different times in order that better known players would be issued football equipment first. The coach even ran out of shoes before he got to Charlie. At practices it was the persistent Justice's job to shag footballs that better known players were kicking. With his feet only in sneakers, Charlie decided to kick a ball back to them. The first kick left his foot like it was out of a cannon, went 65 to 70 yards, and from then on he was the team punter. He does not know to this day how he learned to punt, other than simply to try it, because his red-hot Asheville high school team punted only once in his senior year.

Being called off the bench only to punt got old in a hurry for Charlie, and he nagged the coach for an opportunity to carry the ball in scrimmage. The chance came and he made some good runs, but the coach would only say that he was running through the wrong holes. Then came a scrimmage with the Washington Redskins. Justice scored Bainbridge's only touch-

continued

Charlie Justice met with almost instant success at Chapel Hill on the playing field, and his talents were recognized by others on the team as the key to outstanding accomplishment for the whole squad. Joe Neikirk, Bob Mitten and Bob Cox (left to right) are carrying Charlie off Kenan field after a victory.

The Justice era at UNC was in the late Forties before today's efficiency of high chain link security fences, so every football game in Kenan Stadium was interrupted at least once while game officials and assistant team managers removed a canine fan from the field. The dog then had the best seat in the house from which to watch the rest of the game.

Harry Wismer, the nation's leading radio sportscaster of that day (right), and UNC Head Football Coach Carl Snavely (left) chat with Charlie Justice before the January 1, 1949 Sugar Bowl game against Oklahoma which was won by Oklahoma 14 to 6. Justice played an outstanding game even in defeat, and several hundred autograph-seeking youngsters awaited him outside the Sugar Bowl stadium.

down, averaged 14 yards a carry for four runs, and that earned him a starting position in the backfield, the only high school player in the lineup. Bainbridge went undefeated for two years, with Justice named second string All-Service All-America. He was even nominated for the Heisman Trophy in 1944, although the coveted award ultimately was won by Glenn Davis of the U.S. Military Academy at West Point.

The Justice football reputation in service resulted in his being the most sought-after college recruit in the nation after the war. Much was said about his going to Duke, but that was never a consideration because of advice Charlie received from George McAfee, the Chicago Bears professional star Justice met while in the Navy. Justice says that he and the ex-Duke back McAfee were similar runners, and that he was told by George McAfee, "Charlie, you are not Wallace Wade's kind of runner, and he will just beat you to death."

Justice says that he and his wife, Sarah, had actually decided on the University of South Carolina because they liked Coach Rex Enright, and a man from Florence was at their front door in Asheville to take them to Columbia. At that point Charlie's older brother Jack called Charlie and Sarah into the kitchen and persuaded them they should go to school in the state of North Carolina. Jack went to the front door to tell the Gamecock booster that there had been a change in Charlie's plans, while Charlie and Sarah went out the back door to join Tar Heel enthusiasts in uptown Asheville who took them to UNC. It was the cliff hanger that changed the course and history of athletic events in Chapel Hill.

Justice says that Wallace Wade remained embittered by his decision not to attend Duke, and that Wade never said a kind word after any of the four times Charlie played a major role in beating Duke. As important as the 1949 UNC—Notre Dame game was to the national scene, the importance of the Duke game the next week for UNC alumni was the reason Coach Carl Snavely told Justice he would be held out of the game in Yankee Stadium in New

continued

257

This 1949 picture of Charlie Justice on the sidelines in Yankee Stadium in New York has been published several times, but no one has bothered to explain what was going on. Charlie says he is praying, asking the Good Lord to let the Tar Heels hold their early 6 to 0 lead over Notre Dame. The injured Justice entered the game only once to hold the ball for an unsuccessful place kick, and in spite of the best efforts of the team and his prayers, the game ended Notre Dame 42, Carolina 6.

Charlie Justice (22), Art Weiner (50), and Kenny Powell (53) bubble with enthusiasm after another of their many victories. Justice's pass completion record was helped immeasurably by Weiner and Powell, two of the best pass receivers in the nation. All three players made All-America teams.

Sportswriters Bob Quincy (left) and Julian Scheer (center) show the first copy of *CHOO CHOO* to Justice, and everyone agreed their book was well done. The skilled writers recount Charlie Justice's achievements from high school to Navy, college, and professional football.

York. Charlie says the fact that Wade never voted for him for any of the All-America teams opened up some of the teams for Art Weiner, who Justice thinks should have been on every All-America. Generally, no All-America team included two players from the same college, but Kenny Powell also made All-America, giving that outstanding group two ends and a back on simultaneous All-America teams.

In 1948, a year when Justice was riding high at UNC, he was invited by Mr. Stranahan of Champion Spark Plug Company to the "Banquet of Champions" in Toledo, Ohio. Charlie says he felt out of place in the presence of so many legendary sports figures, and he was sipping a soft drink in the corner when all-time baseball great Stan Musial came in. Musial picked up a drink, then walked up to Justice and said, "Charlie, you probably don't remember me, I'm Stan Musial. I met you when you played on the Navy All-Star Football Team at Pearl Harbor." Justice was struck almost speechless. He considers it one of the greatest compliments of his life.

The stout heart of Charlie Justice came under severe stress in the winter of 1988 when Duke Hospital doctors found the need to replace three blocked bypass arteries that they had installed near Charlie's heart in 1978. The operation went fine, and in 10 days he was released to head home. Three days later, while the Justices were visiting in Greensboro, a staph infection was discovered in Charlie's bypass incision. Dr. D. Patrick Burney at Cone Hospital told Charlie later that during the first two weeks of his 25 days in intensive care his chances "were not worth 15 cents." His heart dropped to 20 beats per minute during the battle to stamp out the infection. Justice is confident he would have departed the earth had not hundreds of people been praying for his recovery, and he is sure Dr. Burney is a miracle man. Friends thought Charlie looked great (weighing 30 pounds less) when he finally made it home to Cherryville in April, ready to continue the good work that made him North Carolina's most admired athlete of all time. *HMM*

The football rivalry between North Carolina and Duke reached its peak during the Charlie Justice years when Wallace Wade (left) coached Duke and Carl Snavely (right) was head football coach at Carolina. The two legendary coaches met four times while Charlie Justice was in school, and all four games were victories for Snavely.

They played together in the College All-Star Game against the pros, Charlie Justice (right) and Eddie Lebaron, The Little General (left), and their friendship was further cemented when both were in the backfield of the Washington Redskins. Forty years later Justice and Lebaron still get together once or twice a year.

Don McCauley (left) was one of several standout backs to play at UNC, after the Justice years. Yet McCauley and all of the later stars combined have not been able to erase many of the Justice records. At the beginning of the 1988 football season, which is 40 years later, Charlie Justice still held 24 of the records in the UNC football yearbook.

Soon after being named UNC's head football coach, Mack Brown contacted Charlie Justice to express his admiration of Carolina's greatest football star. Brown told Justice he actively sought his advice and assistance in building a great football program.

Charlie Justice (right) and SMU's Heisman All-America Doak Walker (second from right) had become close friends. Carolina Coach Carl Snavely (left) gave Doak Walker access to the team meetings in Dallas where UNC was preparing for the Cotton Bowl engagement with Rice University on January 2, 1950. UNC end Kenny Powell is seated on the far side of Walker. Charlie's teammate Paul Rizzo, later a senior executive of IBM, scored Carolina's two touchdowns against Rice. UNC lost 27 to 13.

THE NEWS & OBSERVER
The Newspaper Colossus in Raleigh

There are numerous versions of the story but the advice contained within is always the same.

Governor J. Melville Broughton, speaking to his key administrators, "I don't want any of you to do anything you would be ashamed to read about in *The News & Observer* the next day . . . or that I would be ashamed to read there."

Governor R. Gregg Cherry, to each new appointee after taking the oath of office, "Do a good job and don't ever do anything you don't want to read the next morning in *The News & Observer.*"

These admonitions and warnings are music to the ears of the Daniels family, owners of Raleigh's morning newspaper. According to Sam Ragan, former managing editor, "This is about as high a compliment as a newspaper can receive."

Frank A. Daniels, Jr., president and publisher, does not mince words. "We have no sacred cows—absolutely none," he says, with a grin. "We are in the business of reporting the news and telling people what's going on."

Then he adds, "I subscribe to what my grandfather (Josephus), my father (Frank) and my uncle (Jonathan) have always said—if a newspaper does not have 40 percent of its readers unhappy with it, it is a shoddy newspaper. You hope, of course, that the 40 percent is a moving target." For your information, "shoddy" is a sanitized translation of the word Daniels actually used.

As a top appointee of three North Carolina governors, a former press assistant to a United States senator, and a resident of Raleigh for nearly 20 years, I can verify from personal experience the impact of the newspaper's coverage of politics and government.

As only one example, editor Jonathan Daniels supported the *Brown* decision of the U.S. Supreme Court requiring public school integration in North Carolina and the south. He vigorously opposed the proposed Pearsall Plan supported by Governor Luther H. Hodges, the Pearsall Committee, legislative and school leaders (and ultimately approved by the voters in a state-wide referendum). At the height of the public debate, Daniels ran a barrage of opposition comment which included an editorial each day for 30 consecutive days. It must have been a record—even for the feisty Daniels and the N&O.

Every newspaper worth its salt will agree with *The Chicago Tribune* credo that the press should "inform and lead public opinion and . . . furnish that check upon government which no constitution has ever been able to provide."

It is the job that a responsible newspaper needs to do, and *The News & Observer* takes these responsibilities quite seriously. For over a century it has covered North Carolina politics and government with a consuming intensity—reporting, analyzing, denouncing, supporting, exposing and, on its editorial pages, delivering judgments and commentaries on countless public issues and public officials. It is unwavering in its strong and partisan support for the Democratic party and its nominees.

In recent years, newspaper editorialists and political columnists have complained bitterly about politicians, elected or candidates, who make a practice of "bashing the press." James J. Kilpatrick, the nationally syndicated columnist, writes of "us inkstained wretches of the press" and the indignities they suffer at the hands of irresponsible politicians. "In North Carolina," according to Kilpatrick, "when reason and virtue failed, it was the immemorial custom to assail the Raleigh *News & Observer.*"

Before a tear is shed for the embattled Raleigh newspaper, let it be clearly understood that *The News & Observer* has been "bashing" North Carolina politicians, with impunity, since 1894. North Carolina governors, U.S. senators, congressmen, legislators, appointive and career government employees, city and county officials have all felt the unwelcome sting of the newspaper's editorial attention. Claude Sitton, the flinty, Pulitzer Prize winning editor, hews closely to the N&O editorial and political heritage.

In carrying out its responsibilities to its readers, there is no doubt that much of the "bashing," if it is fair to call it that, deserves to be written. Wrong doers need to be exposed and the electorate should be informed on decisions and actions—right or wrong—of their elected officials. But it should be remembered that those who are treated unfairly or unjustly, *continued*

Frank A. Daniels, Jr., president and publisher of *The News & Observer,* ponders briefly a question during an interview in his office. Such pauses are rare because Daniels, an engaging young man, is outspoken, direct in his speech, and intensely proud of his family and its successful newspaper heritage. He believes fervently in what he is doing to expand *The News & Observer* into a more powerful and profitable media giant in its vast market—Raleigh, the Research Triangle Park region and eastern North Carolina. In recent years the publishing company has acquired several other newspapers and a business magazine. Daniels is the grandson of Josephus Daniels, the founder, and son of Frank A. Daniels, former publisher.

Jonathan Daniels (right), editor of *The News & Observer*, and Governor Luther H. Hodges (left) engage in an animated conversation while John D. Larkins, Jr., state chairman of the Democratic party, listens with interest. The relationship between Daniels and Hodges was complex, reaching back to their student days at the University of North Carolina. Daniels was the son of a wealthy, prominent newspaper publisher. Hodges, the son of a textile worker and storekeeper, was working his way through college. When Hodges became governor, Daniels had returned to Raleigh to take the editorial helm of the family-owned newspaper. Soon the battle on public issues and Hodges' program was joined and continued for years.

whether a governor or a clerk of court, are dealing with a politically powerful daily newspaper operating from essentially a monopoly position in the state capital. As one canny old pol advised, "don't ever get in a cussing contest with someone who buys ink by the barrel."

To understand the editorial and political heritage of the newspaper, it is necessary to consider the founder, Josephus Daniels, who bought control of the enterprise at age 23. At the paper's 100th anniversary in 1965, Vermont Royster, a native Tar Heel, editor of *The Wall Street Journal* and a Pulitzer Prize winner, made these comments about the legendary editor and publisher:

"It's . . . true that some of Josephus' opinions, if read today, would not wear time well. But this is only to say that he was a child of his era, which was the era of Reconstruction when it must have seemed that the Democratic party was the only hope of salvation for the tortured South. It was also an era in which most newspapers were party newspapers, Democratic or Republican, and every editor nailed his dogmas to the masthead and defied the enemy to come tear them down . . .

". . . if Josephus was able to play an influential role at all, it was in part because of his view of what a newspaper is. That view, first of all, led him quite early to the notion that the state capital ought to have a newspaper that would print what went on there whether anybody liked it or not.

Josephus Daniels, founder of *The News & Observer,* and editor and publisher from 1894 to 1948, chats with Dr. Frank Graham, UNC president. A university trustee for 47 years, Daniels had an active interest in university affairs and higher education. Both men, Daniels and Graham, also played important roles in national and international affairs. Daniels served as Secretary of the Navy under President Woodrow Wilson from 1913 until 1921, with Franklin D. Roosevelt as his assistant. In 1933 President Roosevelt appointed him Ambassador to Mexico where he served until 1941. After serving 19 years as UNC president, Dr. Graham served in the United States Senate, as United States Representative on the United Nations Committee of Good Offices in the Dutch-Indonesian Dispute, and as the United Nations Representative for India and Pakistan.

"I suspect this notion, as much as anything else, got the people in Raleigh in the habit of reading the once bankrupt *News & Observer* in preference to the other newspapers. It wouldn't be the first time, nor the last, that this simple journalistic principle turned out to be a good business decision as well.

"I wouldn't be surprised either if this journalistic habit of *The News & Observer* hasn't played some part in the fact that North Carolina, almost alone among the southern states, has never had a shameful and long-continued scandal in its state government.

". . . You have to print the news, but you also have to raise hell. Curiously enough, it doesn't matter too much what you raise hell about, although it's nicer perhaps if you could always be on the side of the angels. The main worth of journalistic hell-raising is that it stirs people up to think for themselves. *The News & Observer* also served if it did nothing more than get people mad at *The News & Observer.*"

Thanks, Vermont Royster, for your observations. If the true goal of a great newspaper is to raise hell and make people mad, *The News & Observer* is in a class by itself—at least in North Carolina. *ELR*

A bronze statue of Josephus Daniels, the work of Janos Farkas and made possible by the Josephus Daniels Charitable Foundation, is dedicated and given to the City of Raleigh in Nash Square, across from *The News & Observer* building. Frank A. Daniels (left) and Frank A. Daniels, Jr., participated in the ceremony on September 24, 1985. That evening the newspaper hosted a gala dinner for hundreds of North Carolinians who had been Tar Heels of the Week, a Sunday feature which had cited over 1,850 North Carolinians for their contributions to their community, state and nation. Hugh Morton and Ed Rankin were among those cited and attending.

A GRANDSON REMEMBERS JOSEPHUS DANIELS

Frank A. Daniels, Jr., was 16 years old when his grandfather, Josephus Daniels, died. While he knew him only in the old gentleman's last years, Daniels has many fond memories of that relationship. They include:

—You should always be proud of earning money with your hands. That's much the better way to earn money. He would match any money young Frank made working with his hands.

—During World War II he had a huge Victory garden and expected his grandson to work it. During harvest time there was plenty of early morning work to pick butterbeans, corn, tomatoes and field peas. The pay was $1 per hour—doubled, of course, because the boy was working with his hands.

—Grandfather never learned to type. No problem. He wrote everything long hand on a tablet with a pencil. Not every compositor in the shop could read his scrawl.

—In later years he was not really interested in day-to-day management of the paper. Frank A. Daniels, the son responsible for the business management, often had a tough time getting his father's attention, and approval, of needed expenditures. Josephus didn't see any sense in buying new presses. So the paper has always gotten by with used equipment.

—The fuel rationing in World War II required Josephus Daniels to ride city buses to work. But he was such a well-known figure in Raleigh that he was often offered a ride when he got to the bus stop. It was not unusual for a city garbage truck to transport the editor/publisher/ex-Cabinet member/ex-Ambassador downtown to his job.

A Bathtub Interview. While Governor R. Gregg Cherry was a student at Trinity College (now Duke University), he set out to attend the national political conventions of both parties. He managed to gain admission to the Republican convention in Chicago, but had no success with the Democrats in Baltimore. While reading a local newspaper, he noted that Josephus Daniels was attending the convention. He didn't know the famous publisher but he hurried to the hotel, found his room and knocked loudly on the door. A voice told him to enter and he went in to find Daniels seated in a bathtub. Cherry quickly explained his problem while the publisher listened calmly. When Daniels understood the young man was from North Carolina, he said he would arrange for admission to all the activities of the Democratic convention . . . and then completed his bath.

A Personal Footnote. In 1941 I worked briefly as a reporter on *The News & Observer.* Josephus Daniels had just returned to Raleigh from his years as U.S. Ambassador in Mexico City, and resumed his work as editor and publisher of the paper. In the fall, with war clouds gathering and Selective Service around the corner, I applied for an officer's commission in the U.S. Navy. This required three letters of recommendation and somehow the former Secretary of the Navy heard about my application. As a fledgling reporter, it would not have occurred to me to approach the publisher. Not only did he write a generous letter of recommendation to the Commandant, Sixth Naval District, he sent me a copy which I still have. It said, in part, "He is a conscientious young man, capable and willing, and I am sure he will do a good job. I am pleased to recommend him and hope that his application will be favorably acted upon."*ELR*

Frank A. Daniels, Jr., glances over an issue of the newspaper, flanked by Hunter George (left), managing editor, and Claude Sitton, veteran editor and Pulitzer prize winner. Sitton came to *The News & Observer* after many years as a reporter with the *New York Times*.

Sam Ragan, managing editor of *The News & Observer* for many years, sits behind his cluttered desk at *The Pilot of Southern Pines*, where he is editor and publisher. A noted poet as well as editor, Ragan's experience spans many of the same decades of this book's authors. Ragan recalls setting up a network of local news correspondents in over 50 counties in eastern North Carolina, including recruiting Tom Wicker, the columnist, who was then working for the *Lumberton Robersonian*. "Not much happened east of Raleigh that we didn't have covered," Ragan says.

As a student photographer, Hugh Morton made this photo of Josephus Daniels, editor, publisher, former Secretary of the Navy, former Ambassador to Mexico and university trustee, speaking over NBC Radio at Memorial Hall, Chapel Hill. Daniels was introducing the man (at left) who is unidentified. Dr. Frank P. Graham, UNC president, is at right.

JAMES B. HUNT
An Acclaimed Governor With 'Missionary Zeal'

James B. Hunt, Jr. has served longer (eight years/1977-85) as Governor of North Carolina than any chief executive to date in the 20th century. He was the first governor elected to two full terms of four years. Counting his four years as lieutenant governor, his service in the state's two top jobs of 12 consecutive years is another record, as well as a tribute to his popularity with voters.

And, for the record, his campaign for the U.S. Senate in 1984 against Jesse Helms makes them co-holders for the most expensive senate campaign to date in U.S. history.

To understand the character, vitality and political ambitions of Jim Hunt, it helps to talk with Bert Bennett, the political godfather to Hunt as well as Terry Sanford. There is no doubt about Terry Sanford's love of elective politics, Bennett says, but "I would say that if there was ever anyone I have met in politics that loved it most it would be Hunt. It's his life."

Hunt's approach to politics has a missionary zeal and "I don't think there is any question he feels he was tapped to at least try to serve," Bennett says. "That's his calling." While no one knows what the future may hold for the former governor, Hunt is a relatively young man and he is looking at the option of running again for the U.S. Senate.

"I think his law business is good, he is enjoying it and probably for the first time he is out of debt," Bennett adds. Whatever choice he makes, the Hunt family will support him completely, as it always has.

While Bennett's candid views are those of an admitted partial observer, William D. Snider, the respected retired editor of the *Greensboro Daily News,* had somewhat similar praise for Hunt when he wrote, "As one who has seen Tar Heel governors in action for over three decades, I must confess that Governor Jim Hunt beats them all for sheer drive and enthusiasm."

Jim Hunt believes that there may be an implication in the term "quality education" as advanced by his friend Terry Sanford which suggests that education is good for education's sake, and Hunt agrees that it is. On the other hand, Hunt believes that his own administration carried education a step further, to emphasize education not for education's sake, but for economic growth.

To amplify this, Hunt says, "There has been sort of a rationale to all I have tried to do, which is that the best jobs generally go to the brightest and best educated people. Then those brightest and best educated people in turn can invent new products and services, make them in a more productive and cost-efficient way, and sell them successfully. Therefore, the economy will grow, and there will be jobs and opportunities. Education and economic growth are inexorably intertwined."

As he was growing up, North Carolina prided itself on being the most progressive state in the south, Jim Hunt says, and that was about as far as it went. By the time he was leaving the governor's office, North Carolina had come into full flower, Hunt adds, and because of the efforts of a lot of people it had literally become one of the leading states in the United States economically.

In early summer of 1977, I was invited by Governor Hunt to have a private lunch with him in Asheville. During the meal the governor outlined the very logical reasons why North Carolina voters should have the right to re-elect their governors and lieutenant governors for a second term. He then expressed the thought that I was the right person to head a statewide committee of business people to campaign for the State Constitution Succession Amendment that the General Assembly had placed on the November ballot.

Knowing how important succession was to him, it was a high compliment, and I agreed to serve. An excellent statewide committee was organized, with both Republicans and Democrats. The key Republican staff member was Phil Kirk, a former legislator and newspaperman. Tom Lambeth, former top aide to Governor Terry Sanford and Congressman Richardson Preyer, was the key staff Democrat. Former Governors Sanford and Jim Holshouser were on the committee.

Around the state there were rumblings in the Republican party that succession was a plot to perpetuate Democratic rule forever, and had it not been for the good work of Governor Holshouser and Phil Kirk, a serious partisan controversy could have developed. Of course, Republican Governor Jim Martin can run for re-election in 1988 because of the 1977 succession amendment.

Looking back 10 years later, how does Governor Hunt feel about succession? He has this to say:

"Succession is absolutely vital. We have not worked the bugs out yet. Historically it is too soon to judge it, but it is not too soon for me to say definitely from my perspective that the North Carolina School of Science and Mathematics, which at least a third of the states are emulating today, would never have happened if I had not had a second term.

"The Microelectronics Center that started a whole new wave of economic development and new industries would not have come about if there had not been a second term.

"The whole State Basic Education Plan that we are in the process of implementing now could not have had the kind of depth and thoroughness that is going to make it successful if we had not had that much time to work on it. North Carolina has been a good state in any event, but the opportunity to have a governor serve two terms is critical to reach the heights we want to reach in this state."

HMM

Jim Hunt was running for lieutenant governor in 1972 when he brought his daughters Rachel (left) and Elizabeth to Grandfather Mountain to meet Hobo, a bear cub. Hobo had just returned from making appearances around the state in behalf of a successful bond issue for the State Zoo in Asheboro.

Some who did not know them marveled that this 1982 scene took place, but Jim Hunt and Jesse Helms are patriotic citizens of North Carolina and the United States who knew that without their cooperation at state and federal levels, Cape Hatteras Lighthouse would be gone. The Committee they co-chaired raised $500,000 in private funds to save the Lighthouse.

Governor Jim Hunt was supportive of annual events and celebrations in all parts of the state. In Wilmington in 1977 he crowns North Carolina Azalea Queen Francesca James, ABC-TV actress in "All My Children."

On November 17, 1982 Governor Jim Hunt speaks at the keel-laying for *Elizabeth II*, a re-creation of similar design to Sir Walter Raleigh's 16th century sailing ships. A large wood carving of Sir Walter faces the Manteo waterfront in the background. Behind Governor Hunt (left to right) are Captain Horace Whitfield of the *Elizabeth II*, 400th Anniversary Director John Neville, and State Cultural Resources Secretary Sara Hodgkins.

Former Governor Jim Hunt is a member of the Raleigh law firm of Poyner and Spruill, which gives him opportunity to discuss legal matters with the firm's senior member, James M. Poyner. Hunt is under pressure to run again for public office, but Poyner says Hunt "is a brilliant lawyer and should continue the practice of law."

Governor Jim Hunt called on Charlotte television performer Arthur Smith to head a statewide campaign to marshall support for a three cents per gallon increase in the state gasoline tax to help maintain highways badly in need of repair. Smith was effective in reaching working people who polls previously had shown not to be in favor of the increase.

As chairman of the "Salute To Terry Sanford" in February 1988, Jim Hunt has to yell to be heard in announcing that the event in the Sir Walter Hotel in Raleigh had raised $550,000 to retire Sanford's 1986 U.S. Senate campaign debt. Behind Hunt (left to right) are U.S. Senator George Mitchell, Governor of New York Mario Cuomo, U.S. Senator Wyche Fowler, and U.S. Senator Daniel Inouye.

When President Jimmy Carter ran for re-election in 1980, Governor Jim Hunt hosted a fund-raiser for the president at Tanglewood Park in Winston-Salem.

When Jim and Carolyn Hunt suited up to suit the weather on Sugar Mountain, few of their fellow skiers recognized them as the Governor and First Lady of North Carolina.

April 1, 1982

August 14, 1983

ANDY GRIFFITH
What It *Truly* Was, Was . . .

How did Andy Griffith get his big break in show business?

Well, what it was, was . . . a lucky combination of things—an engaging young talent, a need for some low-budget entertainment and an enterprising record producer looking for a hit.

Here's the story, as related by Hugh Morton and Orville Campbell:

In 1950, Morton helped found the Southern Short Course in Press Photography and in planning the first meeting in Chapel Hill he asked Russ Grumman, UNC extension director, to suggest some inexpensive entertainment for the dinner meeting. Grumman recommended a young UNC graduate student and PlayMaker who would do some recitations for $25 and he was booked.

Orville Campbell, long-time friend and Chapel Hill newspaper publisher, had printed the Short Course program and Morton invited Campbell to the dinner. Campbell was also a lyric writer, had produced, with Hank Beebe, the successful record, "All the Way, Choo Choo," and was trying to break into the record business in a big way.

When the young graduate student/PlayMaker appeared, he recited "Romeo and Juliet" and "What It Was, Was Football." To quote Morton, "he tore the place up . . . really tore the place up!" Neither Morton nor Campbell had ever heard of Andy Griffith and were overwhelmed with his performance.

Campbell rushed up to Griffith after the program, introduced himself and said, "we've got to make a record of this!" Griffith grinned and replied, "Well, Mr. Campbell, if you've got the money, I've got the time." Campbell admits now he has no idea why he acted so impulsively then—but he is glad he did.

The comedy monologue was recorded at six live performances before Campbell was satisfied that he had captured its rustic humor at its very best. The version selected was actually recorded in Greensboro where Andy Griffith performed before a large and lively audience of insurance sales people and brought down the house with laughter.

The rest is entertainment—and North Carolina—history. The Mt. Airy native and UNC PlayMaker went on to popular and critical acclaim as an actor on Broadway, in the movies and television. He established an enduring place in television and cultural history with "The Andy Griffith Show." More than 25 years since the show was first aired on CBS, reruns of the 249 episodes, featuring the sleepy life in a fictitious North Carolina town, were being shown in over 100 TV markets, not including cable coverage. *ELR*

Andy Griffith, probably the most readily identifiable North Carolinian in the nation, has given his name, time and support for many major public service campaigns in his home state. A home owner in Dare County for 40 years, Griffith helped promote the state and nation-wide campaign to save the historic Cape Hatteras lighthouse. The two photos show graphically how efforts to save the great landmark are building up the shoreline. Hugh Morton, who made this picture, is also chairman of the campaign.

Standing on the turf of Kenan Stadium in Chapel Hill, Andy Griffith delivers "What It Was, Was Football," the comedy-monologue which became a hit record and propelled him to national attention and a starring role on Broadway.

WIWWF was the first talking record to make a hit in 15 years, according to Orville Campbell, the enterprising producer who took a chance on Andy Griffith and his monologue. After orders began to overwhelm Campbell's small company, Campbell and Griffith, who split the profits 50-50, chose Capitol Records to market and sell their hit record.

The lanky, tousel-headed Sir Walter Raleigh is Andy Griffith, a former drama major and PlayMaker at UNC-Chapel Hill. Paul Green's great outdoor drama, *The Lost Colony*, was just beginning its long run to success when Griffith won the audition for the role. He moved to Manteo and played Sir Walter for the next six years. The drama was, and is, valuable experience and summer employment for aspiring actors and actresses. While in Manteo, Griffith created his side-splitting "Romeo and Juliet" monologue which later became a part of the WIWWF record.

The young Tar Heel actor starred with Delores Grey in *Destry Rides Again*, a Broadway success. Griffith was a new talent to Broadway and had his problems with the established star. He became a stage celebrity when Mac Hyman, author of *No Time for Sergeants*, heard his record, "What It Was, Was Football," and picked him for the lead in the Broadway production. Griffith also starred in Paddy Chayefsky's *A Face in the Crowd*.

Andy Griffith admires a Rock City birdhouse from the famous Tennessee attraction which hangs in the backyard of his home in Manteo. During a 40-year career which led to fame and fortune in the entertainment business, Griffith has managed, somehow, to keep (at least figuratively) one foot in North Carolina. He has called Manteo home since graduating from UNC-Chapel Hill in 1947, commuting cross-country in later years from California when his busy career permits the time.

Richard Linke (left) chats with Governor Luther H. Hodges, Orville Campbell and Andy Griffith at a meeting of the Honorary Tar Heels in New York City. Linke, a shrewd, fast-talking New Yorker, first met Griffith when Campbell and Griffith signed a contract with Capitol Records to sell "What It Was, Was Football." Then a top sales executive with Capitol, Linke was so impressed with the talented young Tar Heel that he became his business manager. Linke and Griffith continue this relationship to date. Linke is also a successful Hollywood television and film producer.

THOMAS J. PEARSALL
Courage in Midst of Tumult

It was a balmy spring day—May 17, 1954—when the United States Supreme Court handed down its landmark decision requiring North Carolina, and other southern states, to integrate their public schools. For over 50 years North Carolina had provided its children with a dual system of "separate but equal" school facilities based on race.

State government and public school leaders were stunned by the decree. Governor William B. Umstead, in a carefully worded statement, said the decision ". . . presents complications and statutory problems and difficulties of immeasurable extent" but stated that North Carolina would obey the decision. Unlike some other southern governors, he did not defy the federal government and, in fact, set a tone of reason in a time of political tension and public uncertainty about the future of public education.

In a matter of a few weeks, Umstead chose Thomas J. Pearsall of Rocky Mount to head the Governor's Special Advisory Committee on Education. The state-wide group was asked to study the court decision, the existing dual school system and to make recommendations to the governor on how North Carolina should proceed.

A former speaker of the House of Representatives, Pearsall was a well-known and respected lawyer, businessman, farmer and Democratic party leader. The 19-member committee, which had three black members, was appointed and began its work. Meanwhile, public debate on the school integration question grew heated and, often, inflammatory.

Within less than four months, Governor Umstead died suddenly. Luther H. Hodges, the lieutenant governor, became governor and met with Pearsall, whom he did not know well, to inquire about the committee's work. The 1955 General Assembly would convene in less than two months. Hodges quickly grasped the value of Pearsall's leadership and asked him to continue as committee chairman. Then the governor began an intensive discussion, involving Pearsall and many other state leaders, on how to prepare for the legislature.

As might be expected, the legislators were deeply concerned, divided and confused about what North Carolina could or should do with the obvious crisis in public education. Hodges and the Pearsall group realized clearly they faced an explosive political situation, not only in the General Assembly but in the state-wide political arena where others sought to take personal advantage of the school integration controversy.

The 1955 General Assembly authorized a new committee of seven members and Governor Hodges appointed Tom Pearsall as chairman and the following members: William T. Joyner of Raleigh, R.O. Huffman of Morganton, State Senator Lunsford Crew of Roanoke Rapids, State Senator William Medford of Waynesville, State Representative Edward F. Yarborough of Louisburg and State Representative H. Cloyd Philpott of Lexington (who was elected lieutenant governor in 1960). It was known as the Governor's Advisory Committee on Education.

To understand the complex and sensitive nature of the problem, as viewed from inside the Hodges/Pearsall group, consider this exposition by Paul A. Johnston, the governor's legal assistant who was intimately involved in dealing with the Pearsall committee, the Attorney General's office and with the legislative leaders:

"We found ourselves in a position with segregated schools, with a populace that was, at least for the most part, determined to keep them segregated and with a decision that was going to be binding on all of us that insisted that they not be kept segregated. That was our present position and we knew that any lawyer or right-thinking layman with decent legal advice and honest legal advice, as the Pearsall committee members were given, must conclude that eventually, not when or how, but eventually, there were going to be some Negro children in schools now exclusively for whites.

"That had to come about because of the force of national public opinion and the effectiveness of the decree. How, given those two things of where we were and where we knew we had to come out, the question that remained for us was how to get from where we were to where we had to come out, and not disgrace ourselves. And, of course, a very important fact . . . in order to do any of this . . . (is) leadership. To get from present status to future conclusions, you had to maintain control.

"(The strategy) had to be one of keeping a road open to the eventual conclusion down which public opinion and the force of the decree could force you, but resisting at every point as far as you could legally."

To maintain leadership and control, Hodges and the Pearsall committee had to provide answers to many crucial questions. How to maintain public and legislative support for public schools? How to comply with the court decision to merge dual, long-established, segregated school systems? How to prevent threats of violence and disorder from disrupting the public schools, with one million

continued

Thomas J. Pearsall of Rocky Mount, the father of the "Pearsall Plan," whose calm leadership helped North Carolina and its leaders find a peaceful way to integrate the state's dual system of public schools based on race. A respected lawyer, businessman, farmer and Democratic party leader, Pearsall had served as speaker of the House of Representatives in the General Assembly of 1947.

The opposition to any public school integration included the KKK. The message on this billboard, located on I-95 in Johnston County, reads: YOU ARE IN THE HEART OF KLAN COUNTRY, JOIN THE UNITED KLANS OF AMERICA, INC. This caused grave concern for Governor Luther H. Hodges and law enforcement officials who were responsible for maintaining the public peace.

children enrolled, and the communities involved? How to offset or, at least, dilute the political appeal of opposition leaders who stirred unfounded racial fears and unrest among voters?

With the strong support of Hodges and legislative leaders, the Pearsall committee devised a plan which was adopted by the General Assembly during an historic one-week special session, and included a referendum for an amendment to the state constitution which later received overwhelming support of the voters and carried in all 100 counties.

In brief, the constitutional amendment authorized the General Assembly to establish by statute a means by which local school units could, by popular vote, suspend the operation of their schools, and, under certain circumstances, provide limited public funds for the private education of children.

The final result: the provisions of the Pearsall Plan were never used by any school unit, and North Carolina public schools were gradually integrated without the violence or disruption that closed some public schools in other states. In 1984 historian H.G. Jones wrote, "By the time the (Pearsall) plan was declared unconstitutional in 1966, it had served its purpose as 'a safety valve.' "

As private secretary to Governors Umstead and Hodges, my experience with them and Pearsall clearly showed their commitment to saving the public schools from irreparable harm under existing conditions, while allowing public and legislative support for an integrated school system to develop and solidify. To achieve this goal required time and no one then could predict precisely how

it would evolve (except for a few editorial writers who, of course, can solve complex educational/political/social problems with strokes of their typewriter keys).

Hodges, Pearsall and the committee took a tremendous battering of criticism from those who wanted immediate integration, from those who wanted to resist integration forever and by any means possible, and from those who seemed to say, "let it alone and it will all go away." *The News & Observer,* Raleigh, led by its editor Jonathan Daniels, was a harsh and unrelenting newspaper critic.

As I look back over more than 30 years, I am grateful to these men for their calm courage in leading North Carolina through one of the most tumultuous periods in the state's history. And I marvel that I found no bitterness in any of their later comments about the cascade of criticisms they experienced. I found nothing but their respect for those persons who held different opinions, and a deep gratitude that somehow North Carolina and its people had survived the crisis, saved the public schools and moved forward in compliance with the Supreme Court decree.

Tom Pearsall, in a 1960 interview, said "if anybody is ever going to record the history of this effort in North Carolina . . . the golden thread that ought to run all the way through it is the fact that we have had in this state leadership that was realistic and was determined to preserve the public schools in this state, and would not use the situation to their political advantage or selfish personal advantage."*ELR*

Photo by Charles H. Cooper

HISTORIC GATHERING OF NORTH CAROLINA JUDICIARY
This may be the largest number of judges ever to assemble in the history of North Carolina. They gathered in the Hall of the House at the State Capitol, July 1, 1955, for the swearing in of 15 newly appointed judges of the Superior Court. Seated (left to right) are justices of the Supreme Court: William H. Bobbitt, Jeff D. Johnson, Jr., William A. Devin, Chief Justice Maurice Victor Barnhill, Emery B. Denny, R. Hunt Parker and Carlisle Higgins. Governor Luther H. Hodges stands with his hands on the shoulders of the Chief Justice. Superior Court judges (all standing) are: William Y. Bickett, Walter J. Bone, William J. Bundy, W. H. S. Burgwyn, Hugh B. Campbell, Leo Carr, Francis O. Clarkson, Walter E. Crissman, George M. Fountain, J. Paul Frizzell, P. C. Froneberger, Allen H. Gwyn, Clarence W. Hall, Hamilton H. Hobgood, J. Frank Huskins, Walter E. Johnson, Jr., W. A. Leland McKeithan, Raymond Mallard, Clifton L. Moore, Dan K. Moore, Chester R. Morris, Zeb V. Nettles, Q. K. Nimocks, Jr., Hubert E. Olive, Joseph W. Parker, George B. Patton, Malcolm C. Paul, F. Donald Phillips, J. Will Pless, Jr., L. Richardson Preyer, J. A. Rousseau, Malcolm B. Seawell, Susie Sharp, R. Hoyle Sink, Henry L. Stevens, and Clawson L. Williams. *ELR*

VERMONT CONNECTICUT ROYSTER AT WORK
The editor emeritus of *The Wall Street Journal,* winner of two Pulitzer Prize awards and retired professor of journalism and public affairs at the UNC school of journalism is shown writing at his home in Chapel Hill. A native of Raleigh, his unusual Christian names came from a family tradition of naming the children for U.S. states. He is widely regarded as one of America's most articulate and seasoned writers and commentators on economic, financial and political matters. As a writer or editor, Royster has known and written about every U.S. president from Franklin Roosevelt to Reagan. *North Carolina* magazine described Royster's writing as epitomizing English poet and critic Matthew Arnold's observation that "journalism is literature in a hurry" and used the following passage as typical of Royster's provocative prose: "Nothing is so corrupting to a man as to believe it is his duty to save mankind from man. He comes to evil because he must first usurp the rights of men and finally the prerogatives of God." *ELR*

JESSE HELMS
Senior U.S. Senator, Home-Grown Conservative

Jesse Helms, North Carolina's senior United States Senator, sits in front of a massive display of framed cartoons in his Washington office. It is doubtful that any North Carolina elected official has received so much national, or international, editorial attention, with much of it being critical. The senator, a small town boy who became an influential figure in the nation's capital and in international affairs, does not take himself as seriously as others seem to see him. Possessing a keen wit, Helms obviously enjoys the best efforts of editorial cartoonists to satirize him and his conservative positions.

Senator Helms presents President Ronald Reagan with the first Keeper of the Light certificate, a document used to attract support and funds for the preservation and restoration of the famous and endangered Cape Hatteras Lighthouse. The President also received a Cape Hatteras Lighthouse lamp, another product sold for the same purpose. The presentation by such a powerful political ally of the chief executive, and a North Carolinian, opened doors at the U.S. Department of Interior which had been closed to efforts to save the Lighthouse up to that point. The move by Helms recalls the action by Governor Terry Sanford in making President John Kennedy the first Admiral in the North Carolina Navy, which opened doors at the Defense Department and helped make possible the eventual acquisition of the battleship, U.S.S. *North Carolina.*

In 1941 three young newspaper reporters (*see photo*) met in Raleigh, became friends and roommates and briefly enjoyed life in the state capital before World War II arrived and swiftly ended their civilian employment.

Following the war, two—Jesse Helms and I—returned to Raleigh and resumed civilian lives. Jesse was married to Dorothy Coble of Raleigh, a former classmate of mine in journalism school at UNC-Chapel Hill. Dave Howard settled in Jacksonville, Fla., where he became a successful business journalist and magazine publisher.

During the following years Jesse and I remained friends and our paths crossed from time to time while he worked at *The Raleigh Times,* at WRAL Radio and as executive director of the North

Carolina Bankers Association where his editorials and columns in the association magazine displayed again his skill as a writer and advocate for his employers.

As a life-long Democrat and close associate of three Democratic governors, I saw little of Jesse during the heated Smith-Graham senatorial campaign or his service to U.S. Senator Willis Smith, the Democratic winner. Then came the decision by A.J. Fletcher, owner of WRAL-TV, Raleigh's first TV station, to pioneer in on-the-air editorials on a daily basis.

Jesse Helms, who had won the respect and admiration of Fletcher while employed at WRAL Radio, was chosen to be the writer and voice of WRAL-TV editorials. Fletcher, an attorney, businessman and an active patron of music, drama and the arts, was a strong conservative in political affairs and wanted his station to be an outspoken advocate for his views.

During the next 12 years Jesse worked daily with his employer, who became his close friend and mentor, and produced and aired more than 2,700 editorials. With the title, "Viewpoints," they covered a wide spectrum of conservative and political concerns, were also broadcast on about 70 local radio stations across the state, and were reprinted in 200 newspapers.

Always gifted with words and language, Jesse developed into a television commentator whose forceful comments and slashing attacks on "liberals" and other foes beyond number captured a large and loyal audience of believers and supporters. It is well to remember that there were plenty of targets for an outspoken conservative during those years. But it should also be noted that "Viewpoints" upset, dismayed or enraged thousands of other viewers (especially those attacked) who did not agree with the editorials.

Viewers were experiencing something new on the North Carolina scene, a skilled polemist using the powerful medium of television on a daily basis like it had never been used before in the state. The impact on state politics was significant. And, to coin a phrase, the results are history.

Jesse Alexander Helms, Jr., small town boy, tuba player, sports/news reporter, Navy recruiter, U.S. senator's aide, trade association executive, city councilman, TV executive and commentator, is now serving his third term in the United States Senate. Known nationally and internationally for his outspoken conservative views, Senator Helms remains true to the same basic principles and positions he espoused so vigorously on television.

As the senator has received more and more media attention, I am asked at times about my recollections of the early Jesse Helms. That's easy to answer. Jesse was a tall, skinny fellow who, like

continued

Committees are the most powerful engines of the U.S. Senate organization. Senator Helms, a senior Republican, attends a meeting of the Senate Foreign Relations Committee which was considering confirmation of the new U.S. Ambassador to the Soviet Union, Jack F. Matlock, Jr., a North Carolinian. Helms is flanked by Senator Joseph Biden (left) of Delaware and Senator Richard Lugar of Indiana. Matlock's confirmation was approved at this committee session.

most of us, was happy to have a job, worked very hard, enjoyed life, didn't worry much about having so little money, and lived from pay day to pay day. We were children during the Great Depression of the 1930s but were old enough to remember hard times. Sharing a bathroom at the apartment with six young men was no big deal.

No, we didn't talk much about politics or, for that matter, even about the war going on in Europe. It was a happy time for us in Raleigh and we enjoyed the thrill of seeing our news copy in print. But I do remember that Jesse Helms loved sports and Dot Coble—and that was certainly understandable.

As for Jesse's long and often controversial political career, I am not an authority. His actions and statements often cause grave distress and sharply written and spoken criticism from many North Carolina editorial writers . . . not to mention his political opponents. The publisher of Jesse's home-town newspaper describes him as "the Darth Vader of North Carolina politics." The chairman of the national Democratic party assails him as "the Prince of Darkness."

Then why has Jesse Helms never lost an election? I think it relates to the basic nature of the man. What you see—a decent, honest, hardworking public official, warts and all—is what you get. No matter that he is capable of playing the hardest of hard ball in political campaigns . . . and can raise millions of dollars with his conservative political appeals from in and out of state.

In a time when so many elected officials, especially in the Congress, are perceived as posturing, waffling on issues and testing the political winds constantly with opinion polls, Jesse Helms stands out like a lonesome pine.

He is a small town boy who basically knows where he came from, who helped him along the way, what he believes to be true and who he is. For Jesse, that's enough—for now and the future. *ELR*

Three young newsmen, roommates in a nearby apartment building, stroll down Fayetteville Street in Raleigh in the summer of 1941. Shown (left to right) are Jesse Helms of *The Raleigh Times,* Ed Rankin of *The News & Observer* and Dave Howard of United Press. The photo was made by an enterprising photographer who snapped and sold candid pictures to people on the street.

Junior United States Senator Terry Sanford (left) engages in banter with senior United States Senator Jesse Helms in the hallway outside Helms' office. Despite partisan political and philosophical differences, they both represent North Carolina and maintain an affable relationship. As William D. Snider observed so well in his book, *Helms and Hunt the North Carolina Senate Race*, in North Carolina politics "humor is never far beneath the surface. Informality prevails. Nobody wants to appear too biggety, and there can be aggressiveness even in declarations of modesty."

A FEW Q/A WITH JESSE HELMS

In a brief interview, Senator Jesse Helms answered the following questions:

What person (or persons) had the greatest influence on your life from the standpoint of devoting your career to public service? Briefly, how did this happen?

There are so many, making it difficult to choose, or even narrow the list. Let me try:
R.W. House, my high school principal (Monroe), who encouraged me and counseled me that anybody who tries hard enough, works hard enough, can achieve almost anything provided it's done honestly and consistent with principles consistent with the meaning of America.

Senators Willis Smith and Dick Russell, both of whom told me I "ought to be a senator some day." The truth is, I didn't even *want* to be a senator.

Chief Justice R. Hunt Parker (North Carolina Supreme Court), who spent an inordinate amount of time with me, often inviting me to his office to talk about constitutional principles and the importance of law and justice.

Senator Sam Ervin, who chided me about being a Republican, but who constantly advised me in matters of constitutional principles. (I never moved a peg on any matter involving the constitution without calling and asking his advice.) Moreover, in my 1984 race against Governor Hunt he made a generous statement about me which was enormously helpful. In an interview with a Richmond paper, he said this: "I admire Senator Helms very much. He's one of the few men in public life who's got the courage to stand up for what he honestly believes. Courage is the rarest trait among public men I know of. Many of them are intelligent, but there are very few of them courageous."

Carroll Weathers, who was my across-the street neighbor in Raleigh before he moved to Winston-Salem as dean of the Wake Forest School of Law. Dozens of times, he urged me to run for public office (which I didn't want to do). And when I finally ran in 1972, he was the first to announce his support.

A.J. Fletcher, who was a sort of second father to me. He was owner of WRAL-TV, and WRAL Radio, Raleigh, and gave me the opportunity to write and produce "Viewpoints."

continued

Following a meeting with President Reagan, Senator Helms and Senator Robert Dole of Kansas pause at the White House to chat with associates. Dole is the minority or majority leader of the Senate, depending whether Republicans control the Senate. A presidential contender in early 1988, Dole is married to the former Elizabeth Hanford of Salisbury, who has served as Secretary of Transportation in the Reagan cabinet.

Who do you consider the greatest leaders—public and private—of North Carolina during your lifetime? Briefly, what was, or is their most outstanding contribution?

Again, there are so many.

Senator Josiah W. Bailey because he had the courage to stand up to the prevailing winds. E.g., he opposed FDR on the court-packing scheme. Oddly enough, I never met Senator Bailey.

Archie K. Davis, who has been an effective advocate of the free enterprise system. Good friend, adviser, supporter, I wish Archie could have been governor and/or senator.

Governor Hodges, who believed in innovation. He and Archie Davis are, as you know, fathers of the Research Triangle Park.

Dr. Lenox D. Baker, who taught me the value of self-discipline. The monument to this great man is his compassion for crippled children, and his willingness to sacrifice. His is a largely untold story.

Wallace Wade, also an untold story. Look at the teams he took to the Rose Bowl, including two from Duke. He gave me enormous encouragement for years. He had a superb knowledge of government, yet he was entirely unpretentious.

What would you like to be remembered for when your service in the United States Senate has ended?

I don't know that I'll deserve to be remembered for anything. I've tried to stick with the principles in which I believe, and I have never sought the "popular" course. I have the luxury of not caring whether I stay in the Senate if I have to compromise my principles to do it.

I wish I deserved the kind assessment by Sam Ervin, but I shall always be grateful that he said it.

As a Republican leader, how would you describe your party and its role in governing our state? What do you see in its future in North Carolina?

The future of the Republican North Carolina is yet to be determined. I've tried to convince my fellow Republicans that the GOP will never be a great political party unless and until it realizes that there's no future in trying to be just a little bit less liberal than the other party. We have to offer a choice—not, as the saying goes, an echo. The GOP hasn't learned that— yet. The "liberals" *have* their party. What we need to do is to take a forthright stand on Jeffersonian principles; limited government, cutting down on the bureaucracy, etc.

From your vantage point in Washington, how well has state government—executive, legislative and judicial—served the people of North Carolina during your lifetime?

Very well—because it obviously is nearer the people. The problem with the federal govern-

U.S. Senators from North Carolina and Virginia, Jesse Helms and John Warner, join in laughter on the White House lawn. Both had attended a meeting with the President. Political writers and observers have often noted that Jesse Helms has not freely joined in the "clubbiness" of the United States Senate. As a matter of fact, *Time* magazine, in a 1981 cover article, said that Helms "learned, principally, how to cause a ruckus." He did this, among other actions, by "forcing senators to take stands on issues they would just as soon avoided." *Time* said also that "Helms has a personal following on the right that is second in size and dedication only to that of the President himself—and that trusts him more." A 1988 profile in the same publication said "Few in Congress have been so vilified by the press, and none have been so adept at turning it to political advantage. The darts just seem to pass through him."

ment is that it's so "far away" and so insulated from what the "real America" is all about. On top of that, we've had good government in North Carolina because we've had strong, principled people willing to serve—names that have been forgotten. Ehringhaus, for example; Hoey; Gregg Cherry (who never got his due in terms of his strength of character); Edwin Gill; Sandy Graham. The list is endless

As a WWII veteran and patriot, how would you describe patriotism and love of country in the U.S. today? How can the great words on the monuments be really understood by young Americans—short of the experience of defending our nation at war?

First of all, I believe today's young people are under-rated. The vast majority are bright, they are patriotic, they mostly need role models in terms of courage, fidelity to principle, etc. I meet with them constantly, and they should not be confused with the minority of young people who get most of the media attention. Most of all, to a greater degree than ever existed in my generation, they have a spiritual faith. They understand that this nation was not a happenstance in terms of its creation. They know that the "Founding Fathers" got down on their knees at Philadelphia and prayed for Divine Guidance. And I think they instinctively understand that the survival of America depends upon whether we return to the faith of our fathers.

In short, the majority already understand the blessings of liberty. As I said at the outset, they mainly need more role models who are willing to restate and reaffirm the things said by Jefferson, Washington, Patrick Henry, et al.

What brief word of advice do you have for young people who are considering a career in public service?

If they're looking for a glamorous life, forget it. But if they are willing to sacrifice their time, their hard work on behalf of the fundamental principles on which this nation was based, go to it. First, they need to ask themselves *why* they're interested in public service. Unless they are willing to face up to the fact that this service must be selfless, not selfish, they're kidding themselves.

If they decide to make a commitment, then they should learn everything they can about world history, and especially American history. They've got to understand economics—including the difference between socialism and capitalism. And if they are inclined to measure their achievements by headlines and favorable editorials—my advice is to choose something else for their careers. *ELR*

An experienced reporter and former TV news commentator, Jesse Helms is accustomed to the needs of the news media and to dealing with aggressive competing news people. Here he answers questions following a meeting with President Reagan at the White House in which the president discussed the latest developments in the Iran Contra controversy. Over the years the senator's relationship with North Carolina news media has been mixed, with frequent charges and counter charges at various times, of "Jesse bashing" and "press bashing."

Like all members of Congress, senators greet thousands of visitors to the national Capitol each year, including many school groups. Senator Helms, escorting a group of Tar Heel youngsters down the Capitol steps, enjoys hosting and helping inform them about the historic building and the national government. The visit is usually culminated with a group photograph.

DAVID BRINKLEY
ABC Newsman, Commentator, Author

David Brinkley is without a doubt one of the most respected newsmen in Washington, and a highly regarded professional, according to Thomas B. Cookerly, president and general manager of Station WJLA-TV, the ABC-TV affiliate in Washington, D.C., and former general manager of WBTV Charlotte.

"David Brinkley is held in high regard by the people on Capitol Hill, by his peers at all three networks, and by the viewers," Cookerly says. "We have his 'This Week With David Brinkley' show on our air, and it sells for such a premium you would not believe it. It gets a good rating, and advertisers want to be around it because they know the key opinion makers, the people who count, will be watching that show."

Sam Ragan, editor and publisher of the *Southern Pines Pilot,* is former managing editor of *The News & Observer,* Raleigh, who has also served with distinction as North Carolina's Secretary of Cultural Resources. In 1938, when Ragan was sports editor, city editor, and the only reporter on the *Wilmington Star-News,* he gave high school student David Brinkley his first newspaper job reporting high school sports at $5 per week. Ragan says Brinkley was a quick learner, and a "natural" right from the beginning. Brinkley knew how to get a story, how to write, and had a knack for finding out little things.

Ragan says, "We sent David around to the New Hanover County Courthouse, and there wasn't anything going on at the Courthouse. He decided he would go up and interview people who were in jail. Nobody had ever done that before as far as I know in Wilmington. He quoted them directly on everything they said, and it was a marvelous story."

Brinkley graduated from high school and worked full time for the *Star-News* for a couple of years before being called to active duty in the National Guard in 1940. Sam Ragan recalls, "We covered everything. We had a call about a night-blooming cereus, a flower that blooms one time for about an hour, and doesn't bloom again for years. David and I both went on it, because that was a big story. He thought it was the funniest thing he had ever seen, all these 50 or more people from the neighborhood just sitting there looking at this little plant, waiting for it to bloom. He kept talking about it, and I said you write the story, and he did. He just wrote exactly what had happened, and it was a wonderful piece."

Julian Scheer, now a Washington businessman, was one of North Carolina's best reporters and feature writers in his days with the *Charlotte News.* He became information director for NASA at the peak of United States space activity with an annual budget of $30 million for his division. If the

"it takes one to know one" theory is credible, and many people believe that it is, then reporter Scheer's appraisal of David Brinkley is meaningful when Scheer says, "David is a reporter, first and foremost, and he has always been a reporter. He is polite, but wary of his news sources, because he continues to have a basic reporter's cynicism and skepticism. He has got a great reportorial instinct for honing in on the one or two things that really are important in an interview.

"He is also a guy who still has a sense of what is right and wrong, and what should and should not be seen or talked about on television. David will take a bare script and re-write it, because every word he utters on television has to be his own. He does not like people writing for him, and no one can really write in his style."

When we were raising the money to save the world's greatest battleship, the U.S.S. *North Carolina,* we asked David Brinkley to tape a piece for the television fund-raiser, and he cheerfully complied. A while later David called me, anxious to find a summer job for his teenage son Joel that would take him out of Washington, and he asked if we could use him at Grandfather Mountain. Everything was pretty well set, with a job for Joel at Grandfather and a place for him to stay. Then Joel took out his sharp pencil, and he figured he would make $5 more per week bagging groceries in a Washington neighborhood store, so he passed up his opportunity to enjoy the high hills.

We were able to render a small assist to Joel a couple of years later, however, when David was trying to enter his son in the University at Chapel Hill. David called me to say that even though the boy had excellent grades, the limited number of out-of-state slots was denying him admission. We made some telephone calls, the message being that David Brinkley's job requires that he be in Washington, D.C., but in truth and fact he is from Wilmington, North Carolina, and his highly qualified son should be considered in that light. Joel was admitted, he worked on the *Daily Tar Heel,* and was elected as its editor by the student body. Soon after graduation Joel Brinkley won the Pulitzer Prize while working for the *Louisville Courier-Journal.* In 1988, at 35, he was Jerusalem bureau chief of *The New York Times.* We hope the admissions office at Chapel Hill, which is constantly faced with making difficult judgment calls, feels as good about this as we do.

David Brinkley delivered the Reed Sarratt Distinguished Lecture at UNC-Chapel Hill in April 1988. One of the many stories that delighted the audience was this one: "Many years ago, when I was doing 'The Huntley-Brinkley Report,' I was in an airport lobby somewhere, and I was approached by a gray-haired lady. She said, 'Are you Chet

David Brinkley in the ABC Newsroom in Washington, D.C.

Huntley?' I said, 'Yes, I am.' If I had walked up to Abbott and Costello, I'm not sure I would have known which one was which. The woman in the lobby, still thinking she was addressing Huntley, told me she liked me just fine. Then she said, 'But I don't know how you can stand that idiot Brinkley.' "

When Wilmington held David Brinkley Day I was on the board of the Chamber of Commerce, and was given the job of assembling a "This Is Your Life, David Brinkley" slide show to be presented at the banquet. Al Dickson, executive editor of the *Wilmington Star-News*, who had been on the paper with Brinkley in the early days, was a tremendous help in the research that went into se-curing from David's boyhood friends snapshots that could be made into slides. Wayne Jackson of WECT Television and Allen Jones of WGNI Radio were members of the committee. Wayne made contact with Chet Huntley at the Big Sky development out west, where he had moved when NBC's Huntley-Brinkley team disbanded.

Huntley quite willingly agreed to record our slide show script on audio tape, but on the day of the banquet when the recording arrived from Big Sky, it revealed that Huntley had been out of prac-tice by a few years in making his formerly polished delivery. Allen Jones and his staff at WGNI worked feverishly to spruce up our big surprise for David, and when Huntley's voice boomed over the loudspeaker, all of the hems, haws, and stammers were removed clean as a whistle. We are pretty certain we saw tears on the cheeks of the usually unemotional David Brinkley, once the lights came back on. *HMM*

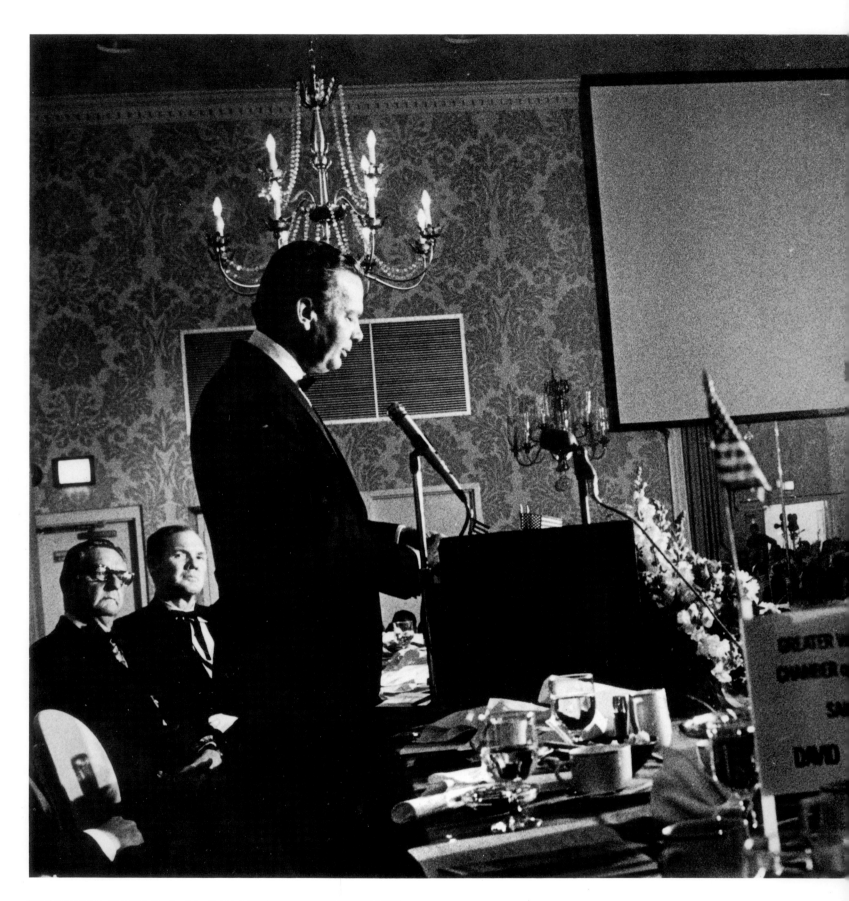

David Brinkley chats with Margie and Sam Ragan following the David Brinkley Day banquet in Wilmington. Brinkley was a student at New Hanover High in Wilmington in the 1930s when managing editor Sam Ragan gave him his first reporting job at the *Wilmington Star-News*.

David Brinkley admires a fat, pond-fed rainbow trout just landed by Governor Luther H. Hodges during a meeting of the Honorary Tar Heels at Cataloochee Ranch near Waynesville.

The screen on the wall in the background is where a "This Is Your Life, David Brinkley" slide presentation has just been shown, and David Brinkley is responding. Wilmington was celebrating David Brinkley Day to honor its distinguished native son.

David Brinkley admires the sleek silhouette of the U.S.S. *North Carolina* Battleship Memorial from the Hilton Hotel pier on the Cape Fear River waterfront at Wilmington. Brinkley did public service television spots used by North Carolina broadcasters during the successful drive to raise funds to save the historic ship.

JAMES G. MARTIN
A Popular, Combative Governor

Three former governors attended a luncheon at the executive mansion hosted by Governor and Mrs. Martin for the Keep North Carolina Beautiful organization headed by Mrs. Jeanelle Moore. Shown (left to right): Dan K. Moore, Governor Martin, Terry Sanford and Robert W. Scott. Pat Holshouser, wife of former Governor Jim Holshouser, also attended the luncheon.

Since the two major political parties became known as Republican and Democrat about 150 years ago, there have been only six Republicans elected as Governor of North Carolina. Only two of these—James E. Holshouser and James G. Martin—were elected in the 20th century. So the average for one and one-half centuries has been the election of a Republican to the state's highest office every 25 years.

Governor Jim Martin is keenly aware of the challenge and opportunity of creating and building support for his program and for the Republican party. His supporters, Republicans and many conservative Democrats, give him high marks for his performance and results to date. His opponents and critics, especially Democrat leaders in the General Assembly, view him as highly partisan and quick to claim credit for what Democrats in the legislature proposed and enacted.

Supporters and opponents, however, will agree that Jim Martin is an intelligent and personable political leader, an effective communicator, with an easy manner and engaging smile, photogenic and a good campaigner. On balance, Martin appears to have much of same popular appeal as President Ronald Reagan, and seems to maintain a relatively high level of public confidence without regard to his actual performance in office.

Under his leadership, Martin says the state has grown in new jobs and economic development while he has tightened up state spending and kept a lid on taxes. He emphasizes a speedier completion of a network of strategic highway corridors which will "tie us together as one united state."

In an interview on his administration, Martin made these comments:

Economic Growth. "Over the last three years (1985—87), North Carolina has had an average $5 billion per year invested in new and expanded manufacturing and non-manufacturing facilities. We have added a net gain of 350,000 jobs in three years. This is a better record, for example, than Massachusetts, a state with approximately the same population, which has had the benefit of the strategic defense initiative investments."

Rural/Urban. "There is an imbalance in jobs between rural and urban areas, and we have been working since 1985 to achieve more balanced growth and to attract new businesses *continued*

Governor James G. Martin is the second Republican governor of North Carolina to be elected in the 20th century. A former Davidson College chemistry professor and six-term member of Congress, Martin is completing his first term and seeks re-election to his office. He is shown speaking at the celebration of the 50th anniversary of the Blue Ridge Parkway at Cumberland Knob.

Virginia and North Carolina share the beautiful Blue Ridge Parkway, one of the nation's great scenic highways. Both states cooperated recently in celebrating the Parkway's 50th anniversary. Virginia Governor Charles Robb (left) visits with Governor Martin while riding in an antique automobile used in the celebration. The Parkway attracts thousands of visitors each year in both states.

Secretary of Transportation Jim Harrington

Like most North Carolinians, the Jim Martin family are sports fans. Although Martin is a former professor at Davidson College, his wife Dottie and son have joined the governor in becoming enthusiastic supporters of the UNC Tar Heel basketball team. At the right is Phil Kirk, the governor's chief of staff. The picture was made at Meadowlands Arena in New Jersey just before Carolina was eliminated from the 1987 NCAA tournament by Syracuse University.

A new report on the magnitude of the motor racing industry in the state brings Governor Martin to the Charlotte Motor Speedway in Cabarrus County for a news conference. He chats with H.A. (Humpy) Wheeler (left), Speedway president, and veteran race driver Dale Earnhardt, 1987 Winston Cup champion. North Carolina is the home of Winston-Cup Motor Racing, and 34 of the top 40 Winston Cup teams were based in the state in 1987. The total economic contribution of motor racing in North Carolina was estimated to be $514.4 million in 1987.

and industries to smaller communities and rural areas. Working with local groups, chambers of commerce and economic developers, and with the bi-partisan support of our legislators, we have put together a package of incentives for businesses to invest in smaller communities (10,000 or less). By 1987 over 60 percent of the new investments were going to smaller communities."

Highways. "I asked for an increase in our motor fuel tax so we could improve our highway system. I guess I'm the only governor ever—or since Governor Cameron Morrison—that didn't go around the state promising everyone a highway. I did promise I-40 because it was badly needed and strategically located. As governor, I went to each region and asked them to tell me what was their major road project so that we could get that four-laned as part of a continuous four-lane system that will come within 10 miles of 90 percent of the population. What an advantage this will be for the entire state."

Public Schools. "We work hard to strengthen our public schools. In the 24 years before I became governor, the percentage of the state budget that went for public schools went down almost every year. The years 1966 (Governor Dan K. Moore) and 1984 (Governor Jim Hunt) were exceptions. The Martin administration has had four years of back-to-back increases. I have proposed budgets that have increased the percentage of general fund revenues going to public schools, and the General Assembly has adopted that percentage each year. That's good. It is a time when we benefit from bi-partisan competition, with the two parties not only cooperating but vying with one another to see who can come up with the best ideas for schools . . . building new schools, paying our teachers better, evaluating them, promoting them."

Veto Power. "The balance of power between the legislative and executive branches of state government is not fundamentally a partisan problem. There is a partisan aspect in that we have now had two Republican governors as one of the consequences of having a state that is evolving into a two-party political system . . . the current power struggle between the legislative and executive branches goes beyond partisan considerations . . . the transfer of day-to-day management of the executive branch over to the legislative branch (can be done) because the North Carolina governor does not have the veto power, never has had the power and the stunning thing is that not once in 212 years have our people ever been allowed to vote on it . . . (the veto power) is a solid part of good government for the governor to have that restraining power to protect his own office and to protect the people from bad legislation . . . the people deserve the right to decide this constitutional question."*ELR*

Governor Martin and Liston Ramsey, Speaker of the House of Representatives, are powerful leaders in Raleigh who are often on opposite sides of political and public issues. Martin, a Republican, and Ramsey, a Democrat, have had their share of differences and criticisms. Speaker Ramsey, a Madison County Democrat, has been a member of the General Assembly since 1960 (with exception of the 1965—66 term), and has served as Speaker of the House since 1981, longer than any person in North Carolina history. A retired merchant, Ramsey has been a full-time legislator for many years.

The voters of North Carolina are expected to elect one of these men governor of North Carolina for the term 1989—1993. Jim Martin (left) is incumbent governor and seeks re-election for a second term. Bob Jordan (right), the lieutenant governor of North Carolina, will face Martin in the November election. A seasoned legislative leader and titular head of the Democratic party, Jordan is a successful businessman from Montgomery County. Both men were attending a basketball game at Dean Smith Student Activities Center, Chapel Hill, when Hugh Morton asked them to pose for this photo. The smiling youngster is unidentified.

The 9th congressional district, which includes Charlotte and Mecklenburg County, has contributed significantly to the fact that North Carolina is a two-party state. Governor Martin (left) served six terms representing the district before winning the governor's office in 1984. Alex McMillan (right), a Charlotte businessman and civic leader, kept the district in Republican hands and is a candidate for his third term. Charles Raper Jonas of Lincolnton captured the seat for the Republicans in 1953, was never defeated and retired voluntarily in 1973.

Governor Martin learns that a quick way to develop an inferiority complex about your height is to be photographed standing beside Tommy Burleson, president of the Avery County Chamber of Commerce, and a former member of the North Carolina State University national championship basketball team. Betty Huskins of the Avery Chamber is at right. Burleson's height is seven feet, four inches.

TAR HEEL ELECTED GOVERNOR OF ALASKA

When the USS North Carolina was berthed in Wilmington in 1961 she collided with the Ark floating restaurant, and Steve Cowper of Kinston, N.C., fresh out of UNC Law School, was sent by the insurance company to represent the Battleship Commission, and he did his job well. In 1987 Steve Cowper took office as Governor of Alaska, where one of his interests is to assure that Alaska's abundant wildlife continues to flourish. As an experienced Alaska outdoorsman, Governor Cowper says: "If you want to keep yourself healthy, the best thing to do is learn a little something about the habits of bears, because they do tend to congregate when the Salmon are running. That's when the fishermen congregate as well." Cowper reached voting age in time to vote for Terry Sanford for Governor of North Carolina in 1960. Mack Pearsall of Rocky Mount and former Governor Jim Hunt were among his classmates in law school. *HMM*

EDWIN GILL — A MAN FOR ALL SEASONS

What is Edwin Gill (wearing glasses), state treasurer, respected financial authority, poet, essayist, bibliophile and life-long bachelor, doing at a gala Hawaiian luau? He was also an astute and successful politician and a leader in the state Democratic party. Gill is enjoying the fun and excitement of a rousing party rally at Atlantic Beach with (left to right) Craig Phillips, state superintendent of public instruction, an unidentified woman and Governor Robert W. Scott. A man of many talents and interests, Gill gets credit for coining, "good government is a habit in North Carolina," and he believed it fervently. Nothing pleased him more than to report that "North Carolina continues to be in excellent financial condition—her budget in balance, her debt within reason, and her bonds rated AAA, the highest rate obtainable." During Governor Luther Hodges' administration, Gill became ill and was forced to remain in bed at his quarters at the Sir Walter Hotel, Raleigh. Hodges decided to cheer him up by having a meeting of the Council of State (all elected state officers) in Gill's bedroom. Shortly after the meeting was called to order around his bed, the proceedings were interrupted by a knock. When the door was opened, an unusually endowed young woman appeared, apologized, and said, "Oh, Edwin, I see you have company. I'll come back later." No one has yet admitted arranging the classic prank. *ELR*

FAREWELL TO THE LEGENDARY 'OLDEST RAT'

Often described (by himself and others) as "the oldest rat in the Democratic barn," Secretary of State Thad Eure will retire in 1988—51 years after he took office in December 1936. At age 88, undefeated at the polls, and having held his office for longer than anyone in the U.S., he will relinquish his position as head of the Department of State and as a member of the Council of State. He will also step down as convener of the State House of Representatives at each first session when the body needs to elect the speaker. And he will no longer be state government's best-known Mr. Democrat. Since 1939 Eure, empowered by a legislative resolution, has assigned the seats of members in both houses of the General Assembly. You would not find any Republicans on the front rows. Well-known for his bow ties, jovial manner and stentorian voice, Eure was a popular master of ceremonies at political rallies and other public events. He will leave the North Carolina political arena with regret—but with many friends and great memories. *ELR*

BELK STORES CELEBRATE 100TH ANNIVERSARY

Paul A. Volcker, former chairman of the board of governors of the Federal Reserve System who served in distinguished posts under five presidents, was guest of honor at the 100th anniversary celebration of Belk Stores Services, Inc., Charlotte, in April 1988. Shown (left to right) are John M. Belk, chairman, Belk Stores Services; Volcker; Thomas M. Belk, president, Belk Stores Services; and John G. Medlin, Jr., chairman/president, First Wachovia. John and Tom Belk are sons of William Henry Belk, founder of the Belk department store organization, who began his first store in Monroe on May 29, 1888 with $750 in savings and $500 that he borrowed. In 1988 there were 350 stores in 16 states, employing 35,000 associates. *ELR*

'KING' RICHARD PETTY AND KYLE
A few days after Richard Petty (left) was photographed with his son Kyle, Richard was in a most unbelievable wreck during the 1988 NASCAR race at Daytona, which the television networks replayed time and again for a large part of the population of the United States. Anyone who witnessed the wreck or the television replay is bound to understand that Richard Petty is brave, lucky, and tough, especially in light of his being in his car whirling around the speedway in Richmond, Va., the following week in the next NASCAR race. May the Lord continue to smile on King Richard, and on Kyle and all of the other drivers who have made racing a great sport and source of entertainment in North Carolina. *HMM*

TWO WORLD CLASS TRACK, FIELD LEADERS
Two track and field luminaries embrace after being inducted into the North Carolina Sports Hall of Fame in 1963. Jim Beatty (left), a native of Charlotte who dominated ACC distance races while a track star at UNC-Chapel Hill, during 1962 was credited with seven American track records. He gained renown as the first runner to break the four minute mile indoors at 3:58:9, set the world record for two miles at 8:29:8, and 3:56:3 for the outdoor mile. Dr. Leroy T. Walker, who came to North Carolina College (now N.C. Central University) at Durham in 1945 when it had no track program and no track, built a nationally known track team that won 11 Olympic medals. Former head coach of the U.S. men's track and field team at the 1976 summer Olympics, Walker has become an international figure in track and field. He may be the most honored sports figure in North Carolina history. In 1987 the U.S. Olympic Hall of Fame became the 12th hall of fame to elect him to its membership. Among his many other achievements, he served three years as chancellor at N.C. Central University. *ELR*

NORTH CAROLINA'S 'THIRD' UNITED STATES SENATOR
That is how many people describe William McWhorter Cochrane, a North Carolinian who has spent more than 30 years working in key appointive positions in the U.S. Senate. He first went to Capitol Hill in 1954 to help W. Kerr Scott open his Senate office and planned to head back to Chapel Hill within a year. But it didn't happen that way. When the 100th Congress began its session, there was only one incumbent senator—John Stennis of Mississippi—who was in office when Cochrane arrived in Washington. After serving with Scott, who died in office, he worked for U.S. Senator B. Everett Jordan for many years. Since 1972 he has been associated with the Senate Rules Committee where he has, among other things, been involved behind the scenes with every major legislative debate of the last three decades. Yet Cochrane, a genial and soft-spoken lawyer, in many ways, has never left Chapel Hill. Recently he was elected president of the General Alumni Association of UNC-Chapel Hill. *ELR*

CHARLES KURALT

CBS 'On the Road' Newsman, Commentator, Author

Charles Kuralt says, "I have friends in New York who think there is not anything out there after you pass the Hudson River, until you get to Hollywood." While friends with that sort of notion may not ever be his best customers, Kuralt believes there will always be a market for television features like his "On The Road" episodes for CBS involving travels around America, as well as books in a similar category.

Not only are there geographical differences in the various parts of the nation that intrigue Americans with their own country, with which not many are completely familiar, there are other regional differences that survive to whet interest. Kuralt says, "You'd have thought we would all talk like television announcers by now, but we don't. The regional accents are still there, and you can tell a New Hampshire man from an Alabaman in the first five seconds of talking with him."

When he expressed those thoughts Charles Kuralt was on a North Carolina Travel Mission to London in November 1987, where he was being interviewed by British journalists. Kuralt told the Britons, "You can close your eyes and stick a pin in the map, then go there and find a good story. I stick to small towns and rural places, because they have more time for you." Kuralt also revealed to the Londoners that he has a whole shelf of books by people who made trips around America, including books by some of their own. "Kipling did it, and Charles Dickens made a grumpy trip around America. He didn't find much to admire."

A recent book with painter Bob Timberlake was great fun, Kuralt says, adding, "I think of myself as a kind of minor league artist, and Bob is a major league one. I was flattered when he wanted me to write some words to go with his pictures. I took still pictures of a lot of his paintings, and stuck them up on a wall in my office at home to contemplate them a few days before I started writing. They are so evocative, especially for anyone who grew up in our region, that it was pretty easy to connect Bob's wonderful paintings with some of my own memories."

After the book with Timberlake, nobody thought there would ever be a North Carolina related project that Charles Kuralt could do for an encore. Happily he found one as a result of an "On The Road" prime time special CBS ran in the summer of 1983. The CBS show needed a theme song, but Charles could find nothing that suited him. He said, "I thought I would write some lyrics myself,

but I needed somebody to write the music, and the only composer I knew was Loonis McGlohon in Charlotte. He enthusiastically agreed, and went even further to find a good group of musicians, some of the best in the country, including Jim Campbell, to record the music in New York.

"It was only a short step the next year, when Governor Jim Hunt was urging his acquaintances to do something to help North Carolina celebrate her 400th birthday. It was Loonis' idea that we go on from the 'On the Road' theme to record what became the album *North Carolina Is My Home*, and give it to the state for her birthday."

The services of McGlohon and Kuralt were free, but the musicians had to be paid. Piedmont Airlines kindly picked up the tab for that, as well as the cost of cutting the records and tapes that were presented to schools and libraries. That was supposed to be the end of it, but request after request came in for public presentations of the program.

McGlohon and Kuralt have appeared with several different symphony orchestras in a number of North Carolina cities. Sponsored by the N.C. Division of Travel and Tourism, *North Carolina Is My Home* has also played New York, Washington, Chicago, Vancouver, London and Tampa, proving to be one of the most effective promotional tools ever utilized by any state.

Its most moving effect, however, is on the every day, ordinary and loyal Tar Heel, of whom there are many. The program is so patriotic, so inspirational, and as Charles says, "so rich and gravy laden," that many a happy tear has been seen on the cheeks of North Carolinians who have witnessed it. It is unforgettable.

Charles Kuralt does not know whether or when he will return to make North Carolina really his home, because he has yet to have made any decisions about retirement. He does, however, spend a great deal of time in North Carolina, possibly more than in his work home of New York City, because his parents live at Kitty Hawk, his brother Wallace lives in Chapel Hill, and Charles has a number of North Carolina projects in the works.

His major North Carolina activity in the spring of 1988 was working to establish the professorship in the University of North Carolina School of Social Work which honors his father, Wallace Hamilton Kuralt. The retired superintendent of public welfare in Mecklenburg County, Wallace Kuralt is beloved by thousands for his outstanding work in that post.

continued

ON THE ROAD

Charles Kuralt leans out of the window of his CBS "On The Road" van in which he has visited all states many times in search of his special kind of non-earthshaking stories that would not otherwise see the glare of network television news. He claims his bosses in New York "never know where I am and don't care."

Anyone who watches the CBS "Sunday Morning" show from beginning to end can usually discern that the part of the show Charles Kuralt personally likes best is the ending. There is always a two-minute series of scenes and sounds from nature, of trout swimming in shallow waters to spawn, of thousands of ducks or geese flying north or south in migration, or of some other natural spectacle. It is a happy and inspiring way to close a Sunday morning program, a reminder that God must have a hand in things, and the viewers obviously approve.

It pleases Charles Kuralt that North Carolina's passion for progress has made a big difference in the lives of individuals, but his knowledge gained in extensive travels elsewhere prompts him to say, "We must not pave every meadow, cut down every forest, terrace every hillside, or pollute every trout river.

"We must not destroy the thing we all love about North Carolina, and that is the natural beauty. It's easy to destroy it, because there is money in it, but cash has never meant quite as much as human relationship and the beauty of the land. Many people back through our history have felt that way."

Pete McKnight, Tom Fesperman, Bill Snider, Roy Parker, Rolfe Neill, and Ed Yoder were journalists who served as an inspiration to Charles Kuralt while he was in college and immediately thereafter. He says, "I have been to every state now, and have gotten to know a lot of journalists. I think North Carolina has been as rich in journalists as any state in the nation. We've really been lucky to have been so well served by our journalists during the civil rights struggles that were so painful in other states, and to some extent in North Carolina.

"The editors of the papers always advised sensibly. We had very few wild-eyed people who urged people on to racial strife, rather they urged brotherhood where it was possible. Everyone I knew about behaved very honorably at a time when to our north the Richmond papers and to our south the Charleston papers were urging their readers on a course that would have been calamitous for them and the country. North Carolina always had that spirit of moderation and good sense."

Wallace Kuralt, younger brother of Charles, remembers when Charles showed his first promise of being a broadcaster at the age of 10. Charlie Justice was setting records on the football field at Chapel Hill, and Charles Kuralt listened intently to Ray Reeve doing the play-by-play on radio. As soon as the game ended, the game would be rebroadcast from memory in the Kuralt front yard, but instead of Ray Reeve, it was 10-year-old Charles Kuralt doing the play-by-play.

By age 14 Charles had persuaded Station WAYS to give him the job of announcing the Charlotte Hornets minor league baseball games on radio. Of course, Charles at that age had no driver's license, so his father drove him to and from Griffith Park each night. Some nights Charles would be the only staff person there, so he handled the radio play-by-play, the scoreboard, and other odd jobs simultaneously. The Charles Kuralt story is a text book example: start young and stay with it if you want to be a success. *HMM*

Charles Kuralt tries clogging with the World Champion Grandfather Mountain Cloggers, directed by David Alexander (third from right). Kuralt did an "On The Road" piece on the clogging team for CBS, but the story wound up featuring Robin Garrison (second from left), a totally deaf member of the team who receives his main signals for dancing by feeling the vibrations on the floor from the other cloggers' feet.

Charles Kuralt and artist Bob Timberlake are at Timberlake's studio in rural Davidson County at the time of publication of their joint literary work, an imposing book featuring words by Charles Kuralt and paintings by Bob Timberlake. The book was a huge success, and glorified North Carolina verbally and pictorially.

Charles Kuralt is married to Suzanna Folsom Baird Kuralt, known to her husband and other friends as Petey. Growing up as the daughter of military parents, Petey learned early that a husband's job may require travel to far away places. She is delighted, however, that Charles can at least come home on weekends to host the CBS "Sunday Morning" show.

Richard Evans Younger, one of America's best wildlife painters, captains the ship as he and Charles head out for a round with the trout in Grandfather Mountain Lake. Younger spent seven years catching and painting the major sports fish of the world for a fishing encyclopedia, so both he and Charles are considered expert anglers. Younger's home is Blowing Rock.

When older newspapermen get together, the stories of the good old days roll on and on. At the left is Furman Bisher, formerly of Kuralt's alma mater paper, *The Charlotte News,* while Kays Gary of the *Charlotte Observer* (right) and Horace Carter, Pulitzer winner from Tabor City, listen. Bisher, sports columnist with the *Atlanta Journal,* has received nearly every award that can come to a sportswriter, and Kays Gary is a legend for his columns in the *Observer.*

Governor James Martin presents the highest honor that the State of North Carolina can bestow, The North Carolina Award, to Charles Kuralt while former Governor James E. Holshouser, chairman of the awards committee, smiles with approval. Kuralt was honored in the category of public service.

Charles Kuralt is speaking about North Carolina to a group of British journalists in the American Club in London in November 1987, where he was introduced as "the most beloved and trusted broadcast journalist in America." He explained that the stories that interest him most "are ones about people doing something unusual, even eccentric," and he said "the charm of North Carolina is in its rural parts."

The sign in Charlotte's Ovens Auditorium stated the situation well, and Charles Kuralt (left) and Loonis McGlohon (right) have been a tremendous hit in every public performance of their album of North Carolina music, narration, and folklore.

Charles Kuralt, slim and with hair, is interviewing Governor Luther H. Hodges on CBS at the 1960 Democratic National Convention in Los Angeles.